中国国情教育地方特色系列教材

总主编　程爱民

# DISCOVERING JIANGSU

主　编　吴　鹏　周桂生

副主编　吴格非　曹力前　陈　俐
编　者　曹力前　朱履骅　杜志峰　储志新
　　　　吴　鹏　周桂生　吴格非　陈　俐
　　　　陈　雪　顾海锋　徐媛媛　叶昕媛
　　　　刘　婷　晏明丽　吴媛媛

上海外语教育出版社
SHANGHAI FOREIGN LANGUAGE EDUCATION PRESS

图书在版编目（CIP）数据

水韵江苏：汉英对照/吴鹏，周桂生主编.
上海：上海外语教育出版社，2024.-- (中国国情教育
地方特色系列教材/程爱民总主编). -- ISBN 978–7
–5446–8361–6

Ⅰ. K925.3
中国国家版本馆CIP数据核字第2024KX7870号

出版发行：**上海外语教育出版社**
（上海外国语大学内） 邮编：200083
电 话：021–65425300 (总机)
电子邮箱：bookinfo@sflep.com.cn
网 址：http://www.sflep.com
责任编辑：王 璐

印 刷：上海锦佳印刷有限公司
开 本：890×1240 1/16 印张 13 字数 366千字
版 次：2024 年12月第1版 2024 年12月第1次印刷

书 号：ISBN 978-7-5446-8361-6
定 价：58.00元

本版图书如有印装质量问题，可向本社调换
质量服务热线：4008-213-263

# 总序

　　《中国国情教育地方特色系列教材》是一套专为国际学生设计的中英双语国情教育教材。这套教材旨在通过各省市的独特视角，向世界展示中华文明的深厚底蕴和东方神韵的独特魅力，同时反映当代中国经济社会发展的巨大成就。教材内容丰富，涵盖了各地的方方面面，依托各学校的学科优势，彰显地域特色。教材采用古今兼顾的视角，以今为主，遵循"三贴近"原则，运用讲故事的手法，生动展现中国的多元面貌。

　　本套教材以"讲好中国故事，传播好中国声音，展示真实、立体、全面的中国"为指导思想，围绕"呈现大美中国、沟通中外文明、构建人类命运共同体"的主题来选择内容。从地方视角出发，注重介绍各省、市、自治区的政治、经济、地理、教育、民生、文化艺术、科技发展等方面的情况与特点，以及当地的名胜古迹、风土人情、传统美食和中外文化交流等诸多方面内容。

　　在编写过程中，我们特别关注了五个要素：国家与社会发展、国情教育主题与范畴、跨文化交际理论与实践、国际学生的特点以及教材编写规范。这五个要素共同构成了教材编写的指导原则，确保了教材的质量和水平，使其能够更好地服务读者，尤其是国际学生和海外读者。

　　本套教材每册分别介绍中国的一个省、市、自治区。每一册都由知名专家和国际中文一线教师精心撰写，内容丰富、语言生动、资料翔实，从不同角度展示了各地的独特魅力。通过阅读和学习本套教材，您将了解到：

1. 自然环境与地理位置：各地区的自然环境、地理位置及气候特征等；

2. 历史文化：各地的历史背景、文化传统、名胜古迹和节庆风俗等；

3. 经济发展：各地经济发展状况，包括支柱产业、知名企业、对外贸易等；

4. 社会生活：教育、医疗、民生、交通及日常消费等；

5. 最新发展动态：各地的重大工程、城市规划、科技创新等。

此外，为了使您能够更加直观地了解中国相关地区的情况，每册教材还配有大量精美图片、视频和其他数字资源。总之，此套地方特色系列教材通过一个个微观景象或故事，帮助您更好地了解中国各地的风土人情、文化教育、科技经济发展及社会生活等方面的情况，让您在学习和生活中能更快地融入中国这个大家庭。我们相信，有了这套教材的陪伴，您在中国的学习和生活将会变得更加愉快和充实！预祝您在中国一切顺利！

程爱民

2024年9月

目
录

# Contents

## PART 1

## 江苏概况 Overview of Jiangsu

# PART 2

城市名片 City Showcase

第一章　南京：六朝古都

Chapter 1　Nanjing: Ancient Capital of the Six Dynasties

## 第四章　常州：中华龙城
## Chapter 4　Changzhou: The Dragon City of China

第五章　镇江：城市山林

Chapter 5　Zhenjiang: Urban Mountains and Forests

第七章　南通：中国近代第一城

Chapter 7　Nantong: The First City of Modern China

**第八章　徐州：楚韵汉风**
Chapter 8　Xuzhou: Strategic Place of Chu and Han

第九章　淮安：壮丽东南第一州
Chapter 9　Huai'an: The Most Magnificent City in Southeast China

第十章　连云港：新亚欧大陆桥东方起点
Chapter 10　Lianyungang: The Eastern Starting Point of the New Eurasian Land Bridge

第十一章　盐城：黄海明珠　湿地之都
Chapter 11　Yancheng: Pearl of the Yellow Sea, Capital of Wetlands

Part 1

江苏概况

OVERVIEW OF JIANGSU

# 一、引言

江苏在中国东部沿海地区，地处富饶的长江三角洲，地理位置极为重要。丰富的自然资源和独特的地理环境为江苏的经济发展、农业生产、旅游开发以及与周边地区的经济合作提供了有力的支持。作为中国重要的经济大省、工业大省、农业大省和制造业大省，江苏为中国的现代化建设和对外交往作出了重要贡献，在海内外也产生了广泛的影响。江苏的省会是南京，省花是清香淡雅的茉莉花。

## 1. 地理位置

江苏位于中国的东部，东临黄海，北邻山东，东南与浙江和上海相接，西与安徽相邻，总面积约为10.72万平方公里。江苏是中国地势最低平的省份之一，平原面积占全省87%，地势从东向西逐渐升高。全省最高点是连云港云台山的玉女峰，海拔624.4米。江苏是中国唯一同时拥有大江、大河、大湖、大海、大运河的省份。水资源丰富，沿海平原广阔，这为江苏提供了良好的港口条件和海运资源，对发展水利航运十分有利，促进了外贸和海洋经济的发展。

# I. Introduction

Jiangsu Province is located along the Yangtze River Delta on China's eastern coast and benefits from its rich natural resources and distinctive geographical setting, which have provided a strong foundation for Jiangsu's economic growth, agricultural production, tourism, and economic collaboration with neighboring regions. With its significant contributions in economy, industry, agriculture, and manufacturing, Jiangsu has played a crucial role in China's modernization and international exchanges, and has exerted a substantial influence at home and abroad. Nanjing is the provincial capital, while the fragrant and elegant jasmine represents the provincial flower.

## 1. Geographical Environment

Jiangsu, situated in the eastern part of China, is bordered by the Yellow Sea to the east, Shandong to the north, Zhejiang and Shanghai to the southeast, and Anhui to the west. It covers a total area of approximately 107,200 square kilometers. Jiangsu is one of the lowest-lying provinces in China, as 87% of its area is flatland that gradually slopes up from east to west. The highest point in the province is the Yunv Peak of the Yuntai Mountain in Lianyungang, standing at an altitude of 624.4 meters. Jiangsu stands out as the only province in China that boasts a large river, a large lake, a long coastline, and a grand canal. Its abundant water resources and extensive coastal plain provide excellent port conditions and shipping facilities, which are highly beneficial for the advancement of water conservation and shipping, and promoting international trade and the maritime economy.

The Yangtze River, the Huaihe River and the northern section of the Beijing-Hangzhou Grand Canal flow through Jiangsu. The Yangtze

长江、淮河和苏北运河是江苏境内的主要河流。长江是中国最长的河流，流经江苏的南部地区。淮河是江苏的北部边界，它向东南流入黄海。苏北运河是京杭大运河最繁忙的航段之一，连接了淮河与长江。江苏拥有大量湖泊，湖泊率约为6%，居全国之首。全国五大湖，就有两个位于江苏。太湖是中国第三大淡水湖，也是江苏最大的湖泊，以其优美的湖光山色和灿烂的人文景观闻名中外，是中国著名的风景名胜区。江苏的矿产种类多，非金属矿多，岩盐、芒硝、水泥用灰岩、陶瓷土等是江苏的特色矿产。"苏湖熟，天下足。"江苏自古以来就是富庶之地、鱼米之乡。中国两大主要粮食作物——水稻和小麦，江苏的产量均稳居全国前列。江苏也是南方蔬菜产量最大的省份之一。

### 2. 重要影响

从古至今，江苏一直是中国非常重要的一个省份，在经济、文化、教育和科研等方面都发挥着重要作用。

River, the longest river in China, traverses the southern part of the province. The Huaihe River serves as the northern border of Jiangsu and flows southeast into the Yellow Sea. The northern section of the Beijing-Hangzhou Grand Canal is one of the busiest segments of this ancient waterway, connecting the Huaihe River with the Yangtze River. Lakes account for about 6% of Jiangsu's area, the highest in all of China's provinces and regions. In fact, two of the five largest lakes of China are located in Jiangsu. The Taihu Lake, the third largest freshwater lake in China and the largest lake in Jiangsu, is renowned for its scenic beauty and cultural legacy. The province is rich in minerals, particularly non-metallic minerals like rock salt, mirabilite, limestone for cement production, and ceramic clay. Jiangsu is rich in agricultural produce, as reflected in the saying, "So long as Suzhou and Changzhou remain productive, the whole country shall be full." The province ranks among the country's top producers of rice and wheat, the two staple foods in China, and is also one of the largest production base of vegetables in southern China.

### 2. Key Contributions

An important province in China since ancient times, Jiangsu plays a vital role in the country's economy, culture, education, and scientific research.

Jiangsu stands out as one of China's most economically advanced provinces, as it consistently holds the second place in terms of economic output nationwide, thus laying a strong foundation for the steady and continuous growth of the country's economy. The province boasts numerous economic hubs and industrial zones which encompass a wide range of sectors including manufacturing, information technology, biopharmaceuticals, chemicals, and modern services. Notably, Changzhou, dubbed

江苏是中国经济最发达的省份之一，其经济总量长期稳居全国第二，为国家经济的持续稳定增长奠定了坚实的基础。省内拥有众多经济中心和工业基地，涵盖制造业、信息技术、生物医药、化工、现代服务业等诸多行业。例如，被誉为"新能源之都"的常州就汇聚了3400多家新能源产业链相关企业。

江苏在中国文化史上也扮演着十分重要的角色，是中国古代文化的重要发源地之一。这里孕育了丰富多彩且独具特色的地域文化，金陵文化的庄重、吴文化的婉约、淮扬文化的细腻与楚汉文化的豪迈，交相辉映。中国共有142座历史文化名城，其中江苏有13座，数量位居全国之首。每一座城市都是历史与文化的凝结，从南京六朝古都的庄重肃穆，到苏州园林的精巧雅致，再到扬州古运河岸的流水人家与徐州汉风古韵的悠悠往事，都承载着千年的历史，诉说着城市的辉煌与变迁。这些城市，还有镇江、淮安、无锡、南通、泰州、常州以及常熟、宜兴、高邮等地，共同构成了江苏丰富多彩的文化版图。江苏名胜古迹繁多，江南园林和水乡古镇最为人称道；而昆曲、古琴、云锦、苏绣等各类非物质文化遗产更是不胜枚举。这些都吸引了大批国内外游客前来参观"打卡"。江苏深厚的历史文化底蕴不仅对海外华人的文化根源探寻与传承产生了重要影响，还促进了国际友好交流与互动。

江苏在教育与科研领域同样展现出强劲的实力，拥有众多高等院校和先进的科研机构，在中国教科领域具有显著地位。如南京大学、东南大学、苏州大学和南京航空航天大学等高校不仅享誉国内外，还携手众多顶尖科研机构和前沿创新实验室，共同构建了江苏强大的教育科技生态系统，为培养高素质人才以及推动科技创新奠定了坚实的基础。

the "new energy capital", hosts over 3,400 businesses linked to the new energy sector.

Jiangsu Province holds a significant place in Chinese culture, as it is one of the important birthplaces of the country's ancient culture. It has nurtured diverse and vibrant regional cultures, including the Jinling, Wu, Huaiyang, Chu, and Han cultures. Of the 142 historical and cultural cities in China, Jiangsu is home to 13, ranking the first in the country. Each city is a testament to the rich tapestry of history and culture, from the ancient capital of the Six Dynasties in Nanjing and the elegant gardens in Suzhou to the ancient canal in Yangzhou and the ancient Han legacy of Xuzhou. These cities, along with Zhenjiang, Huai'an, Wuxi, Nantong, Taizhou, Changzhou, Changshu, Yixing, Gaoyou, and other places, form the vibrant cultural map of Jiangsu. The province is home to numerous attractions and historic sites, while its classical gardens and ancient waterside towns are particularly famous. Jiangsu also boasts a wide range of intangible cultural heritage, including Kunqu opera, Guqin (an ancient plucked instrument), Yunjin (cloud brocade), and Suzhou embroidery, which draw the attention of domestic and international tourists. With its profound historical and cultural heritage, Jiangsu is an intriguing place for overseas Chinese trying to explore their origin, and for people from different countries seeking to establish friendly ties.

In addition, the province has developed an impressive strength in education and scientific research with a number of universities and advanced scientific research institutions, which take up prominent positions in China's education and science sectors. Renowned universities such as Nanjing University, Southeast University, Soochow University, and Nanjing University of Aeronautics and

江苏在中国改革开放的历史进程中有着举足轻重的地位，它不仅是国家对外开放的重要窗口，也是经济转型与升级的活跃示范区。省内不同区域的发展策略也显示了江苏对外开放的多元化路径：苏南地区的外向型经济，苏中地区的产业结构优化与升级，苏北地区的基础设施建设和外资项目引入，江苏自贸试验区的设立更是标志着江苏的对外开放进入了新阶段。江苏在国际交流与合作方面也展现出了非凡的活力，通过与多国政府的广泛联系，与国际企业、研究机构的紧密合作，不断拓宽国际合作的广度与深度，努力将江苏建设成具有"世界聚合力的双向开放枢纽"。不仅要"引进来"外资与先进经验，也要推动本土企业"走出去"，吸引全球范围的资源要素，成为连接国内外市场的关键通道，促进全球经济的互利共赢、共同发展。

总而言之，江苏作为中国东部沿海的重要省份，地理位置优越，不仅是国家经济发展的关键支柱，也是文化传承与创新的重要基地，长期以来在海内外都具有重要的影响力，吸引着全球的目光。随着时间的推移，江苏以深厚的历史底蕴和蓬勃的现代活力，不断地提升其在全球的影响力和吸引力。不仅深化国际经济合作与文化交流，促进全球产业链和创新链融合，还努力构建绿色的、可持续的发展模式，吸引着更多的全球合作伙伴共谋发展，共创美好未来。

Astronautics have collaborated with top scientific research institutions and cutting-edge innovative laboratories to foster a robust educational technology ecosystem in Jiangsu, thus creating a strong foundation for training high-quality talents and driving scientific and technological innovation.

Furthermore, Jiangsu plays a pivotal role in China's reform and opening-up process. It serves as an important gateway for the country's opening up and acts as a dynamic demonstration area for economic transformation and upgrading. The development strategies implemented in the different regions of Jiangsu showcase the diverse paths towards opening up: southern Jiangsu focuses on an export-oriented economy, central Jiangsu emphasizes industrial structure optimization and upgrading, and northern Jiangsu prioritizes infrastructure construction and the attraction of foreign investment projects. The establishment of the Jiangsu Pilot Free Trade Zone marks a new phase in Jiangsu's opening up. The province has also demonstrated remarkable vitality in international exchanges and cooperation as it cooperates with foreign government offices, collaborates with international enterprises and research institutions, and continuously expands the scope and depth of international cooperation. Jiangsu aims to become a "two-way open hub bringing the world together" by attracting foreign investment and advanced experience, as well as by encouraging the global expansion of local enterprises, attracting global resources, and serving as a vital channel connecting domestic and foreign markets. This approach aims to promote the mutually beneficial development of the global economy.

Jiangsu, as an important province on China's east coast, plays a crucial role in the country's economic growth and serves as a hub for cultural

## 二、历史文化

### 1. 历史沿革

早在新石器时代晚期，江苏及周边地区就有人类活动的踪迹。春秋时期，这里成为吴国和越国这两个重要诸侯国的核心区域。公元前221年，秦始皇统一六国，建立了秦朝。在秦朝的行政区划中，江苏地区属于扬州郡的管辖范围。而后，历经多个朝代的更替，江苏地区因为优越的地理位置、发达的水路网络、富饶的物产资源，逐渐成为南方的政治、经济和文化中心。

江苏于1667年正式建省，"江苏"这一名称取自江宁府（今南京市）的"江"字和苏州府（今苏州市）的"苏"字。江苏简称"苏"，繁体字写为"蘇"，包含了草、鱼、禾三个部分，象征着江苏不仅有兴旺的渔业资源，还有肥沃的土地，适合农作物生长，自古以来就是"鱼米之乡"。

1842年，随着第一次鸦片战争的结束，中国被迫签订了《南京条约》。这一事件标志着中国近代史的开端，也促使江苏地区逐渐成为东西方文化交流与碰撞的前沿。中华

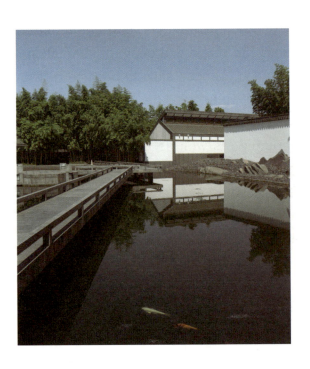

preservation and innovation. Over the years, it has garnered attention and exerted a positive influence at home and abroad. Leveraging its rich historical heritage and dynamic modernity, the province actively engages in global economic cooperation, cultural exchanges, and the integration of global industrial chains and innovation chains. Additionally, it is committed to establishing a sustainable and environmentally friendly development model in order to attract global partners and promote mutual growth for a brighter future.

## II. History and Culture

### 1. Development

As far back as the late Neolithic period, there were traces of human activities in Jiangsu and its surrounding areas. It was the central region for the two big vassal states of Wu and Yue during the Spring and Autumn Period. In 221 BC, when Qin Shihuang (the first emperor of China) unified the six states to found the Qin Dynasty, Jiangsu fell under the jurisdiction of Yangzhou County in the Qin administrative divisions. With the rise and fall of successive dynasties, Jiangsu gradually became the political, economic, and cultural hub of the south due to its advantageous geographical location, well-developed waterway network, and rich natural resources.

In 1667, Jiangsu was officially established as a province, and the name "Jiangsu" actually came from the two Chinese characters representing Nanjing and Suzhou. Jiangsu is commonly referred to as "Su". The traditional version of the Chinese character contains three parts: grass, fish, and grain, symbolizing the province's thriving fishery resources and fertile land as the "land of fish and rice", a moniker it has borne since ancient times.

The year 1842 marked a significant turning

人民共和国成立初期，为了适应国家发展的需要，江苏进行了重要的行政区划调整，撤销苏南、苏北行署区，设立了无锡、徐州、苏州、常州等多个专区作为地级行政单位。

1953年，确定南京为江苏的省会城市，江苏省人民政府也正式成立。此后，江苏的经济、文化和教育等领域发展迅速，成为中国东部地区最重要的省份之一。改革开放以后，江苏积极响应国家政策，进行了经济体制改革，并大力推行对外开放，出台了一系列吸引国内外投资的政策和措施，成为中国改革开放进程的重要推力。

1984年以来，苏南、苏中、苏北三大区域根据各自优势，实施了不同的发展战略。特别是自2010年起，在跨境电商领域，南京、苏州和常州等地相继成为跨境电子商务综合试验区，进一步推动了江苏的经济发展。随着扬子江城市群的崛起，江苏不断调整经济结构，着重发展高端制造业、战略性新兴产业和现代服务业，巩固了其在中国众多省份中的领先地位。与此同时，江苏非常重视传统文化的挖掘、保护传承和创新发展，积极促进文化与经济的融合，提升了文化产业的整体实力和影响力。

point for China as the First Opium War came to an end and China was forced to sign the Treaty of Nanjing. The event marked the start of China's modern historical period and pushed Jiangsu to the forefront of cultural exchanges and interactions between the East and the West. In the early years of the People's Republic of China, Jiangsu's administrative divisions underwent adjustment to meet the demands of national development. The southern and northern Jiangsu administrative districts were abolished, and cities such as Wuxi, Xuzhou, Suzhou, and Changzhou were established as prefecture-level administrative units.

In 1953, Nanjing was designated as the provincial capital of Jiangsu, and the Jiangsu Provincial People's Government was officially established. Since then, Jiangsu has experienced rapid growth in economy, culture, and education, before finally becoming a key province in eastern China. After the launch of reform and opening-up, Jiangsu actively responded to national policies by implementing economic structural reforms, promoting openness, and attracting domestic and foreign investments. These efforts have played a significant role in China's reform and opening-up process.

Since 1984, southern, central, and northern parts of Jiangsu have pursued distinct development strategies based on their respective advantages, particularly in the field of cross-border e-commerce, where Nanjing, Suzhou, and Changzhou have emerged as comprehensive pilot zones since 2010, further driving Jiangsu's economic development. With the emergence of the Yangtze River city clusters, Jiangsu has continuously adjusted its economic structure and focuses on high-end manufacturing, strategic emerging industries, and modern service sectors, in order to solidify its position as a leading province in

当前，江苏不仅经济持续快速增长，形成了以先进制造业为基础，高新技术产业与服务业等多元化发展的经济结构，还在文化教育与科技创新等方面蓬勃发展，塑造了江苏作为中国东部核心省份的领先地位，也在中国的现代化进程中发挥着不可或缺的重要作用。

## 2. 文化印记

在江苏这块历史悠久的土地上，曾发生过很多重要的历史事件，留下了极为丰富的文化遗产。其中，京杭大运河对江苏影响深远，这条水上通道从开凿到现在已经具有2500多年的历史，不仅是水利工程的奇迹，也极大地促进了江苏地区沿岸城市的经济发展和文化交流，是江苏历史不可或缺的一部分。大运河也影响了江苏许多城市的布局和建设，沿河形成了独特的水乡风貌。比如苏州的古典园林、扬州的盐商宅邸都与运河有着密不可分的关系。运河周边形成了独特的商业网络和市场体系，改变了人们的生活方式和社会结构，也促进了商人阶层等新兴社会阶层的出现和崛起。如今，作为南水北调东线工程的一部分，大运河仍发挥着极其重要的水资源调配功能，满足了江苏乃至华北地区的农业灌溉、工业生产、居民生活用水等多方面需求，同时也成为一项重要的文化旅游资源。

江苏除了举世闻名的园林艺术，还历来是培养文人墨客的摇篮。如施耐庵、唐寅

China. Simultaneously, Jiangsu places great importance on the preservation, promotion, inheritance, and innovative development of its traditional culture. It actively promotes the integration of culture and economy in an effort to enhance the overall strength and influence of the cultural industry.

In its continuous and rapid economic growth, Jiangsu has established an economic framework centered around advanced manufacturing and supported by the diversified development in high-tech and service industries. It has also thrived in culture, education, and scientific and technological innovation. As a result, Jiangsu has emerged as a prominent province in eastern China and played a crucial role in China's modernization efforts.

## 2. Cultural Impressions

Important historical events that took place in Jiangsu have left behind a remarkably rich cultural heritage. The Beijing-Hangzhou Grand Canal, with a history of over 2,500 years, has had a far-reaching impact on Jiangsu. This water passage not only showcases remarkable achievements in hydrological engineering but also has greatly contributed to the economic development and cultural exchanges of riverside cities in Jiangsu. Now, it is an indispensable part of Jiangsu's history. For example, the classical gardens in Suzhou and the salt merchants' mansions in Yangzhou are inextricably linked to the canal. Along the canal, unique commercial networks and market systems have been formed to shape people's lifestyles and social structures, and new social classes have emerged, such as merchants. Today, the canal continues to play a vital role as a part of the eastern route of the South-to-North Water Diversion Project. It effectively allocates water resources to meet the demands of agricultural irrigation, industrial production,

（唐伯虎）、郑板桥、徐霞客和朱自清等名家，都在江苏留下了深刻的足迹，他们在文学、绘画、教育等领域都作出了杰出贡献，丰富了江苏的文化底蕴。此外，江苏还保留着大量传统民间艺术和丰富多样的音乐表演艺术形式，如扬州剪纸、惠山泥塑、漆器、南京大鼓、苏州评弹等。这些独特的文化表现形式不仅富有地方特色，更是世代江苏人民智慧结晶和创造精神的体现，深入了解并传承这些宝贵的文化遗产，能帮助我们更好地了解江苏的悠久历史和人文风貌。

### 3. 旅游资源

江苏拥有丰富的旅游资源，包括自然景观和人文景观。江苏有三大旅游区：以太湖风光和古典园林等著称的太湖风景名胜旅游区；包括南京、扬州、镇江和南通的长江风景名胜旅游区，以造型生动的六朝陵墓石刻，宏伟浩荡的长江和近现代革命纪念地为特色；包括徐州、连云港、淮安和盐城在内的徐淮风景名胜旅游区，特色在于自然山水和历史古迹。这些旅游区凭借着悠久历史和深厚的文化底蕴吸引了众多国内外游客。

此外，江苏还有许多古色古香的古镇和村落，如周庄、同里、陆巷古村、明月湾村

residential water supply, etc. in Jiangsu and even northern China. Meanwhile, it is an important site of cultural tourism that attracts visitors from around the world.

In addition to its world-renowned classical gardens, Jiangsu has also been a cradle for intellectuals and artists. Shi Nai'an, Tang Yin (Tang Bohu), Zheng Banqiao, Xu Xiake, and Zhu Ziqing, all big names in literature, painting, and education, lived in Jiangsu for a time and left a lasting impact on Jiangsu's cultural heritage. The province boasts a wide array of traditional folk arts, as well as a diverse range of musical and performing arts, including Yangzhou paper-cutting, Huishan clay sculpture, lacquerware, Nanjing drums, and Suzhou Pingtan, which help to express Jiangsu's local characteristics and show the wisdom and creative spirit of generations of people.

### 3. Tourism Resources

Jiangsu is endowed with rich tourism resources, including both natural scenic spots and cultural attractions. The province is home to three large tourist areas: the Taihu Lake Scenic Area, famous for its beautiful views and classical gardens; the Yangtze River Scenic Area, including Nanjing, Yangzhou, Zhenjiang, and Nantong, famous for intricate stone carvings, scenery of the magnificent Yangtze River, and modern revolutionary memorial sites; and the Xuhuai Scenic Area, including Xuzhou, Lianyungang, Huai'an and Yancheng, famous for natural landscapes and historical monuments. The historical and cultural heritage and stunning natural scenery of these tourist areas are an irresistible attraction for domestic and international tourists.

In addition, Jiangsu boasts a number of charming ancient towns and villages, such as Zhouzhuang, Tongli, Luxiang, and Mingyuewan,

等。这些地方完好保存着古朴的建筑风格和传统的生活方式，让游客沉浸在江南古韵之中。江苏的美食同样令人向往，精致的淮扬菜、南京的盐水鸭和扬州的炒饭等，每一道都吸引着无数美食爱好者前来品尝。

江苏以其悠久的历史文化、多姿多彩的自然风光、丰富的地方美食和完善的旅游服务设施，成为独具魅力的旅游目的地。无论是文化追寻者、自然爱好者还是美食品尝者，都可以在江苏拥有令人难忘的旅行体验。

## 三、经济科技

### 1. 经济腾飞

2023年，江苏的地区生产总值稳步增长，达到了12.82万亿元，同比增长5.8%，在全国范围内排名第二，仅次于广东省。省内地区生产总值达万亿的城市增加到5个，分别为苏州、南京、无锡、南通及常州。

2023年，江苏的粮食总产量759.5亿斤，创造了新的纪录。进出口总值5.52万亿元，实际使用外资规模保持全国首位。制造业高质量发展指数达91.9，居全国第一，社

where ancient architectural styles and traditional ways of life have been preserved, so that visitors can have an opportunity to experience the quaint charm of Jiangnan (south of the Yangtze River). Jiangsu's cuisine is equally desirable, as gourmets flock to the province for the exquisite local dishes such as salted duck from Nanjing and fried rice from Yangzhou.

Jiangsu stands out as a distinctive tourist destination due to its extensive history, vibrant culture, picturesque natural landscapes, diverse local dishes, and top-notch tourist amenities. Whether you are interested in exploring culture, enjoying nature, or indulging in local cuisine, Jiangsu promises an unforgettable travel adventure.

## III. Economy and Technology

### 1. Economic Takeoff

In 2023, Jiangsu's gross domestic product (GDP) experienced a steady growth and reached 12.82 trillion yuan, registering a 5.8% increase from the previous year and ranking second in the country behind Guangdong Province. The number of cities with a GDP of one trillion yuan in the province has increased to five, namely Suzhou, Nanjing, Wuxi, Nantong, and Changzhou.

The province's total grain output for 2023 was 75.95 billion tons, setting a new record. The province recorded a total import and export value of 5.52 trillion yuan, and kept its position as the top recipient of foreign investment in the country. The manufacturing industry in Jiangsu achieved a high-quality development index of 91.9, ranking first in the country, while the total retail sales of consumer goods ranked second in the nation. Additionally, all the 13 prefecture-level cities in Jiangsu were recognized as top 100 national cities in advanced manufacturing.

Jiangsu highlights a diversified economic

会消费品零售总额居全国第二。13个设区市全部入选国家先进制造业百强市。

江苏的经济产业发展多样化，尤其是制造业，在全国长期处于领先地位。江苏制造业的优势在于其持续的创新能力和产业升级转型。同时，在新能源和智能制造等方面，江苏也取得了显著进展。光伏产业更是在全球处于领先地位。生物医药、高端装备、新材料等战略性新兴产业的蓬勃发展，进一步丰富了江苏的产业生态。政府正在积极推动新兴产业的发展，计划到2025年初步形成"10+X"未来产业体系。

江苏的经济呈现出产业结构持续优化、新兴产业快速崛起、服务业迅速发展的健康发展态势。

### 2. 科技经纬

江苏在科技创新领域持续发力，发展质量与效益不断提升。2023年，江苏全社会研究与试验发展活动经费支出占省内地区生产总值达3.2%，万人发明专利拥有量达61.5件，连续8年在全国各省区中排名第一。江

and industrial development, especially in the manufacturing industry, which has long held the leading position in the country. The advantage of Jiangsu's manufacturing industry lies in the continuous innovation and the industrial upgrading and transformation. At the same time, Jiangsu has seen significant progress in new energy and intelligent manufacturing, while its photovoltaic industry takes a leading position in the world. The province's industrial landscape has been further shaped by the rapid growth of strategic emerging sectors such as biopharmaceuticals, high-end equipment, and new materials. The provincial government is actively promoting the development of these industries and aims to establish a "10+X" future industrial system composed of 10 emerging industries and a group of cutting-edge industries by 2025.

Jiangsu's economy has demonstrated a positive growth trajectory characterized by a consistent focus on industrial structure improvement, a rapid surge in emerging industries, and significant advancements in the service sector.

### 2. Scientific and Technological Innovation

Jiangsu Province continues to make efforts in the field of scientific and technological innovation, and sees the improvement in the quality and efficiency of development. In 2023, Jiangsu's expenditure on research and experimental development (R&D) activities accounted for 3.2% of its regional GDP, and the number of invention patents per 10,000 people reached 61.5, ranking first among all provinces and autonomous regions in the country for 8 consecutive years. Jiangsu has achieved significant milestones in cutting-edge fields: the Zijinshan Laboratory of Network Communication and Security is included in the national laboratory strategic plan; the

苏在多个科技前沿领域取得了令人瞩目的成果，如网络通信与安全紫金山实验室被纳入国家实验室战略布局；江苏太湖实验室牵头研发的"奋斗者"号潜水器完成了极限深潜任务；高效率全钙钛矿叠层电池技术入选中国科学十大进展。

此外，江苏拥有科技型中小企业9.4万家；苏州实验室总部基地开工建设；全省的国家重点实验室总数已达31个，新获评国家专精特新"小巨人"企业795家，这两项数量均位列全国第一。截至2023年年底，江苏的高新技术企业超过5.1万家，人才总量超1560万人，形成了强大的科技创新人才支持体系，为持续推动高质量的科技创新发展提供了有力的智力资源保障。

江苏将进一步推进科技管理职能的改革，让科研机构、科研工作者有更多的自主权，继续加大自主培养高层次创新人才的力度，为我国高水平科技自立自强提供人才支持。

"Fendouzhe" (Striver) submersible, developed by the Jiangsu Taihu Laboratory, successfully completed extreme deep diving missions; the high-efficiency all-perovskite tandem cell technology is recognized as one of China's top 10 scientific advances.

Additionally, Jiangsu boasts 94,000 small and medium-sized technological enterprises. The base for laboratory headquarters has recently started construction in Suzhou. Jiangsu is home to 31 national key laboratories and 795 newly recognized "little giant" enterprises, ranking first in the country on both counts. Over 51,000 high-tech enterprises with an employment of more than 15.6 million help to build a robust support system for scientific and technological innovation in Jiangsu and to provide the intellectual resources for the high-quality development in scientific and technological innovation.

Jiangsu aims to encourage the reform of science and technology management, so that research institutions and workers can enjoy more autonomy. The focus will be on nurturing high-level, innovative talents through independent training programs, thereby contributing to China's self-reliance in scientific and technological advancements.

## IV. Social Welfare

In Jiangsu Province, the well-being of the people is always prioritized, and ensuring people's livelihood through social welfare has been a policy highlight. The province is dedicated to fulfilling the basic living requirements of its residents, enhancing their quality of life, and contributing to the overall advancement of the population. These efforts serve as a strong basis for driving forward Chinese-style modernization.

## 四、社会民生

江苏始终坚持"以人民为中心"的价值导向，高度重视社会福利和民生保障，致力于满足人民的基本生活需求，提升人民的生活质量，提高人口整体素质，为推进中国式现代化建设奠定了坚实基础。

在医疗保障方面，江苏建立了全覆盖的基本医疗保险制度，包括城镇职工基本医疗保险和城乡居民基本医疗保险，确保每位居民都能享有基本的医疗服务保障。

在养老保险方面，江苏积极推动进一步改革，不仅建立了城乡居民基本养老保险体系，还不断完善个人账户制度。同时，加大对养老服务设施建设的投入，提供一系列养老服务和救助措施，形成了综合的养老保障体系，确保老年人安享晚年。

除了医疗和养老等焦点问题，江苏也积极应对教育、就业、住房等领域的挑战，努力创造就业创业机会，并出台多项住房保障政策。这些举措旨在缩小城乡和不同群体之间的福利差距，促进社会公平和稳定发展。同时，江苏不断完善终身教育体系，加强现代医疗卫生服务网络，推进生态文明建设和人文环境优化，以更好地适应和满足人民日益多元化的需求。

In terms of healthcare, a comprehensive system of basic medical insurance has been established in the province. This system includes basic medical insurance for urban employees, basic medical insurance for urban and rural residents. It aims to provide every resident with access to essential medical services.

Through active reform in endowment insurance, a basic endowment insurance system for both urban and rural residents has been established in Jiangsu, while the personal account system has seen continual improvement. Investments in the development of eldercare facilities have been increased and a range of services and relief measures have been provided to ensure a comprehensive old-age safety net that allows older members of society to enjoy their retirement years.

In addition to key issues such as healthcare and eldercare, various challenges in education, employment, and housing have been addressed with systematic measures. Employment and entrepreneurship opportunities have been created and housing security policies have been introduced. These measures aim to bridge the gap in social welfare between urban and rural areas and between different social groups, so that the society may develop in a just and stable way. The province has continued to improve its lifelong education system, strengthen its modern medical and health service network, and promote the construction of ecological civilization and a humanistic environment in order to meet the evolving needs of its residents.

## 五、当代江苏

### 1. 现代化建设

自古以来，江苏便是中国经济与文化都非常繁荣的地区。改革开放以来，江苏更是充分利用自身地域优势，在推进现代化进程与城市发展中都取得了显著成就，展现出蓬勃的活力和广阔的发展前景。

（一）经济增长

丰富的自然资源、优越的地理位置为江苏的经济发展提供了良好的基础。近年来，江苏的国内生产总值一直保持全国第二。先进制造业、高新技术产业和现代服务业快速发展。随着新一代信息技术与制造业的深度融合，江苏的工业体系正经历智能化升级，为经济的高质量发展开辟了新的路径。机械制造、电子信息、钢铁、纺织等，江苏在多个支柱产业上都展现了明显的竞争优势。近年来，人工智能、生物医药等新兴战略产业的持续壮大更是为江苏的经济发展按下了"加速键"。

（二）城市建设

随着经济的飞速发展，江苏的城市建设也发生了日新月异的变化。交通网络更加完善，高速公路、铁路、水运和航运构成了立体化的交通体系，提供了方便快捷的出行方

## V. Jiangsu Today

### 1. Modernization

Throughout history, Jiangsu has stood out as a hub of economic and cultural prosperity in China. Since the reform and opening-up, taking advantage of its strategic location, Jiangsu has excelled in advancing modernization and urban growth, a process characterized by great vitality and promising development opportunities.

(1) Economic Growth

Jiangsu's abundant natural resources and strategic geographical location provide a good foundation for its economic development and have made it the second leading province in China in terms of GDP in recent years. The province's focus on advanced manufacturing, high-tech industries, and modern services has propelled its economic development. While a new generation of information technology is being integrated with traditional industries, the industrial system of Jiangsu experiences an intelligent upgrade. The province's competitive advantages are evident in key industries such as machinery manufacturing, electronic information, steel, and textiles. In recent years, the growth of emerging sectors like artificial intelligence and biopharmaceuticals further bolster Jiangsu's economic progress.

(2) Urban Construction

This sector is experiencing significant transformations due to the rapid growth of the economy. The province's transportation infrastructure has become more advanced, as well-developed highways, railways, water routes and shipping routes form a comprehensive transportation system. The convenient travel helps to boost economic interactions and cultural exchanges inside and outside the province. In particular, the introduction of high-speed rail has further enhanced connectivity between Jiangsu and other provinces.

式，极大促进了省内外的经济互动和人文交流。特别是高铁的开通，使江苏与其他地区的联系更加紧密。

江苏的城市面貌焕然一新，环境更加优美、城市规划更加科学化、城市管理更加人性化，也更加注重生态平衡和可持续发展。近年来，通过应用人工智能、大数据和物联网等高科技手段，城市管理效率显著提高，公共服务水平更加贴心、高效。这不仅增强了城市综合竞争力，还极大地提升了民众生活的便利性和幸福感，推动了江苏在智慧城市建设和现代化城市治理方面更上一个台阶。

在快速发展经济的同时，江苏注重生态文明建设，践行绿色发展理念。习近平总书记的指示为江苏的绿色发展指明了方向。通过实施一系列生态环境治理项目，江苏的水环境和空气质量得到了显著改善，长江沿岸地区焕发新生，使江苏的城市更加美丽宜居。

（三）教育投入

江苏历来重视教育事业的发展，作为中国教育资源大省，江苏拥有南京大学、东南大学等众多知名高等院校。通过不断加大对教育的投入、优化教育资源配置、加强师资队伍培养等措施，江苏的教育质量不断提升，确保教育公平，为社会输送了大量高素质人才。

Cities in Jiangsu have taken on a new look, with beautiful environments, scientific urban planning, improved urban management practices, and a focus on ecological balance and sustainable development. In recent years, thanks to the use of high technology such as artificial intelligence, big data, and the Internet, the urban management sees great improvement and the public services become more personalized and efficient. As a result, cities in Jiangsu boast all-round competitiveness, residents enjoy a convenient and happy life, and the province goes up a level in smart city development and modern urban governance.

While Jiangsu's economy is in rapid development, much emphasis has been put on ecological protection and "green development" practices under CPC Secretary General Xi Jinping's instructions. After the completion of a series of ecological projects, the qualities of water and air see considerable improvement, the areas along the Yangtze River have been revitalized, and the cities of Jiangsu become more beautiful and livable.

(3) Investment in Education

The development of education has always been a top priority in Jiangsu. The province boasts some of China's top educational resources, including prestigious higher education institutions such as Nanjing University and Southeast University. Through continued investment in education, effective distribution of educational resources, and enhanced teacher training, Jiangsu has significantly improved the overall quality and equality in education. As a result, a large number of high quality talents have been produced for the betterment of the society.

## 2. 发展潜力

江苏是中国经济最发达的省份之一，凭借坚实的产业基础、强大的经济实力、丰富的科教资源和优越的地理环境，不仅在国内经济格局中占据重要的地位，而且在教育、公共卫生和社会保障等领域也展现出领先全国的水平。江苏致力于产业转型升级，通过发展先进制造业、服务业和新兴产业，提升产业附加值和国际竞争力，同时，积极推进绿色低碳发展，注重环境保护和可持续发展，有望成为中国绿色发展的示范区域。

此外，江苏拥有优良的港口和发达的交通网络，对外贸易发展潜力巨大。在此基础上，江苏坚持经济发展、科技创新和开放合作，积极推动文化产业发展，更好满足居民的物质和精神文化需求，不断增强居民的获得感、幸福感和安全感。

展望未来，江苏将继续坚持以人民为中心，全面对外开放合作，促进区域协调发展，加大人才引进和培养力度，开辟新的发展领域和增长点，推动绿色低碳转型及农业农村现代化建设，同时大力推动文化事业的发展。通过不断的探索与创新，江苏有望将自身打造成中国东部地区的重要经济枢纽。

## 2. Development Potential

As one of the most economically developed provinces in China, Jiangsu is celebrated for its robust industrial base, economic prowess, ample scientific and educational resources, and favorable geographical conditions. It plays a significant role in the national economic landscape and excels in providing high-quality education, public health services, and social welfare. The province is committed to industrial transformation and upgrading by increasing industrial added value and global competitiveness through the development of advanced manufacturing, services, and emerging industries, while prioritizing green and low-carbon growth, emphasizing environmental conservation and sustainable development, and aiming to be a model for eco-friendly development in China.

Furthermore, excellent ports and a well-developed transportation network make Jiangsu an ideal hub for developing international trade. Building upon this foundation, the province is committed to fostering economic growth, promoting scientific and technological innovation, opening up for cooperation, and actively supporting the development of cultural industries to meet the diverse material and spiritual needs of its residents, thereby enhancing their overall well-being and sense of contentment.

Looking to the future, Jiangsu will continue to open up for comprehensive cooperation based on the human-oriented ideals, promote coordinated regional development, attract and nurture talents, explore new growth opportunities, and promote green and low-carbon transformation, agricultural and rural modernization, and cultural development. Through continuous exploration and innovation, Jiangsu aims to establish itself as a prominent economic hub in eastern China.

## 练习

### 一、判断题

1. 江苏位于中国的西部地区。　☐

2. 江苏的自然地理特点是以丘陵和山地为主。　☐

3. 长江不流经江苏省。　☐

4. 江苏省素有"鱼米之乡"的美称，是中国最富裕的省份之一。　☐

5. 江苏以淮扬菜闻名。　☐

6. 江苏省拥有世界一流的高等教育机构，如南开大学、东南大学、苏州大学、江苏大学等。　☐

7. 2023年江苏省的地区生产总值（GDP）达到了12.82万亿元，位居全国第一。　☐

8. 地区生产总值（GDP）达到万亿的城市有苏州、南京、无锡、南通、常州。　☐

9. 江苏还保留着大量的传统民间艺术，如剪纸、刺绣、泥塑、漆器、篆刻等。　☐

10. 机械制造、电子、钢铁、纺织等都是江苏的优势产业。　☐

### 二、思考题

1. 除了长江和苏北平原，江苏还有哪些地理特征？

3. 江苏有哪些音乐表演形式？

4. 请说说江苏省医疗保障制度的特点。

5. 除了医疗保障和养老保险，你知道江苏省还有哪些社会福利政策吗？

6. 江苏的什么总产量创造了新的记录？

7. 在未来产业方面，江苏计划到2025年初步形成什么样的未来产业体系？

三、拓展题

1. 根据江苏的地理特点，你认为该地区能发展哪些经济产业？

2. 介绍一下江苏著名的文化遗产和建筑风格。选取其中一个，介绍一下它的特点和重要性。

3. 请介绍一位与江苏有关的重要文化人物。

4. 请简要介绍江苏的一项非物质文化遗产。

5. 除了南京，你知道江苏还有哪些值得一游的城市或景点？

6. 向同学们介绍自己家乡的经济发展状况与特点。

7. 你认为江苏在社会福利和民生保障方面还有哪些可以改进的地方？

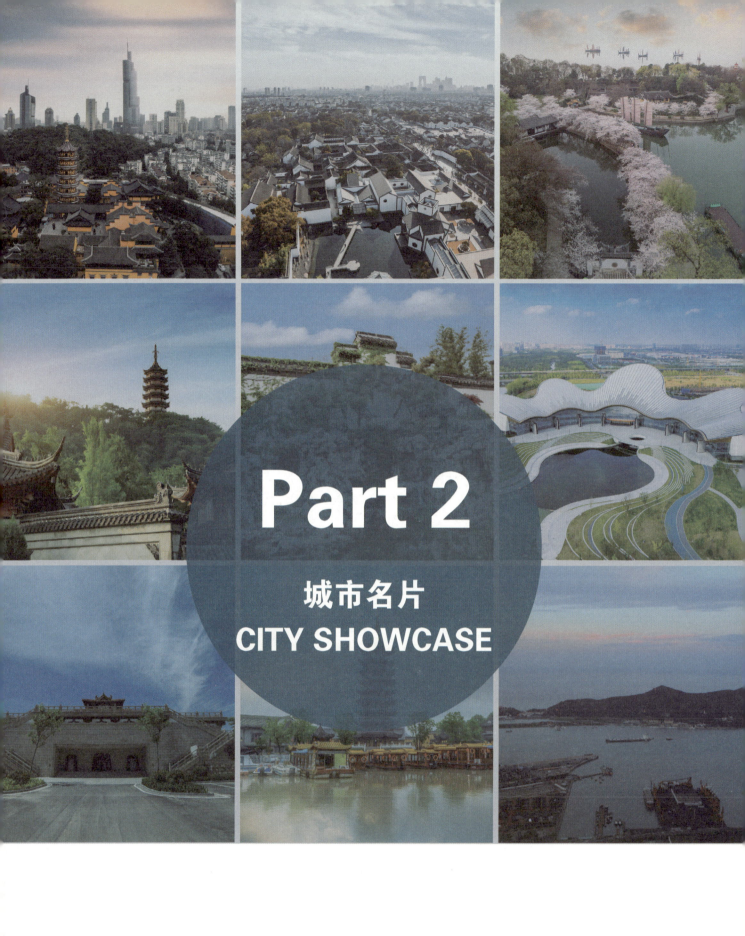

Part 2

城市名片
CITY SHOWCASE

# Chapter 1

南京

NANJING

第一章

六 / 朝 / 古 / 都
Ancient Capital of the Six Dynasties

南京简称"宁",是江苏的省会,城市常住人口接近1000万,集省会城市、中心城市和特大城市三重身份于一身,也是全国重要的科研教育基地和综合交通枢纽。

## 一、城市概况

### 1. 地理环境

南京位于江苏西南部、长江下游，奔腾的长江水穿城而过。南京是中国东部地区重要的中心城市，历史上一直有"东南第一重镇"之称。

南京东、南、北三面环山，西临长江。城市内交错分布着平原与丘陵，河流和湖泊。最高山峰是位于南京东部郊区的紫金山，最大的城市湖泊是玄武湖，流经主城区的秦淮河被称为南京的母亲河。

南京的气候特点是四季分明，雨水充沛。春季温暖湿润，秋季凉爽宜人，春季和秋季是这座城市最舒适的季节；南京的夏季非常炎热，但遍布全城的高大梧桐树可以为人们带来绿荫和清凉；冬季气温一般在2～10℃，偶尔下雪，雪后的南京城银装素裹，别有风情。

南京是中国最有名的园林城市之一，绿树成荫，繁花似锦，环境优美。南京还拥有许多独特的地貌，如江宁火山群、汤山温泉、溧水天生桥等。特别值得一提的是雨花石，这种带有美丽色彩和花纹的天然玛瑙石具有非常高的文化审美价值。

南京是首批国家历史文化名城和全国重点风景旅游城市。"江南佳丽地，金陵帝王州"是对南京这座城市的最好描述。

## I. Overview

### 1. Geographical Environment

Nanjing is located in the southwestern part of Jiangsu Province. It is situated by the lower reaches of the Yangtze River, whose rushing waters pass through the city. Nanjing is a key city in the eastern part of China, historically known as the "First Important Town in the Southeast".

Nanjing has mountains on its eastern, southern, and northern sides and bordered by the Yangtze River to the west. The city is interspersed with flat and hilly areas, as well as rivers and lakes. The highest mountain is the Zijin Mountain in the eastern suburb; the largest lake in the urban area is the Xuanwu Lake; the Qinhuai River, known as the mother river of Nanjing, flows through the downtown area.

Nanjing's climate is characterized by four distinct seasons and abundant rainfall. Spring is warm and humid, while autumn is cool and pleasant: these are the pleasant seasons. Summer in Nanjing is very hot, but the tall plane trees all over the city provide green shade. In winter, the temperature is generally between 2–10°C with occasional snow. After snowfall, Nanjing, blanketed by a glistening layer of white, has a unique charm.

Nanjing is one of the most famous garden cities in China. It features an exquisite natural environment filled with beautiful trees and blossoming flowers. Nanjing is also home to many unique landforms, such as the Jiangning Volcanic Cluster, the Tangshan Hot Spring and the Lishui Natural Bridge. The Rain Flower Stones, a kind of natural agate stones with beautiful colors and patterns, are a specialty of Nanjing with high cultural and aesthetic value.

Nanjing is one of the first group of national historical and cultural cities and an important

## 2. 城市变迁

南京是中国四大古都[1]之一，有长达50万年的人类活动史，将近2500年的建城史，以及大约450年的建都史。

修筑于2500多年前的"越城"，位于现今中华门外，被认为是南京建城史的起点，是南京城市文明的起源。

历史上，南京曾经是多个王朝或王国的都城。公元229年，东汉末年三国的东吴在南京建立都城，这是南京成为都城的开始。接着东晋，南北朝时期的宋、齐、梁、陈，连续在这里建都，前后共计320多年，因此南京被称为"六朝古都"。

南京在历史上曾经有过70多个名字或别称，如金陵、建康、石头城等。南京城市旧称之多，不仅在中国而且在世界上也属罕见。名称的繁多，表明南京这座城市经历了漫长的历史岁月和兴衰起伏。

## 3. 今日南京

南京地处长江黄金水道与京沪大动脉的交汇点，是中国重要的综合交通枢纽，与邻近的上海、杭州、苏州等城市一起，构成了长江三角洲核心城市群。

---

[1] 中国四大古都：西安、南京、洛阳和北京。
China's four great ancient capitals are Xi'an, Nanjing, Luoyang and Beijing.

---

tourist destination in China. It is best described as "a beautiful place south of the Yangtze River, an imperial state of Jinling".

## 2. Development

Nanjing is one of the four great ancient capitals[1] of China. It has a history of 500,000 years of human activity, nearly 2,500 years of urban history, and about 450 years as a capital city.

Built about 2,500 years ago, the Town of Yue, located outside the present-day Zhonghua Gate, is considered the starting point of Nanjing's urban history and the origin of the city's civilization.

Historically, Nanjing was the capital of several dynasties or kingdoms. In 229 A.D., Wu, one of the Three Kingdoms after the Eastern Han Dynasty, established its capital in Nanjing, marking the beginning of Nanjing's status as a capital city. Then, the Eastern Jin Dynasty and the four Southern and Northern Dynasties Song, Qi, Liang and Chen consecutively built their capitals here for a total of more than 320 years. This is why Nanjing is known as the "Ancient Capital of the Six Dynasties".

Nanjing has had more than seventy names or aliases, such as Jinling, Jiankang, and Stone City. This number of former names is rare not only in China but also in the world. The variety of names also shows that Nanjing has endured a long history of repeated rise and decline.

## 3. Nanjing Today

Located at the intersection of the golden waterway of the Yangtze River and the Beijing-Shanghai Railway, Nanjing is an essential comprehensive transportation hub in China, and together with the neighboring cities of Shanghai, Hangzhou, and Suzhou, it forms the core metropolitan cluster of the Yangtze River Delta.

Today, Nanjing has a strong cultural atmosphere and impressive educational

今天的南京文化气息浓厚，教育实力强劲，是全国重要的科研教育基地。发达的经济实力、优美的自然环境、现代化的城市布局、众多的历史文化遗迹，让南京这座历史名城充满了独特的魅力。

prowess, it is also an important scientific research hub in China. Thanks to its flourishing economy, beautiful environment, modern cityscape, and various historical and cultural relics the ancient city of Nanjing is reinvigorated.

## 二、文化印象

## II. Cultural Impressions

### 1. 美丽古都

南京是中华文明的重要发源地之一，在历史上长期是中国南方的政治、文化中心。南京的建城历史非常悠久，是著名的古代都城，也是中国四大古都中唯一位于长江流域的城市。在汉语里，带有"京"字的城市都有过作为都城的历史。但像南京这样，有6个古代王朝在此建都，并且累计时间长达300多年，是很少见的。

丰厚的文化积淀和独特的人文景观，是南京人最为自豪的古都气质。在南京，保存着许多重要的历史遗迹。位于钟山风景名胜区内的明孝陵，是世界文化遗产；城东中山门外高大威武的神兽——南朝石辟邪，是南京人最喜爱的城市标志；流传至今的老地名，乌衣巷、常府街、四望山、三步两桥，都蕴藏着丰富的历史典故。古时候的南京，城内的街道布局和功能区域划分，也是根据丘陵和河道的走向巧妙安排的。如今，行走在南京城中，常常有新旧时空穿越之感。第一次来到南京的人，沿着秦淮河，可以探访

### 1. A Beautiful Ancient Capital

Nanjing is one of the important birthplaces of Chinese civilization and has long been the political and cultural center of southern China. It is a famous ancient capital with a long history and the only one of the four ancient capitals of China to be located in the Yangtze River Basin. In Chinese, all cities with the name of Jing have a history as a capital. However, as is the case of Nanjing, it is rare for a city to have been the capital for over 300 years and for six ancient dynasties.

The abundance of rich culture and historical sites add to the ancient city's unique appeal, which is the pride and joy of the local Nanjing people. In Nanjing, many important historical sites have been well preserved. The Ming Xiaoling Mausoleum, located in the Zhongshan Scenic Spot, is a World Heritage Site. The tall and mighty "Bixie" stone beast statues from the Southern Dynasties, located outside the Zhongshan Gate on the east side of the city, are a city emblem cherished by the people of Nanjing. History resonates in the old place

弯曲幽深的古街小巷；登上明城墙，可以眺望湖山环绕的城市风光。

中国三大博物馆①之一的南京博物院中，众多精美、珍贵的文物让人们深刻地感受到，"六朝古都"不只是一个历史概念。而今天的南京，正在为历史文化名城的高质量发展探路，也力求向世界展示历史底蕴与时代潮流相结合的"美丽古都"。

### 2. 博爱之都

如果说"美丽"是南京的颜值，"博爱"就是南京的内核。"博爱"是中国民主革命的伟大先驱孙中山先生提出的理念。在钟山风景区中山陵的入口处，有一座高大的牌坊"博爱坊"，上面就刻着孙中山先生手书的这两个大字。

---

① 中国三大博物馆：故宫博物院、南京博物院和台北故宫博物院。
The three biggest museums in China: the Beijing Palace Museum, the Nanjing Museum and the Taipei Palace Museum.

names handed down through generations, such as the Lane of Black Garments, the Street of the Chang's Residence, the Stone City, the Mountain with Four Views, and the Two Bridges in Three Step. In ancient Nanjing, the layout of the streets and the division of functional zones within the city were skillfully arranged according to the directions of the hills and rivers. Nowadays, walking in Nanjing, you often have a sense of time travel between the old and the new. If you come to Nanjing for the first time, travelling along the Qinhuai River, you can explore the deep, winding ancient streets and alleys, or you can climb the Ming City Wall and look out over the cityscape surrounded by lakes and hills.

The Nanjing Museum, one of the three biggest museums in China[1], has many exquisite and precious cultural artefacts, which help visitors understand that the "Ancient Capital of the Six Dynasties" is not just a historical concept. Today, while protecting cultural relics and architecture, Nanjing focuses on upgrading its urban functions, exploring ways for high-quality development as a historical and cultural city, and striving to show the world a "beautiful ancient capital" that combines historical heritage with current trends.

### 2. The City of Fraternity

If "beauty" is the outward appearance of Nanjing, then "fraternity" is the inner core. The concept of "fraternity" was put forward by Dr. Sun Yat-sen, the great pioneer of China's democratic revolution. In fact, the word "Fraternity" written by Dr. Sun Yat-sen himself is engraved on a tall arch at the entrance of the Sun Yat-sen Mausoleum in the Zhongshan Scenic Area.

Fraternity is the embodiment of the Chinese values since ancient times. It emphasizes the harmony and cooperation between people,

博爱，是中国人自古以来价值观的体现，不仅强调人与人之间的和谐互助，还将视野投向整个社会和大自然，代表着"天下为公"的思想和构建人类命运共同体的愿望。"博爱"象征着南京博大、包容的城市文化和市民精神。南京是一座拥有"大爱"的城市。"博爱之都"由一个个实实在在的文明细节所组成。南京人真诚友善，热心公益，积极参加志愿服务，注册志愿者超300万人，彰显着市民的文明素养；市政建设坚持"以人为本"，努力打造出行方便的无障碍城市,为人们的交通、购物、游览提供便利；截至2023年，南京已与23个国际城市缔结友好城市关系，在经贸、文化、教育等方面开展全方位的交流合作，国际"朋友圈"越来越壮大。

山水城林，人文历史，富裕便利，博爱包容，把南京塑造成了中国最具幸福感的宜居城市。

and envisions society and nature as a whole, representing the idea of "the whole world as one community" and the aspiration for "a community with a shared future for humanity". Fraternity symbolizes the extensive and inclusive urban culture and civic spirit of Nanjing, a city of great love. The "city of fraternity" is built on a foundation of many tangible acts of civility. The people of Nanjing are sincere and friendly, enthusiastic about public welfare, and active in volunteer services. There are more than 3 million registered volunteers in Nanjing, and the city's municipal construction adheres to a people-oriented philosophy, striving to build a barrier-free city with easy accessibility to facilitate people's transportation, shopping, and sightseeing. As of 2023, Nanjing has entered into sister-city relationships with 23 foreign cities and has carried out comprehensive exchanges and cooperation in such areas as economy, trade, culture, and education, growing its international "circle of friends".

The landscape and city greenery, humanistic culture and history, affluence and convenience, and fraternity and inclusivity have shaped Nanjing into one of China's happiest and most livable cities.

## 三、教育交流

### 1. 高等教育概况

南京是中国重要的科教中心，高等教育资源丰富，高校实力强劲，是除了北京、上海以外的中国"高教第三城"。

南京拥有不同办学层次、不同办学类型的高校共51所，专业覆盖面很广，几乎包含了所有的学科和专业；办学特色鲜明，科研实力强劲，在国内外有着广泛的影响力和很高的声誉。每年5月20日，南京有7所高校共同庆祝生日。这些高校都拥有一个共同的源头——国立中央大学。该大学曾经是亚洲排名第一的大学，1949年更名为国立南京大学、南京大学，1952年拆分、重组后，形成了现在的7所高校。

南京是国际学生理想的求学地，入选QS"全球最佳留学城市"前一百强。在南京学习的国际学生，占江苏国际学生总人数的一半以上，"一带一路"共建国家的国际学生人数持续增加。丰富的教育资源、深厚的文化底蕴、便捷的交通、适宜的居住环境、包容的城市氛围，都是吸引国际学生的重要因素。南京积极搭建国际青年交流平台，每年组织多项国际交流活动，打造了多条"外国友人看南京"国际交流参访路线，路线聚焦人文历史、科技创新、绿色生态、和平友好、社会治理等主题，展现真实、立体、全面的南京形象。

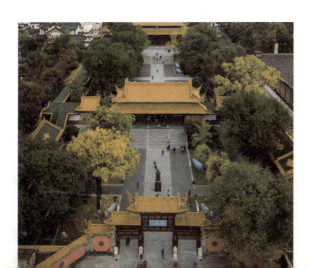

## III. Education and International Exchanges

### 1. Overview of Higher Education

Nanjing is an important hub of science and education in China, rich in higher education resources and influential universities, and is ranked "third city of higher education" in China, only behind Beijing and Shanghai.

Nanjing has a total of 51 higher education institutions of different levels and types, with a comprehensive coverage of specialties, including almost all disciplines and majors. Nanjing's higher education institutions have distinctive schooling traditions and are strong in scientific research, hence they enjoy great influence and an outstanding reputation nationally and even worldwide. Every year on May 20th, seven colleges and universities in Nanjing celebrate their shared birthday. These colleges and universities all share a common origin: National Central University. Once the top-ranking university in Asia, National Central University was renamed National Nanjing University and Nanjing University in 1949. In 1952, it was split and reorganized to form the current seven colleges and universities.

Nanjing is an ideal place for international students to study in China, ranking in the QS Top 100 "World's Best Destinations for Students". International students studying in Nanjing account for more than half of the total number of international students in Jiangsu Province, and the number of international students from "Belt and Road" countries continues to increase. The abundant educational resources, rich cultural heritage, convenient transportation, suitable living environment and tolerant city atmosphere of Nanjing attract international students. Nanjing is actively building a platform for international

## 2. 高校介绍

### 1）南京大学

南京大学（www.nju.edu.cn）是南京最著名的高校，是中国教育部直属的重点综合性大学。它的前身是创建于1902年的三江师范学堂，这是中国办学历史悠久的高校之一。南京大学为国家富强和科技进步作出了重要贡献。学校目前拥有仙林、鼓楼、浦口、苏州4个校区，有40个院系，学科覆盖文理工医，本、硕、博学生共4万余人，其中国际学生1300多人。

南京大学是开展国际交流与合作最活跃的中国大学之一，与世界众多一流大学和高水平科研机构建立了紧密的协作关系。其中，南京大学－约翰斯·霍普金斯大学中美文化研究中心是中国改革开放以后最早实施的高等教育国际合作长期项目之一，至今已成功运行了30多年，为中美文化交流培养了众多骨干人才，在海内外产生了巨大的影响。

youth exchange programs by organizing several international exchange activities annually and creating a number of international exchange visits called "Foreign Friends See Nanjing", which aim to show an accurate and comprehensive image of Nanjing on the themes of humanities and history, science and technological innovation, green ecology, peace and friendship, and social governance.

## 2. Introduction to Universities

### 1) Nanjing University

Nanjing University (www.nju.edu.cn), the most famous university in Nanjing, is a key comprehensive university directly under the Ministry of Education of the People's Republic of China. Its predecessor, the Sanjiang Normal School founded in 1902, is one of the oldest universities in China. In more than a century of existence, Nanjing University has made important contributions to the country's growth and prosperity as well as scientific and technological progress. Nanjing University currently has four campuses (Xianlin, Gulou, Pukou, and Suzhou), 40 departments covering liberal arts, science, technology and medicine, and over 40,000 Bachelor's, Master's and PhD students, including more than 1,300 international students.

Nanjing University is active in international exchange and cooperation, establishing close collaborative relationships with many of the world's leading universities and high-level research institutions. Among them, Nanjing University-Johns Hopkins University Center for Chinese and American Cultural Studies, one of the earliest long-term projects of international cooperation in higher education after China's reform and opening-up, has been running for more than 30 years and produced many talented people for important positions in the China-US cultural exchanges and having

a significant impact both domestically and internationally.

Nanjing University is also one of the earliest universities in China to provide education for international students. With a wealth of experience in international student education and excellent operational conditions, Nanjing University has educated tens of thousands of international students from more than 100 countries and regions, and many of its global alumni have been active in various fields, such as in academia, public service and non-governmental organizations. The School of Overseas Education (SOE), the administrative department for international students, is located on the Gulou Campus of Nanjing University, adjacent to the "International Youth Art District" on Jinyin Street.

### 2) Southeast University

Southeast University (SEU, www.seu. edu.cn) is a comprehensive, research-oriented university directly under the Ministry of Education of the People's Republic of China and co-built with Jiangsu Province. Its strong suit is engineering. It shares a common origin with Nanjing University, both formerly known as the Sanjiang Normal School. Southeast University currently has five campuses (Sipailou, Jiulonghu, Dingjiaqiao, Wuxi and Suzhou), 34 departments, over 40,000 Bachelor's, Master's and PhD students, including nearly 2,000 international students. Among the many disciplines at Southeast University, Engineering, Computer Science, Material Science and Chemistry rank among the top in the world.

Adhering to the principle of "honoring the world with science and serving the country with talents", Southeast University boasts an outstanding reputation in education and teaching and is an essential base for scientific

南京大学也是中国最早开展国际学生教育的高校之一，有着丰富的来华留学教育经验和良好的办学条件，已培养了来自100多个国家和地区的数万名国际学生，许多校友活跃在全世界的学术界、公共服务和非政府组织等各个舞台。国际学生的管理部门海外教育学院位于南京大学鼓楼校区，紧邻金银街"国际青年艺术街区"。

### 2）东南大学

东南大学（www.seu.edu.cn）与南京大学同出一源，前身也为三江师范学堂，是直属中国教育部并与江苏省共建的，以工科为主要特色的综合性、研究型大学。东南大学目前拥有四牌楼、九龙湖、丁家桥、无锡、苏州5个校区，有34个院系，本、硕、博学生4万余人，其中在校国际学生近2000人。在东南大学的众多学科中，工程学、计算机科学、材料科学和化学均位居世界前列。

东南大学坚持"以科学名世、以人才报国"，不仅教育教学声誉卓著，而且是中国科学技术研究的重要基地。学校坚持产学研相结合，获得了多项国家级科技奖项，参与了"探月计划""三峡工程"、港珠澳大桥、高铁技术等多项国家级重大工程项目。学校的中国发明专利申请、专利授权数量位列中国高校第二位，有效发明专利位列中国高校第三位。

东南大学与美国麻省理工学院、英国剑桥大学、德国慕尼黑大学、法国巴黎高科等全球18个国家或地区的47所世界一流大学和高水平研究机构建立了紧密的合作关系。2017年，东南大学发起成立了"中英大学工程教育与研究联盟"，这是中国与英国合作建立的首个以工程教育与研究为特色的大学联盟。此外，学校还与澳大利亚蒙纳士大学合作建立了东南大学—蒙纳士大学苏州联合研究生院，这是中国教育部批准的我国第一所中外联合研究生院。

and technological research in China. The university has strived for a combination of industry, academia and research and has won several national scientific and technological awards, and participated in major national projects such as the Moon Exploration Program, the Three Gorges Project, the Hong Kong-Zhuhai-Macao Bridge, and the high-speed rail technology. Southeast University ranks second among Chinese universities for the number of patents applied for and granted, and third among Chinese universities for the number of patents successfully developed.

Southeast University has established close cooperative relationships with 47 world-class universities and high-level research institutes from 18 countries and regions, including the Massachusetts Institute of Technology (MIT) in the United States, the University of Cambridge in the United Kingdom, the University of Munich in Germany, and the Paris Institute of Technology in France. In 2017, Southeast University initiated the establishment of the "Sino-British University Alliance for Engineering Education and Research", the first university alliance featuring engineering education and research between China and the United Kingdom. The university also cooperates with Monash University in Australia to establish Southeast University-Monash University Suzhou Joint Graduate School, the first Sino-foreign joint graduate school approved by the Ministry of Education of the People's Republic of China.

## 四、科技创新

近年来，南京的经济保持稳定且高速增长，2020年，经济总量进入中国大中城市前十。南京也是中国的科教重地和人才高地，拥有一大批高水平的科研院所和国家级研发平台，其科研综合实力位居中国前列。

推动科技创新是南京经济发展的必由之路。南京的目标是建设成具有全球影响力的创新名城，打造综合性科学中心和科技产业创新中心。

### 1. 创新名城

优越的区域环境、雄厚的经济实力、现代化的城市建设和强大的人才吸引力，是南京建设创新型城市的重要基础。

2021年，南京正式获批建设引领性国家创新型城市，高新技术企业多达7800余家。

## IV. Technology Innovation

In recent years, Nanjing's economy has been growing steadily and rapidly, and as of 2020, it entered the list of the top ten large and medium-sized cities in China in terms of economic output. Nanjing is also China's science and education center, boasting a large talent pool in a number of high-level scientific research institutes and state-level R&D platforms; the overall strength of scientific research ranks among the top in China.

Driving scientific and technological innovation is a must for Nanjing's economic development. By developing as a comprehensive center for scientific, technological, and industrial innovation, Nanjing aims to become a globally renowned and influential city.

### 1. Renowned City of Innovation

A favorable regional environment, tremendous economic strength, modern city construction and a large talent pool are what make Nanjing an innovative city.

In 2021, Nanjing was officially approved to build a leading national innovative city with as many as 7,800 high-tech enterprises. Unicorn enterprises[1] are a vital new force to promote industrial science and technology innovation as well as the development of the new economy. As of 2023, there are 17 unicorn enterprises in Nanjing. The creation of Zijinshan Laboratory, a leading scientific and technological innovation platform in Jiangsu Province, demonstrates Nanjing's innovative capabilities. The laboratory attracts top scientific research talents to conduct research on information technology and has already achieved a series of breakthrough results. Nanjing ranked sixth in the world according to the "2023 Global Nature Index — Research Cities", behind Beijing and Shanghai, as well as the New York

独角兽企业①是推动产业科技创新和新经济发展的重要新生力量，截至2023年，南京共有独角兽企业17家。江苏省和南京市共建的紫金山实验室展示了南京的创新能力，已逐渐成为江苏重大基础科研创新平台的"佼佼者"，聚集顶尖科研人才，在信息技术方面的研究已经取得了一系列突破性成果。在"2023年全球自然指数—科研城市"排行榜上，南京位列全球第六，仅次于北京、上海以及美国纽约都市圈、波士顿都市圈和旧金山湾区。在2023年全国创新型城市排行榜上，南京位列第四。

南京的国际化程度也吸引了众多海内外高层次人才。自2010年起，由在华外国人每年投票评选的"魅力中国—外籍人才眼中最具吸引力的中国城市"，南京7次位居前十名。如今，南京正以其独特的魅力，吸引着越来越多的优秀人才和创新项目。

## 2. 产业强市

南京是中国重要的制造业基地，在长期发展过程中，形成了汽车制造、电子信息、钢铁和石化四大支柱产业。近年来，南京致力于制造业的转型升级，积极发展新兴电子信息、绿色智能汽车、高端智能装备、生物医药与节能环保新材料四大先进制造产业。2023年，南京地区生产总值超过了1.7万亿元，继续走在全国高质量发展的前列。

---

① 独角兽企业是指创办时间比较短，企业估值超过 10 亿美元的未上市企业。

Unicorn enterprise is an unlisted company that has been founded for a relatively short period of time and has an estimated value of more than $1 billion.

metropolitan area, the Boston metropolitan area and the San Francisco Bay Area in the United States. Nanjing also ranked fourth in the list of innovative cities in China in 2023.

The internationalization of Nanjing has also attracted many high-level talents from home and abroad. Since 2010, Nanjing has ranked in the top ten in "Charming China — Most Attractive Chinese Cities in the Eyes of Foreign Talents" seven times, voted annually by foreigners in China. In recent years, Nanjing has attracted more and more talented individuals and innovative projects.

## 2. A Powerful Industrial City

Nanjing is a substantial manufacturing base in China and, throughout long-term development, has formed four cornerstone industries: automobile manufacturing, electronic information, steel industry, and petrochemicals. In recent years, Nanjing has committed itself to transforming and upgrading its manufacturing industry, actively developing the five major advanced manufacturing industries of emerging electronic information, eco-friendly intelligent vehicles, high-end intelligent equipment, biomedicine, and energy-saving and environmentally friendly new materials. In 2023, Nanjing's GDP exceeded 1.7 trillion yuan, and the city continues to be at the forefront of the country's high-quality development.

Nanjing is striving to build two globally competitive major industrial clusters: software and information services, and new electric power (smart grid). It is seeking a leading position in the domestic market in the fields of clean energy vehicles, intelligent manufacturing equipment, integrated circuits, biomedicine, new materials, and aerospace. In the future, Nanjing aims to advance sectors such as

南京正努力打造具有全球竞争力的软件和信息服务、新型电力（智能电网）两大产业集群；积极争取在新能源汽车、智能制造装备、集成电路、生物医药、新型材料、航空航天等产业领域取得国内领先地位。未来，南京将重点发展新一代人工智能、第三代半导体、基因与细胞、元宇宙、未来网络与先进通信以及储能与氢能等产业。

new-generation artificial intelligence, third-generation semiconductors, genes and cells, meta-universes, future networks, advanced communication, and energy storage and hydrogen energy.

## 练 习 一

### 一、判断题

1. 南京的70多个城市名称表明南京拥有悠久的历史。☐

2. 南京目前是中国南方的政治、文化中心。☐

3. 独角兽企业数量的多少，可以说明这座城市对人才、项目的吸引力。☐

### 二、思考题

1. 南京经济发展的目标是什么？

2. 南京的四大支柱产业是什么？

3. 你认为南京建设创新名城的基础是什么？

## 五、特色美食

南京菜也被称为"金陵菜""京苏大菜",是江苏菜系(简称苏菜)的四大代表菜之一。由于南京靠近长江,原料多以水产品为主,擅长炖、焖(mèn)、烤、煨(wēi)等手法,注重食材的新鲜和时令,菜品细致精美,口感鲜香酥嫩。

发达的水陆交通、独特的地理位置以及包容的民风民俗,决定了南京饮食口味是"兼取四方特色,适应八方之味",具有大气、平和的古都风范。

### 1. 盐水鸭

南京人一直以喜鸭而闻名,全市一年鸭产品销量7000万只以上。"没有一只鸭子能游出南京"的调侃,生动形象地表现了南京人对鸭子的喜爱。南京的鸭食品制作技艺精湛,享誉世界的北京烤鸭,据说正是起源于南京。盐水鸭是南京最著名的美食之一,至今已有2000多年的历史,是南京人餐桌上最常见的菜肴。

每年农历八九月,桂花盛开时制作的盐水鸭味道最佳,所以也被称为"桂花鸭"。

### 2. 皮肚面

皮肚面是南京的特色小吃之一,因为通常有皮肚、猪肝、肉丝、木耳、西红柿和青菜六种配料,也被称为"六鲜面"。皮肚实

## V. Specialty Food

Nanjing cuisine, also known as "Jinling cuisine" and "Jing-Su cuisine", is one of the four primary cooking styles representative of Jiangsu cuisine. Due to Nanjing's proximity to the Yangtze River, aquatic products are a staple ingredient, and stewing, braising, roasting, simmering and other techniques are commonly used. With a focus on freshness and seasonality, the dishes are delicate and exquisite, with a fresh and crisp taste.

Since Nanjing has advanced land and water transportation, an advantageous geographical location, and inclusive folk customs, its food boasts characteristics from all over and easily adapts to the tastes of people from all places with all the style of an ancient capital.

### 1. Boiled Salted Duck

Nanjing has always been famous for its love of ducks, and more than 70 million ducks are sold annually in the city. The joke "no duck can swim out of Nanjing" perfectly expresses the local people's love for duck. With more than 2,000 years of history, the skill in producing Nanjing duck products is second to none; even the world-renowned Peking duck is originally from Nanjing. Boiled salted duck, one of the most famous delicacies in Nanjing, is the most common dish on the table of Nanjing people.

Boiled salted duck tastes best from the eighth to the ninth month of the lunar calendar. It is also known as "osmanthus duck" because it is made when osmanthus flowers are in full bloom.

### 2. Pork Rind Noodles

Pork rind noodles are one of Nanjing's specialties. It is also known as "six-fresh noodles" because it usually contains six fresh ingredients: pork rind, pork liver, shredded meat, wood ear mushrooms, tomatoes and bok

际上就是猪皮，油炸后变成金黄色，放入面汤中能充分吸收汤汁，口感松软爽脆、入口即化。

皮肚面的面条都是小锅现煮的，因此也叫"小锅面"，一锅就是一碗，用大碗装盛。面条的口感软中带有弹性，汤料爽口醇香，味道鲜美可口。在南京人的心里，皮肚面就是家的味道。

## 六、名胜古迹

悠久的历史和灿烂的文化，为南京留下了大量名胜古迹。南京自古就有金陵四十八景的说法。截至2023年底，南京有国家等级旅游景区52家，其中4A级以上景区29家，钟山风景名胜区—中山陵园风景区、夫子庙—秦淮风光带风景名胜区均为国家5A级旅游景区，并被评为"中国旅游胜地四十佳"。

### 1. 明孝陵

明孝陵在钟山的南面，中国明朝开国皇帝朱元璋和皇后马氏合葬在这里。马皇后的谥号为"孝慈高皇后"，又因朱元璋提倡孝治天下，所以名为"孝陵"。明孝陵是中国规模最大的帝王陵寝之一，规模宏大，气派恢宏。陵区内的主体建筑和石刻代表了明初石刻艺术的最高水平。

明孝陵改变了之前皇帝的陵墓布局，此后500余年20多座帝王陵寝都按照明孝陵的模式建造，因此，明孝陵也有"明清皇家第

choy. The pork rind is fried until golden brown. When placed into the noodle soup, the pork rind absorbs all of the flavor and giving it a soft and crisp taste.

The noodles are cooked in small pans, hence the alternative name "small pan noodles". When cooking is done, the noodles are served in large bowls. The texture of the noodles is soft and elastic, and the soup is refreshingly mellow and flavorful. In the hearts of Nanjing people, pork rind noodles represent the idea of home.

## VI. Historical Sites and Scenic Spots

The long history and vibrant culture of Nanjing have given the city many scenic spots and historical monuments. Nanjing has been known as the "Forty-eight Scenic Spots of Jinling" since ancient times. As of the end of 2023, Nanjing had 52 national-grade tourist sites, including 29 of 4A grade or above. Dr. Sun Yat-sen's Mausoleum at Zhongshan and the Confucius Temple near the Qinhuai Scenic Belt are both 5A grade national tourist sites and are listed in the top 40 "Best of China's Tourist Attractions".

### 1. Ming Xiaoling Mausoleum

Located on the south side of the Zhongshan Mountain, the Ming Xiaoling Mausoleum is where the founding emperor of the Ming Dynasty, Zhu Yuanzhang, and his empress, Empress Ma, are buried together. It was named after Empress Ma's posthumous title "Xiao" (filial piety), which Zhu Yuanzhang advocated as a way to rule the world. The Ming Xiaoling Mausoleum, with its immense scale and magnificent grandeur, is one of the largest imperial mausoleums in China. The main building and stone carvings exemplify the highest level of stone carving craftsmanship in the early Ming Dynasty.

In the 500 years after the Ming Xiaoling

一陵"的美誉。

明孝陵是首批全国重点文物保护单位和首批国家5A级旅游景区。2003年，明孝陵被列入《世界遗产名录》，这也是目前南京唯一的世界文化遗产。

## 2. 夫子庙

夫子庙位于南京城南、秦淮河畔，又叫孔庙或文庙，是用来供奉和祭祀孔子的地方。夫子庙其实是一组规模宏大的古建筑群，由孔庙、学宫、江南贡院三大建筑群组成，占地面积非常大。它始建于东晋，经历四毁五建，是秦淮风光带上的一个重要景点。

夫子庙已经由明清时期的文教中心，演变成了繁华闹市，是享誉海内外的旅游胜地、文化长廊、美食中心、购物乐园。夫子庙供应的传统食品和风味小吃不下200种，以"秦淮八绝"为代表的秦淮风味小吃最为著名；夫子庙灯会是南京的特色民俗文化活动，在每年的春节至元宵节期间举行，是中国首批国家级非物质文化遗产。

Mausoleum was built, more than 20 emperors' mausoleums were modeled after it; therefore, the Ming Xiaoling Mausoleum has had the reputation of "the first mausoleum of the Ming and Qing Dynasties".

The Ming Xiaoling Mausoleum is one of the first key national cultural relic protection sites and one of the first 5A-level national tourist attractions. In 2003, the Ming Xiaoling Mausoleum was added to the World Heritage List, making it the only World Heritage Site in Nanjing.

## 2. The Confucius Temple

Located in the south of Nanjing, along the Qinhuai River, the Confucius Temple, also known as the Temple of Literature, is dedicated to the ancient Chinese thinker Confucius.

The Confucius Temple is actually a large complex of ancient buildings. It covers a vast area and consists of three parts: the Confucius Temple, the Palace of Learning, and the Jiangnan Examination Hall. Originally built in the Eastern Jin Dynasty, it has undergone four destructions and five reconstructions. It is an important attraction on the Qinhuai Scenic Belt.

The Confucius Temple has evolved from a cultural and educational center in the Ming and Qing Dynasties into a bustling downtown area. It is a renowned tourist attraction, cultural promenade, gourmet center and shopping paradise. The Confucius Temple serves more than 200 kinds of traditional food and flavorful snacks, including the most famous "Eight Wonders of Qinhuai". A lantern festival is held there between the Spring Festival and the Lantern Festival every year; it is a folk event unique to Nanjing, and one of the first national intangible cultural heritage customs in China.

## 七、文学之都

南京文脉悠长、文学底蕴深厚。虽然历史上的朝代不断在此更替，但是文化与文明几千年来传承不息，南京作为中国教育文化名城的影响力一直延续至今。

### 1. 天下文枢

在南京夫子庙江南贡院正门前有"明经取士、为国求贤"八个大字，这是古代中国科举考试的宗旨。这里长期作为官方教育机构，贡院是中国最大的"公务员"考场，选拔了大量的政治、科学和文化人才，有"东南第一学"之称。尤其是在明、清两朝，江南贡院选拔了全国半数以上的官员。在夫子庙大成门南面的牌坊上，刻着"天下文枢"四个大字，意思是"天下文化的中心"，这是对南京在中国文化史上地位的崇高赞誉。

南京是中国文学大师的聚集地，是重要文学著作的生产地，许多文人墨客都在此留下了著名的文学作品。在中国文学发展史

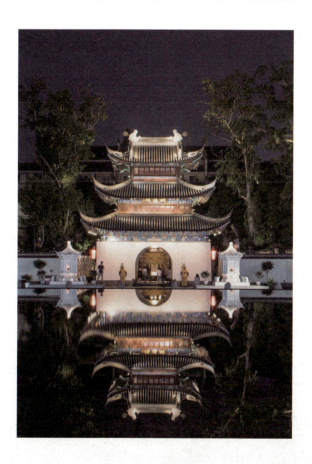

## VII. Literary Center

Nanjing has a long cultural lineage and rich literary heritage. Although the dynasties have come and gone throughout history, the civilization has been passed on for thousands of years, and Nanjing's influence as a famous city of education and culture in China continues to this day.

### 1. The Literary Capital of China

In front of the main gate of the Jiangnan Examination Hall in the Confucius Temple, there is a plaque, "Recruiting talent and seeking the virtuous for the good of the country", which was the purpose of the imperial examinations in ancient China. A large number of political, scientific and cultural talents were selected through the imperial examinations in this place, which was also an official educational institution and China's largest imperial examination site with the title of "the first school in the southeast". In the Ming and Qing Dynasties, more than half of the country's government officials came from the Jiangnan Examination Hall. A plaque saying "Cultural Center of China" hangs on the South Dacheng Gate of the Confucius Temple, praising Nanjing's leading position in China's cultural history.

Nanjing is the place where many Chinese literary masters lived and many important literary works were created; it is where the Chinese literati left their mark. In the history of Chinese literature, many "firsts" were born in Nanjing, such as the first professional literary education institution, the Literature Institute, and the first reading material for children, *The Thousand-Character Essay*. About 10,000 works of literature were written in or about Nanjing. The world's largest encyclopedia, *The Yongle Canon*, was compiled in Nanjing. The Kunqu Opera classic *Peach Blossom*

上，许多"第一"都是在南京诞生的，如第一个专业文学教育机构文学馆，第一部儿童启蒙读物《千字文》等。大约有1万部文学作品是在南京写成或者是与南京相关，如世界最大的百科全书"万书之书"《永乐大典》在南京编写；昆曲经典作品《桃花扇》讲述了明朝末年在南京发生的故事；"我买几个橘子去，你就在此地，不要走动。"朱自清《背影》中描写的场景正是南京浦口火车站。南京是中国四大名著之一《红楼梦》的作者曹雪芹的出生和成长之地；美国作家、诺贝尔奖得主赛珍珠也在南京生活并进行创作。

南京不仅有丰厚的文学遗产，在文学传播、文学教育普及等方面都无愧于"天下文枢"这一赞誉。2019年，联合国教科文组织授予南京"世界文学之都"的称号。南京成为中国第一个获此称号的城市。

## 2. 书香南京

崇文重教的悠久传统，熏陶出南京市民热爱学习的良好风尚。

南京有博物馆、纪念馆和美术馆84家，公共图书馆及分馆736家，实体书店近千家，公共文化设施遍布全市。南京图书馆是

*Fan* tells the story of Nanjing at the end of the Ming Dynasty. The famous scene "I'm going to go buy a few oranges; you stay here and don't move" depicted in Zhu Ziqing's *Father's Back* is set in Nanjing's Pukou Railway Station. Cao Xueqin, the author of *Dream of the Red Chamber*, one of the Four Classical Novels of China, was born and raised in Nanjing. American writer and Nobel laureate Pearl S. Buck also lived in Nanjing and created some of her works there.

Nanjing has a rich literary heritage and deserves praise as "the literary capital of China" in terms of its literary communication, widespread literary education, etc. In 2019, UNESCO awarded Nanjing the title of "World Literature Capital", making it the first city in China to be bestowed such a prestigious title.

## 2. A City in Love with Reading

The long tradition of respect for literature and education has fostered a fantastic culture of love for learning among the citizens of Nanjing. Nanjing has 84 museums, memorial halls and art galleries, 736 public libraries and branches, nearly 1,000 bookstores, and public cultural facilities all over the city. Nanjing Library

中国第一所公共图书馆，是中国第三大图书馆，亚洲第四大图书馆。南京先锋书店（五台山总店）被《国家地理》杂志评为"全球最美十大书店"的书店。

南京是中国出版和翻译最具活力的城市之一。南京的江苏凤凰传媒出版集团实力雄厚，近年来持续排列在"全球出版50强"前十名。

崇尚文学、酷爱读书是南京人鲜明的精神气质。文学与阅读已成为广大市民的一种生活方式。南京每年都举办丰富多彩的主题阅读活动，各种读书节、文化讲座、书籍分享活动随处可见。2024年2月，南京入选联合国教科文组织发布的"全球学习型城市网络"名单。今天的南京积极推动学习型社会建设，将文化发展融入城市发展战略，书香气息更加浓郁。

## 八、和平城市

2017年，经国际和平城市协会批准，南京成为中国首个"国际和平城市"。在漫长的城市发展历史中，南京饱受战火的摧残。对南京来说，和平，具有特别的意味。

### 1. 遇难同胞纪念馆

1937年12月13日，日军侵占南京后，公然违反国际公约，大肆屠杀中国百姓，南京遭受了一场空前的劫难，死难者总数达30万以上。在侵华日军南京大屠杀遇难同胞纪念馆中，12秒一次的水滴，象征着在1937

is the first public library in China, the third largest in China and the fourth largest in Asia. Nanjing Pioneer Bookstore (Wutaishan Main Store) is recognized by *National Geographic* magazine as one of the "Top Ten Most Beautiful Bookstores in the World".

Nanjing is one of China's most dynamic cities for publishing and translation. Nanjing's Jiangsu Phoenix Media Publishing Group has a strong presence globally and has consistently ranked in the top ten of the "Global 50 Publishing Ranking" in recent years.

The admiration for literature and love of reading is a part of the spirit of the Nanjing people. Reading has become a way of life for the general public. Every year, themed reading activities, various reading festivals, cultural lectures, and book-sharing activities can be found everywhere in the city. In February 2024, UNESCO put Nanjing in the "Global Network of Learning Cities" list. Today, Nanjing encourages the construction of a well-learned society and tries to integrate cultural development into the city's overall development strategy.

## VIII. A City for Peace

In 2017, Nanjing became China's first "International City of Peace", as approved by the International Cities for Peace. During its long history of urban development, Nanjing has seen the ravages of war. For Nanjing, peace means something special.

### 1. Memorial Hall for the Victims of the Nanjing Massacre

Over 300,000 Chinese people were massacred in Nanjing by Japanese invading troops who broke into the city on December 13th 1937 and acted against international conventions in the ensuring atrocities. It was an unprecedented catastrophe. In the Memorial Hall for the Victims of the Nanjing Massacre,

年，每12秒就有一个生命逝去。

"南京大屠杀档案"中包括美国牧师约翰·马吉拍摄的历史影像资料，已经被联合国教科文组织列入《世界记忆名录》。约翰·拉贝是南京人无法忘却的名字。这名德国人和其他国际友人一起，在南京大屠杀期间共同组建南京国际安全区，保护了超过25万中国人的生命。位于南京大学校园里的拉贝故居至今保存完好。

尊重生命、保卫和平，不仅是南京人民、中国人民的愿望，更是全人类的共同追求。中国把每年的12月13日定为南京大屠杀死难者国家公祭日，提醒后人：只有牢记这段历史，才能珍视来之不易的和平。

## 2. 珍爱和平

中华民族是热爱和平的民族。和平共处、和平交流、和平发展，一直是中国人强调的和平外交理念。坐落在长江边的南京宝船厂遗址，见证了明朝郑和率领庞大船队七下西洋，开辟海上丝绸之路的故事；雨花台外的渤泥国王墓，见证了古代中国与周边国

the 12-second water drop symbolizes that a life was lost every 12 seconds in 1937.

The "Nanjing Massacre Archives" include historical footage taken by American pastor John Magee, which has been entered into UNESCO's Memory of the World Register. John Rabe is another name that the people of Nanjing will never forget. The German, along with other international friends, co-organized the Nanjing International Safety Zone during the Nanjing Massacre, which protected more than 250,000 Chinese citizens. Rabe's former residence on the campus of Nanjing University is well preserved to this day.

Safeguarding life and peace is the unanimous aspirations of the people of Nanjing and China, as well as all humanity. By designating December 13th of each year as the National Day of Public Memorial for the Victims of the Nanjing Massacre, China reminds future generations that only by remembering history can we cherish hard-won peace.

## 2. Cherishing Peace

China is a peace-loving nation. Peaceful coexistence, peaceful exchanges, and peaceful development have always been the cornerstones of China's peaceful diplomacy. The ruins of the Nanjing Treasure-ship Shipyard, situated along the Yangtze River, witness the story of Zheng He's seven voyages to the Western Seas as the head of a huge fleet in the Ming Dynasty, which opened up the Maritime Silk Road. The Tomb of the King of Boni, situated outside Yuhuatai, bears witness to China's friendly exchanges with neighboring countries in ancient times. The Meiyuan Xincun on Changjiang Road is a record of the efforts made by the CPC delegation, headed by Zhou Enlai, in striving for peace.

Starting in 2020, the Nanjing Peace Forum, held in Nanjing for three consecutive years,

家友好交往的历史；长江路上的梅园新村，记载了以周恩来为首的中共代表团在争取和平方面所做的努力。

自2020年起，连续三年在南京举办的"南京和平论坛"围绕自然环境与人类命运、全球绿色复苏、文化交流、国际和平行动、青年行动等主题，把和平与可持续发展作为关注点，推动人与自然和谐发展，诠释并传播"共建人类命运共同体"的理念。

has focused on the themes of the natural environment and human destiny, global environmental recovery, cultural exchange, international peace action and youth action. By bringing peace and sustainable development to the forefront, the Forum promotes the harmonious development of human beings and nature, and promotes the concept of "building a community with a shared future for mankind".

## 九、风尚地标

南京是引领中国经济、文化发展的现代化大都市之一。在日新月异的城市发展变化中，不断涌现的南京地标吸引着众多的游客和创业者。

### 1. 新街口

有"中华第一商圈"称号的新街口，位于南京市中心，是拥有超过百年历史的中国著名商业中心。新街口商圈是中国百货业最发达、商贸密集度最高的地区之一，商业资源非常丰富。在这片不到0.3平方公里的土地上，汇集了多家购物中心、百货商场、特色街区等，是市民、游客购物、休闲、娱乐的好去处。新街口的营业额长期位居中国各商业街区之首，是我国唯一一个拥有4个销售额达40亿元以上的百货购物中心的商圈。

## IX. Stylish Landmarks

Nanjing is one of the modern metropolises leading China's economic and cultural development. Amidst ever-changing urban development, Nanjing sees the emergence of landmarks attracting many tourists and entrepreneurs to the city.

### 1. Xinjiekou

Xinjiekou, located in the center of Nanjing, is a famous shopping district with over 100 years of history, known as "China's first shopping district". Xinjiekou is one of the most developed areas in China in terms of shopping venues. On this land of less than 0.3 square kilometers, there are a number of shopping centers, department stores, and unique neighborhoods, which make it an ideal place for shopping and leisure. Xinjiekou's turnover has long ranked

新街口广场中央竖立着孙中山铜像。这是中国众多孙中山铜像中最为著名的一座。

## 2. 紫峰大厦

紫峰大厦是一座由中国全额投资并建造的摩天大楼，高450米，是南京最高的建筑。该大厦的外形新颖独特，因为顶部针管状的设计，被南京人亲切地称为"注射器"。大厦外立面采用绿、蓝两色玻璃勾画出龙的形象，融入了中国元素。站在72层的观景平台远眺，南京城尽收眼底，可以看到传统与现代融合的独特风貌，更可以看到南京生机勃勃的发展潜力。

## 3. 南京南站

南京南站是亚洲最大的高铁站，是华东地区最重要、最繁忙的铁路枢纽之一，发车班次数量常年位居中国前三名。依照"古都新站"的设计理念，车站主体以中国古典元素为主。而车站采用的垂直换乘方式，实现了交通"零换乘"，这一内部构造也在其他城市迅速推广应用。步入宽敞的候车大厅，走向宏伟的列车站台，这种古今融合、中西合璧的设计，将中国古典建筑与现代化车站相结合，打造出彰显南京独特气质的新地标。

first among all commercial districts in China, and it is the only shopping district in China where four department stores and shopping centers boast a combined sales volume of more than 4 billion yuan.

In the center of Xinjiekou Square is a bronze statue of Dr. Sun Yat-sen. This is the most famous of Dr. Sun Yat-sen's statues in China.

## 2. Purple Peak Tower

The Purple Peak Tower is a skyscraper invested in and built entirely by Chinese resources. At 450 meters high, it is the tallest building in Nanjing. The shape of the building is so unique that it is affectionately called the "syringe" by the locals. The facade of the building incorporates Chinese elements with two sets of green and blue glass outlining the shape of a dragon. Standing on the 72nd-floor observation deck, you can enjoy a panoramic view of Nanjing. Looking out across the city, you will see a unique fusion of tradition and modernity, as well as a city teeming with life and development potential.

## 3. Nanjing South Railway Station

Nanjing South Railway Station is the largest high-speed railway station in Asia and one of the most important and busiest railroad hubs in East China, ranking in the top three nationally in the number of trains. Its design adheres to the concept of "a modern station in an ancient capital", and the main body features classical Chinese elements. The interior of the station adopts the "vertical transfer" mode for a "zero transfer" experience, which has been widely used in other cities. Boasting spacious waiting halls and grand platforms, the station offers a fusion of ancient and modern, Chinese and Western elements, thus turning into a new landmark that encapsulates Nanjing's unique atmosphere.

## 练习二

### 一、判断题

1. 北京烤鸭的历史比南京烤鸭悠久。　□

2. 南京是一座中国教育文化名城。　□

3. 南京是全世界唯一一个获得"世界文学之都"称号的城市。　□

4. 约翰·拉贝在南京大屠杀期间组建了南京国际安全区，保护了很多中国人的生命。　□

5. 新街口是"中华第一商圈"，新街口商圈是中国百货业最发达、商贸密集度最高的地区。　□

### 二、思考题

1. 明孝陵名字的由来是什么？

2. 南京的书香气息体现在哪些方面？

3. 南京的哪些历史遗迹可以体现这是一个珍爱和平的城市？

### 三、拓展题

1. 你觉得南京城的独特魅力是什么？一座城市的哪些方面，可以吸引你来学习和工作呢？

2. 结合自身经历，描述一个你曾经在中国生活中感受到"博爱"的经历故事。

3. 查阅资料，了解约翰·拉贝的故事，参观拉贝故居。

# Chapter 2

苏州

第二章

人 / 间 / 天 / 堂

Heaven on Earth

"上有天堂，下有苏杭"。苏州不仅是一座历史文化名城，保留了精美的古典园林、悠久的丝绸织造传统，也是备受欢迎的旅游目的地。同时，它还是一座经济强市和现代化都市，高新技术产业蓬勃发展，融合了传统与现代之美。

## 一、城市概况

### 1. 地理环境

"上有天堂，下有苏杭。"苏州地处长江三角洲中部，江苏东南部，东面是上海，南面是浙江，西面是太湖，北面是长江。苏州气候温和，雨量充沛，土地肥沃，物产丰富，优越的自然条件使得其成为中国最宜居的城市之一。

苏州古称"姑苏"，以水闻名，是著名的"东方水城"。全市约三分之一面积被水域覆盖。苏州古城区河道总长35公里，桥梁170多座，是中国河、桥最多的城市。众多的历史古迹和园林散布在苏州城的各个角落，构成了"江南水乡"特有的美丽画卷。

### 2. 城市变迁

苏州的历史起源于2500年前春秋时期的吴国。公元前514年，吴王阖闾命令伍子胥建造吴国的都城。伍子胥根据苏州一带的地理和气候特点，选中了姑苏山（今灵岩山）东北30里（15公里）的地方，建成了一座周长47里（23.5公里）的大城，并开凿了一条护城河来保护城市。直到今天，苏州城的位置几乎没有变化，仍然坐落在当时的位置上，这在人类历史上是非常罕见的。

## I. Overview

### 1. Geographical Environment

"Just as there is paradise in heaven, there are Suzhou and Hangzhou on earth." Located in the central part of the Yangtze River Delta in southeastern Jiangsu Province, Suzhou is bordered by Shanghai to the east, Zhejiang to the south, the Taihu Lake to the west, and the Yangtze River to the north. The city boasts a mild climate, abundant rainfall, fertile land, and rich resources, and is one of the most livable cities in China.

Suzhou was known in ancient times as "Gusu". Often referred to as "the Venice of the East", Suzhou has water bodies covering one-third of the city's area. The ancient city has a total of 35 kilometers of waterways and more than 170 bridges — the largest numbers of rivers and bridges in all Chinese cities. Its most distinctive feature is "rivers running parallel to streets and waterways flowing next to alleys," where numerous historical monuments and gardens are scattered throughout Suzhou, forming the unique landscape of a Jiangnan water town.

### 2. Development

The history of Suzhou dates back to the State of Wu of the Spring and Autumn Period 2,500 years ago. In 514 BC, King Helü of Wu ordered his minister Wu Zixu to build the capital of the State of Wu. Taking into consideration the geography and climate of the Suzhou area, Wu Zixu selected a location 30 *li* (15 km) northeast of Mount Gusu (today's Lingyan Mountain) to build a large city with a circumference of 47 *li* (23.5 km) and dug a moat for protection. To this day, the location of Suzhou has remained almost unchanged, and it still sits on its original site, something of a rarity in human history.

隋唐时期，随着大运河的开通，苏州成为连接中国南方和北方最重要的水陆交通枢纽之一。唐朝中后期，由于北方战乱不断，大量人口南迁，带来了当时最先进的技术和劳动力，苏州的土地资源得到了广泛的开发，手工业和商业也日益繁荣。宋朝时期，苏州成为国家主要的粮食产区，绢绸的产量名列前茅。"苏湖熟，天下足"的说法就是出自此时。到了明清时期，苏州已经成为全国的经济中心，不仅是全国最大的商业城市，也是最大的工业城市，人口和财富在当时的中国城市中位居第一。当时的苏州还是中国对外贸易的中心口岸，也是东半球第一商业大都会。明朝著名航海家郑和七次下西洋，都是从苏州太仓的刘家港出发的。

1949年以后，苏州进入了新的发展阶段，特别是改革开放后，苏州的经济高速发展。1990年起，苏州在城西建设了国家级的高新技术产业开发区，简称"高新区"。1994年，苏州工业园区在城东建立，简称"园区"。苏州依靠"高新区"和"园区"，成功吸引了大量的外资，外来人口纷纷来苏就业，苏州成为当代中国经济最活跃的城市之一。

With the opening of the Grand Canal during the Sui and Tang dynasties, Suzhou became one of the most important water and land transportation hubs connecting southern and northern China. In the middle and late Tang Dynasty, continuous wars in northern China led to a large population migration to the south, which brought the most advanced technology and labor force. Suzhou's land resources were extensively developed, and handicraft and commerce flourished. In the Song Dynasty, Suzhou became one of the main grain-producing areas in the country and a leading silk producer. This period also gave rise to the saying, "Good harvests in Suzhou and Huzhou (a city close to Suzhou) promise wealth and abundance for all to enjoy." By the Ming and Qing Dynasties, Suzhou had become China's economic center and the largest commercial and industrial city, with its population and wealth ranking first among Chinese cities at the time. Suzhou was also the center of China's foreign trade and the first commercial metropolis in the Eastern Hemisphere. The famous navigator Zheng He launched all seven of his voyages to the Western Seas from Liujiagang in Taicang, Suzhou.

After 1949, Suzhou entered a new development phase, especially after China's reform and opening-up when Suzhou's economy experienced a period of rapid growth. In 1990, Suzhou began to build a national high-tech industrial development zone in the west of the city, known as the High-Tech Zone. In 1994, the Suzhou Industrial Park was established in the east of the city. Thanks to the High-Tech Zone and the Suzhou Industrial Park, Suzhou has attracted significant foreign investment and provided a lot of jobs. Now, Suzhou is one of the most economically active cities in China.

### 3. 今日苏州

目前，苏州全市面积8657.32平方公里，常住人口1296万（截至2023年底）。2023年，苏州的生产总值超过了2.4万亿，经济总量在全国城市排名第六位，江苏第一位，号称中国"最强地级市"。

在城市发展的同时，苏州非常重视对古城的保护。早在1986年，苏州就确立了"保护古城，发展新区"的规划，并推出了一系列管理方法，在保护文化遗产的同时，进行城市改造开发。苏州有一个著名的规定，护城河以内的新建建筑高度不得超过24米，以确保古城整体风貌不受高大建筑的影响。因此，苏州也成为全国唯一全面保护古城风貌的历史文化名城，拥有"世界遗产典范城市""世界特色魅力城市""世界花园城市"等多项荣誉。

如今的苏州，既保留着古城千年的传统文化魅力，又展现了现代城市的繁华景象，是名副其实的"人间天堂"。

### 3. Suzhou Today

Suzhou currently has a total area of 8,657.32 km² and a permanent population of approximately 12.96 million (as of the end of 2023). In 2023, Suzhou's GDP exceeded 2.4 trillion yuan, ranking sixth in the country and first in Jiangsu, earning it the title of "China's strongest prefecture-level city".

While developing the city, Suzhou has paid great attention to conserving the ancient city. In 1986, Suzhou began applying the principle of "protecting the ancient city while developing new areas" in urban planning and implemented various management strategies. To protect its cultural heritage while developing and transforming the city, Suzhou enacted a renowned regulation limiting the height of new buildings the ancient city's moat to 24 meters at most to ensure that the overall appearance of the ancient city is not affected by tall buildings. Suzhou has become the only historical and cultural city in the country that comprehensively protects the ancient skyline, and has been honored as a "World Heritage Model City", a "World Distinctive Charm City", and a "World Garden City".

With its mix of millennium-old traditional cultural charm and bustling modernity, today's Suzhou truly lives up to its name as "heaven on earth".

## 二、文化印象

苏州古称"吴"，是吴文化的发祥地。吴文化是江南文化的主要来源，以其细腻、精致、开放和包容的特点著称。苏州古典园林、昆曲、苏绣都是吴文化的典型代表。

### 1. 园林之城

"江南园林甲天下，苏州园林甲江南。"中国古典园林通常分为皇家园林、私家园林和寺庙园林3种。苏州是私家园林保留最多、最完整的城市，被誉为"园林之城"。目前苏州全市保留下来的园林有100余处，其中拙政园、留园等9座园林被联合国教科文组织列入《世界遗产名录》。

苏州园林始于春秋，唐宋时期开始增多，明清时期达到巅峰。适宜的气候、丰富的物产，较少遭受战乱和自然灾害，使得当时社会的富有阶层（主要是退休的官员和富有的商人）纷纷选择到苏州定居。他们往往选择远离市中心的郊区来建造自己的住所。在满足居住的同时，建造一座大花园来追求自然山水的乐趣。苏州园林的主人往往具有

## II. Cultural Impressions

Historically known as "Wu", Suzhou is the birthplace of the Wu culture in southeast China. This culture is noted for its delicacy, sophistication, openness, and inclusiveness. Important icons of the Wu culture include Suzhou's classical gardens, the Kunqu Opera, and Suzhou's embroidery.

### 1. The City of Classical Gardens

"The gardens in Jiangnan are the best under heaven, and those in Suzhou are the best of Jiangnan." Chinese classical gardens are divided into three categories: imperial gardens, private gardens, and temple gardens. Suzhou, known as the "City of Classical Gardens", hosts the largest and most complete collection of private gardens. Currently, Suzhou boasts over a hundred gardens, among which nine, including the Humble Administrator's Garden and the Lingering Garden, are recognized as UNESCO World Heritage Sites.

Suzhou's gardens were first created in the Spring and Autumn period. The number of gardens increased during the Tang and Song dynasties and peaked in the Ming and Qing dynasties. Thanks to its favorable climate, abundant resources, and relative peace from wars and natural disasters, Suzhou was settled by affluent people (mainly retired officials and wealthy merchants). Preferring

很高的文学和艺术修养。他们亲自参与设计，在园林里加入了自己的审美理念和人生感悟。他们在园林里赏花、饮酒、写诗、作画，享受属于自己的诗意人生。这种园林生活既能入朝为官，又能在家"游山玩水"，是中国古代知识分子的理想人生。

与富丽堂皇、规模宏大的皇家园林不同，苏州园林往往占地不大，讲究"天人合一"——人与自然和谐共生。为了达到这样的境界，苏州园林往往因地制宜，利用现有的树木和流水进行设计，讲究自然之趣，避免对称或规整。设计师和工匠们努力确保游览者无论站在哪里，眼前总有一幅完美的图画。人在园中走，如在画中游，美不胜收。

the quiet suburbs far from the bustling city center for their residences, they built extensive gardens that met their living needs and allowed them to indulge in the beauty of natural landscapes. The owners of these gardens, usually highly educated, participated in the designs to incorporate their aesthetics and life philosophies. In these gardens, they enjoyed flowers, poetry, drinking, painting, and leading a poetic life. This garden lifestyle represented the ideal life of ancient Chinese intellectuals.

Unlike the grand imperial gardens, Suzhou's gardens are usually smaller and emphasize the harmony between man and nature. To achieve this harmonious coexistence, Suzhou's gardens were tailored to the local landscape to account for existing trees and water bodies. They enhance natural charm by avoiding strict symmetry and uniformity. Designers and craftsmen worked to ensure that visitors to the gardens could always enjoy a perfect view from any angle. Walking in the garden is like wandering in a painting, a feast for the eyes.

## 2. The City of Silk

Silk is one of the symbols of ancient Chinese civilization and an important representation of Chinese culture. Ancient Chinese craftspeople invented and mass-produced silk products, thus starting what became known as the "Silk Road", the first trade route between the East and the West in world history. Suzhou is one of the birthplaces of China's sericulture and has been reputed as the "Capital of Silk and Land of Riches". Artifacts such as ramie cloth and spinning wheels unearthed at the Caoxie Mountain Site indicate that people in this area had already begun sericulture and silk reeling and had mastered professional weaving techniques five to six thousand years ago.

Suzhou's development flourished along with the silk industry. As early as the Qin and Han

### 2. 丝绸之都

丝绸是中国古文明的标志之一，是中国文化的重要体现。中国古代劳动人民发明并大规模生产丝绸制品，开启了世界历史上第一次东西方大规模的商贸交流，这一贸易路线被称为"丝绸之路"。苏州是中国蚕桑文明的重要发祥地之一，有"丝绸之府，锦绣之地"的美誉。在苏州草鞋山遗址中出土的葛布、纺轮等文物，表明早在五六千年前，生活在这片区域的华夏先民就已经开始养蚕、取丝，并掌握了专业的纺织技术。

苏州的发展与丝绸业的兴盛紧密相连。早在秦汉时期，苏州就已经成为养蚕织丝的重要地区，唐宋时期更是成了全国丝绸中心。公元1276年，意大利人马可·波罗来到中国，描绘"苏州是一座美丽的大城市。这里盛产生丝，人们用生丝纺织出成品，不仅供自己消费，使人人都穿着绫罗绸缎，而且还销往外地市场。这里人口稠密，商业和手工业都很发达，实在令人惊叹。"

到了明清时期，苏州的丝绸生产和贸易达到高峰，皇家高级丝绸织品大多出自苏州织工之手。丝绸业的发展促进了城市日益繁华，城市人口迅速增长，城区逐渐向郊区扩展，新兴了一批市镇，如吴江的盛泽镇，就是著名的"绸都"。丝绸产业还带动了苏州其他行业和整个社会的发展，使苏州在近代成为我国工商业最为发达的城市之一。

如今，丝绸产业仍然是苏州最具代表性的特色产业之一，国内外的游客来苏州，常会选择丝绸制品作为礼品带回家乡馈赠亲友。

Dynasties, Suzhou emerged as a major silk production and weaving center. During the Tang and Song Dynasties, it was firmly established as the center of China's silk industry. In 1276, Marco Polo came to China from Venice and described Suzhou as "a beautiful large city. Here, silk is produced in great quantities, and the people weave it into various goods. The silk produced is not only used locally, ensuring that everyone is clothed in fine silks, but is also exported to markets abroad. The city is densely populated, and both commerce and handicrafts are highly developed. It is truly astonishing."

During the Ming and Qing Dynasties, Suzhou's silk production and trade reached a peak, and high-grade silk products weaved in Suzhou were used by the imperial family. The growth of the silk industry spurred the city's prosperity, leading to a population boom and a gradual expansion of the urban area into the suburbs. This expansion gave rise to new towns like Shengze in Wujiang. The silk industry also drove the development of other industries in Suzhou, making it one of the most developed industrial and commercial cities in modern China.

Today, silk continues to be one of Suzhou's most characteristic industries. Domestic and international tourists often buy silk products when they visit Suzhou, taking them back home as gifts for their families and friends.

## 三、教育交流

### 1. 高等教育概况

苏州自古人才辈出，有着崇文尚教的优良传统，教育事业一直非常发达，有"状元之城"和"院士之乡"的美誉。

名城名校融合发展是苏州市近年来全力推进的发展战略。目前，苏州全市共有包括苏州大学、苏州科技大学在内的26所高校，另有南京大学等9所高校在苏州设有分校区。全市在校大学生约30万名，研究生超过2万人，国际学生3000余人。自2002年起，苏州市开始建设独墅湖科教创新区。该创新区以合作办学和科技创新为特色，吸引了中国科学技术大学、中国人民大学以及牛津大学、蒙纳士大学等33所中外知名院校来苏州办学，在校生人数近8万。该创新区被评为中国首个"高等教育国际化示范区"。

### 2. 高校介绍

#### 1）苏州大学

苏州大学（www.suda.edu.cn）是苏州市规模最大的综合性大学，也是中国历史悠久的名校之一。作为国家"双一流"建设

## III. Education and International Exchanges

### 1. Overview of Higher Education

With a strong tradition of valuing education, Suzhou boasts a highly developed educational system. Historically a cradle of education, the city has earned the reputation as the "City of Top Scholars" and "Hometown of Academicians".

In recent years, Suzhou has vigorously promoted an integrated development strategy linking the city and its educational institutions. Suzhou has 26 higher education institutions, including Soochow University and Suzhou University of Science and Technology, and nine branches of out-of-town universities, such as Nanjing University. The city has about 300,000 undergraduates, over 20,000 graduate students, and over 3,000 international students. Since 2002, Suzhou has been developing the Dushu Lake Science and Education Innovation District, which focuses on cooperative education and technological innovation, and attracts 33 renowned domestic and overseas institutions such as the University of Science and Technology of China, Renmin University of China, the University of Oxford, and Monash University. With nearly 80,000 students studying onsite, the district has earned the reputation as China's first "International Higher Education Demonstration Zone".

### 2. Introduction to Universities

#### 1) Soochow University

Soochow University (www.suda.edu.cn) is not only the largest comprehensive university in Suzhou but also one of the oldest ones in China. A national "Double First-Class" initiative university and a "211 Project" university, Soochow University has made remarkable achievements in teaching, scientific research, and social services.

高校和"211工程"大学，苏州大学在教学、科研和社会服务方面都取得了显著成就。

苏州大学拥有完善的学科体系，纳米科学与技术、材料科学与工程、生物医学工程、能源科学与工程等领域的学科实力处于国际领先水平。学校目前在苏州市共有4个校区，在校生近5万人。

作为一所具有国际化视野的大学，苏州大学与全球240余所高校和科研机构建立了广泛的合作关系，开展了形式多样的国际交流与合作。学校现有来自70多个国家的1200余名国际学生，分布在全校22个学院，涵盖本科和研究生层次的100多个专业。苏州大学也是中国第一家在境外办学的高校。2011年，老挝苏州大学在老挝首都万象成立，成为中国"一带一路"的重要驿站和文化名片。

自2017年起，苏州大学设立了"苏州大学外国留学生奖学金"，吸引了全球数千名外国学生申请攻读硕、博士学位。纳米科技、材料学、生物医药、临床医学以及汉语、新闻传播等成为国际学生申请的热门专业。

Soochow University offers a comprehensive range of disciplines, with world-leading areas such as Nano Science and Technology, Materials Science and Engineering, Biomedical Engineering, and Energy Science. The university has nearly 50,000 students in its four campuses in Suzhou.

As a globally oriented university, Soochow University has established extensive partnerships with more than 240 universities and research institutions worldwide, engaging in a wide range of international exchanges and collaborations. The university hosts over 1,200 international students from more than 70 countries across 22 colleges and over 100 undergraduate and graduate programs. The university was also pioneering as the first Chinese University to establish a campus abroad. In 2011, Lao Soochow University was established in Vientiane, the capital of Laos, as a significant milestone and cultural emblem for China's Belt and Road Initiative.

The "Soochow University International Student Scholarship", established in 2017, has empowered thousands of foreign students to apply for master's and doctor's degree programs. Popular majors among these students include Nano Science and Technology, Materials Science, Biomedicine, Clinical Medicine, Chinese Language, and Journalism and Communication.

### 2) Suzhou University of Science and Technology

Suzhou University of Science and Technology (www.usts.edu.cn), located southwest of Suzhou, is the second largest university in Suzhou, with Environmental Engineering as its strongest discipline. Since 1993, the university has hosted annual foreign-oriented human resource training classes sponsored by China's Ministry of Commerce. These sessions have trained over 2,000

**2）苏州科技大学**

苏州科技大学（www.usts.edu.cn）位于苏州市的西南部，是苏州在校生规模第二的高校，环境工程专业为该校的特色专业。学校自1993年以来每年承办由中国商务部主办的援外人力资源培训班，已为120多个"一带一路"共建国家和发展中国家培训了2000余名环保、能源和物流等领域的官员和技术人员。

**3）西交利物浦大学**

位于苏州工业园区独墅湖畔的西交利物浦大学（www.xjtlu.edu.cn）是中国目前规模最大的中外合作大学，由西安交通大学与英国利物浦大学于2006年合作创办。国际化是西交利物浦大学最大的特色。学校外籍教师的比例很高，除了公共基础课以外，所有课程都是全英文授课。毕业生可以获得两所高校颁发的学位证书。相比英国利物浦大学，西交利物浦的学费和生活费用更为优惠，吸引了不少国际学生前来就读。

officials and technicians from more than 120 Belt and Road partner countries and developing countries in environmental protection, energy, and logistics.

### 3) Xi'an Jiaotong-Liverpool University

Xi'an Jiaotong-Liverpool University (www.xjtlu.edu.cn), located on the shores of the Dushu Lake in the Suzhou Industrial Park, was established in 2006 through a partnership between Xi'an Jiaotong University and the University of Liverpool in the UK and is now the largest Sino-foreign university joint venture in China. Internationalization is its most distinctive feature. Foreign experts account for a high percentage of its faculty, and except for public basic courses, all courses are taught in English. Graduates are awarded degrees from both partnering institutions. Compared to the University of Liverpool's home campus, Xi'an Jiaotong-Liverpool has more preferential tuition and living expenses, so it attracts many foreign students.

## 四、经济腾飞

苏州不仅有着悠久的历史和灿烂的文化，同时也是中国经济最发达的城市之一。改革开放以来，苏州充分发挥紧邻上海的区位优势，积极发展外向型经济和开放型创新经济，成为中国"最强地级市"。

### 1. 开放创新的园区经济

改革开放以来，苏州提出了"从五湖四海走向五洲四洋"的战略，通过建立经济开发区和工业园区，成为"世界工厂"，确立了以加工贸易为主的外向型经济龙头地位，多项经济指标位居全国前列。

苏州工业园区创建于1994年，这是中国和新加坡两国政府间的首个合作项目，被誉为"中国改革开放的重要窗口"和"国际合作的成功范例"。园区是中国首个开展开放创新综合实验区域，吸引了大量跨国企业的投资。经过多年的发展，苏州工业园区已拥有国家高新技术企业近2800家，科技创新型企业超万家，成为中国开放程度最高、发展质效最好、创新活力最强、营商环境最优的区域之一。2019年，中国（江苏）自由贸易试验区苏州片区在工业园区落户，为苏州进一步发挥开放优势、推进创新发展提供了新的机遇。

苏州还积极参与"一带一路"建设，加强与共建国家的经贸合作。例如，埃塞俄比亚东方工业园、印尼吉打邦农林生态产业园等境外开发区和产业园已成为苏州参与"一带一路"建设的重要载体，为"一带一路"贡献了"苏州力量"。

## IV. Economic Takeoff

Suzhou is renowned not only for its long history and splendid culture but also for being one of China's most economically developed cities. Since China's reform and opening-up began, Suzhou has fully capitalized on its strategic location near Shanghai, actively developed an open and innovative economy, and been recognized as China's "strongest prefecture-level city".

### 1. Industrial Parks of Openness and Innovation

Since China's reform and opening-up, Suzhou has adopted an international development strategy, establishing economic development zones and industrial parks to become the "world's factory". This strategy has cemented its position as a leader in an open and innovative economy and its focus on the processing trade, with its key economic indicators consistently ranking among the country's best.

The Suzhou Industrial Park, established in 1994 as the first inter-governmental cooperation project between China and Singapore, is hailed as an important window into China's reform and opening-up and a successful example of international cooperation. The park is China's first comprehensive experimental area for open innovation and attracts investment from many multinational corporations. After years of development, the Suzhou Industrial Park now hosts nearly 2,800 national high-tech enterprises and over 10,000 technological innovation enterprises, and boasts the highest degrees of openness, the best development quality, the strongest innovation vitality, and the most optimal business environments in China. In 2019, the establishment of the China (Jiangsu) Pilot Free Trade Zone Suzhou

## 2. 崛起的制造业

作为中国最重要的制造业基地之一，苏州的工业门类包括电子、汽车、机械、化工等多个领域。超过150家世界五百强企业落户苏州，苹果、索尼、英特尔等跨国公司都在苏州设立了生产基地，为苏州制造业注入了新的发展动力。

生物医药是苏州重点发展的新兴产业之一，苏州的生物医药产业已经处于全国领先地位，创新企业数量、人才规模、企业融资总额均占全国总量的20%以上。纳米技术也是苏州近年来重点发展的领域。苏州工业园区的苏州纳米城是全球最大的纳米技术应用产业综合社区，拥有1000余家纳米技术企业，2023年全年产值1460亿元。人工智能产业是苏州经济发展的新引擎，目前苏州已聚集了人工智能相关企业近1000家，在语音识别、计算机视觉、自动驾驶、大数据、工业互联网等领域形成了一定的产业优势。

Area within the Industrial Park opened new opportunities to enhance Suzhou's openness and foster further innovative development.

Suzhou actively engages in the Belt and Road Initiative to strengthen the economic and trade cooperation with partner countries. Key platforms like the Eastern Industrial Zone in Ethiopia and the Ketabang Eco-Agricultural Park in Indonesia, where Suzhou can channel its energies into the Initiative, are pivotal in Suzhou's contribution to the Initiative.

## 2. Emerging Manufacturing Center

As one of China's most important manufacturing hubs, Suzhou hosts various sectors, including electronics, automobiles, machinery, and chemicals. Over 150 Fortune 500 companies, including major multinationals such as Apple, Sony, and Intel, have established production bases here, injecting fresh momentum into the city's manufacturing sector.

Biopharmaceuticals have become one of Suzhou's key emerging industries in recent years. Suzhou's biopharmaceutical industry is now a national leader, accounting for over 20% of the national totals in innovative enterprises, employment scale, and financing. Nanotechnology is also a key area of development in Suzhou. The Suzhou Nanopolis is the world's largest community in nanotechnology application industry, hosting over a thousand nanotechnology enterprises with an annual output of 146 billion yuan in 2023. Another new engine for Suzhou's economic development is the artificial intelligence industry. Suzhou has gathered nearly a thousand AI-related enterprises, establishing significant industrial strengths in voice recognition, computer vision, autonomous driving, big data, and industrial Internet.

### 3. 领跑的科技创新

作为中国科技创新的重要城市之一，苏州拥有高新技术企业1.5万余家。

苏州与260多家国内外高校建立了稳定的合作关系，建有产学研机构160多家。众多的高校和科研机构，为科技人才的培养和科研成果的转化提供了坚实基础。

苏州还发布了极具吸引力的人才政策，面向全球积极引进高水平人才，为未来的经济发展奠定了坚实基础。未来，随着中国经济的持续发展和长江三角洲区域一体化发展的加速推进，苏州将迎来更加辉煌的发展前景。

### 3. National Technological Innovation Leader

One of China's key cities for technological innovation, Suzhou has over 15,000 high-tech enterprises.

The city prioritizes the development of education and international openness, having established stable partnerships with over 260 universities worldwide and boasting more than 160 industry-university-research institutions. The city's many universities and research institutes provide a solid foundation for training scientific and technical talents and transforming research into practical applications.

Suzhou has also implemented highly attractive talent policies and actively recruits high-level talents worldwide, thus paving the way for its future economic development. As China's economy continues to develop and the regional integration of the Yangtze River Delta picks up pace, Suzhou's future growth prospects are even more promising.

## 练习一

### 一、判断题

1. "上有天堂、下有苏杭"，这里的"苏"指的是江苏。　☐

2. 苏州是中国桥、河最多的城市。　☐

3. 苏州工业园区是中国与新加坡政府的合作项目，是中国改革开放的窗口。☐

### 二、思考题

1. 请举例说明吴文化的特色是什么？

2. 丝绸的发展对苏州城市的发展有什么影响？

3. 苏州为什么能被评为中国首个"高等教育国际化示范区"？

## 五、特色美食

苏州不仅拥有悠久的历史，也有着灿烂的美食文化。苏州人遵循自然之道，吃东西讲究应时令、按季节，到什么时候，吃什么东西。苏州的本地菜叫苏帮菜，用料精细、做工细致，注重菜品的色、香、味、形，追求视觉和味觉的双重享受。

### 1. 松鼠鳜鱼

作为"鱼米之乡"，苏州的水产资源非常丰富。苏州人爱吃鱼，也擅长做鱼。松鼠鳜（guì）鱼就是苏帮菜中一道经典名菜，它的造型像一只松鼠，鱼肉外脆里嫩，酸甜可口。这道菜有着悠久的历史，据说清朝乾隆皇帝在苏州品尝过这道菜，并大加赞赏。有了来自皇帝的好评，松鼠鳜鱼变得更加有名，来苏州的游客都会去品尝一下这道菜。

## V. Specialty Food

Alongside its long history, Suzhou also boasts a splendid culinary culture. The locals adhere to the principles of eating according to the season and choosing foods that harmonize with the current time of a year. Suzhou's local cuisine is characterized by its fine ingredients, meticulous preparation, and emphasis on dishes' color, aroma, taste, and shape, aiming for both visual appeal and exquisite flavor.

### 1. Sweet and Sour Mandarin Fish

Known as a "land of fish and rice", Suzhou has abundant aquatic resources. The people of Suzhou have a deep love for fish and excel in its cooking. Sweet and sour mandarin fish is a classic dish in Suzhou cuisine. It is shaped like a squirrel, tastes crispy outside and tender inside, and has a sweet and sour flavor. The dish has a long history, and it is said that even Emperor Qianlong of the Qing Dynasty once tried this dish in Suzhou and highly praised it. Thanks to this imperial stamp of approval, sweet and sour mandarin fish has been a must-try dish for tourists visiting Suzhou.

### 2. 奥灶面

苏州人爱吃面，苏州街头到处可以看到各式各样的面馆。苏州面条的特点在于面条细而筋道，面汤鲜美可口，配料丰富多样。起源于苏州昆山的奥灶面是苏州面条的代表之一。奥灶面的面汤要用多种原料精心熬煮，另外还有"三烫"的特点——"面烫、汤烫、碗烫"。在冬天的早晨吃上一碗热气腾腾的奥灶面，能让人一整天都充满活力。

### 3. 碧螺春茶

碧螺春是中国传统名茶，已有1000多年的历史了。它产于苏州市吴中区的太湖边，因茶叶颜色碧绿、形似螺蛳而得名。太湖边种植了大量桃树、柑橘树、枇杷树等果树。当地的农民将茶树种在果树下，茶叶吸收了花香和果香，因此带有清新的水果气息。据说，清明节前茶叶品质最好，此时采摘和制作出来的茶被称为"明前茶"，是碧螺春中的珍品。

## 六、名胜古迹

### 1. 拙政园

拙政园是苏州现存最大的古典私家园林，被誉为江南古典园林的代表作。明朝正德八年（1513年），御史王献臣官场失意回到家乡，建造了拙政园作为养老之所。王献臣用西晋潘岳《闲居赋》中的"拙"和

### 2. Aozao Noodles

Suzhou people love noodles, and there are numerous noodle shops lining the city's streets. Suzhou noodles are renowned for their fine, chewy texture, flavorful broth, and various rich toppings. Among the local varieties, the Aozao noodles from Kunshan stand out. The soup is meticulously prepared with various ingredients, and the dish is cooked with the "three scalds" technique, where the noodles, soup, and bowl are all scalded. A bowl of hot Aozao noodles on a winter morning can energize one for the whole day.

### 3. Biluochun Tea

Biluochun is a renowned traditional Chinese tea with over a thousand years of history. It is grown and processed on the banks of the Taihu Lake in Wuzhong District and is named for its green color and the snail-like shape of its leaves. The banks of the Taihu Lake are lined with numerous peach, tangerine, loquat, and other fruit trees. Local farmers plant tea shrubs under these fruit trees, where the tea leaves absorb the fragrances of flowers and fruits to send out a fresh, fruity aroma. The leaves picked and processed before the Qingming Festival are considered the finest and are highly prized by connoisseurs.

## VI. Historical Sites and Scenic Spots

### 1. The Humble Administrator's Garden

The Humble Administrator's Garden is the largest extant classical private garden in Suzhou and is considered a masterpiece of Jiangnan classical gardens. In 1513, during the Zhengde era of the Ming Dynasty, the censor Wang Xianchen, disillusioned with officialdom, returned to his hometown and built a garden to enjoy his retirement. Wang named his garden "humble administrator", from Pan Yue's "Essay on Idleness" in the

"政"二字命名自己的园子，表达了自嘲和隐逸的情感。

据说建造拙政园的时候，吴门画派最著名的画家文征明曾经参与设计。如今，拙政园中还有一株他亲手种植的紫藤，距今已有400多年的历史，被称为"活着的文物"。拙政园以水为中心，所有建筑都依水而建，水边的假山和花木也尽可能地模仿江南水乡的风光。荷花是拙政园的一大特色。园内的水池里种满荷花，建筑也多以荷花命名。每年夏天，拙政园都会举办荷花旅游节，吸引众多游客前来观赏。

### 2. 网师园

网师园是苏州园林中较小的一座，虽然面积不到拙政园的六分之一，但布局巧妙、建筑精致，别具一格。"网师"的意思是"渔翁"，代表园林主人归隐山林的情怀。

网师园是中国第一个走出国门的园林。1978年，美国博物馆代表团来苏州参观，决定仿照网师园西面的庭院——殿春簃建造一座古典庭院。来自苏州的工匠们带着所有材料，包括从四川采来的楠木和苏州相城御窑

Western Jin Dynasty, poking fun at himself and expressing his desire for seclusion.

Legend has it that Wen Zhengming, Suzhou's most renowned painter at the time, played a role in designing the Humble Administrator's Garden. Today, a wisteria, over four hundred years old and planted by Wen Zhengming, still stands in the garden and is known as a "living cultural relic". The garden is designed around water, with every building harmoniously aligned along the water's edge. The artificial hills and plants by the water attempt to mimic the scenery of a Jiangnan water town as much as possible. Lotuses are a defining feature of the garden, filling the ponds and inspiring the names of numerous buildings. The garden celebrates this icon with a Lotus Tourism Festival each summer, drawing crowds of admirers.

### 2. The Garden of the Master of Nets

Although the Garden of the Master of Nets is one of Suzhou's smaller gardens, at less than one-sixth the size of the Humble Administrator's Garden, it is cleverly laid out, exquisitely built, and has a unique style. "Master of Nets", a fancy reference to "fisherman", represents the

烧制的砖瓦，漂洋过海。1980年3月，一座
与殿春簃几乎一模一样的庭院在纽约大都会
艺术博物馆成功落户，并在美国引起了轰
动。因为是按照明朝建筑设计的，庭院名为
"明轩"。前总统尼克松、国务卿基辛格等
数次前往参观，前去参观的美国民众更是络
绎不绝。

### 3. 虎丘

　　位于苏州城西北角的虎丘被称为"吴
中第一名胜"。宋朝著名诗人苏东坡曾经说
过，到苏州不游虎丘，是一件非常遗憾的事
情。据《史记》记载，在2500年前的春秋时
期，吴王阖闾死后被葬在虎丘山，3天后，
有一只白虎蹲在山上，"虎丘"由此得名。

　　虎丘的高度只有34.3米，但是历朝历代
留下的名胜古迹非常多，其中最出名的是剑
池和虎丘塔。剑池的形状像一把剑，传说吴
王阖闾墓的入口处就在这里，与吴王一起入
葬的还有3000把宝剑和许多财宝。出于保护
虎丘塔的目的，剑池至今没有被发掘，可以
说是虎丘最为神秘的地方。

　　虎丘塔是江南现存最早的佛塔，距今
已有1000多年的历史。这座塔有7层，塔高
47.7米。由于地基的问题，虎丘塔自明朝开

garden owner's aspiration for a reclusive life.

The Garden of the Master of Nets was the first Chinese garden to be replicated abroad. In 1978, a delegation from an American museum visited Suzhou and decided to replicate the courtyard on the west side of the Garden of the Master of Nets, the Dianchun Hall, in a classical courtyard design. Suzhou craftsmen and materials, including nanmu wood from Sichuan and bricks and tiles from Suzhou's Xiangcheng Imperial Kiln, were sent to the US. In March 1980, a courtyard almost identical to the Dianchun Hall was built in the Metropolitan Museum of Art in New York. Since it was designed in the style of the Ming Dynasty, it was named "the Ming Pavilion." It caused a sensation in the United States, attracting visits from dignitaries such as former President Nixon and Secretary of State Kissinger.

### 3. The Tiger Hill

The Tiger Hill, located in Suzhou's northwest corner, is celebrated as "the number one scenic spot of Wu". The famous poet Su Dongpo once said that it would be a great shame not to visit the Tiger Hill when in Suzhou. According to *Records of the Grand Historian*, 2,500 years ago, during the Spring and Autumn Period, King Helü of Wu was buried on the Tiger Hill. Three days after his burial, a white tiger was spotted on the hill, hence the name.

Although only 34.3 meters high, the Tiger Hill is rich in historical and cultural sites from various dynasties, most notably the Sword Pool and the Tiger Hill Pagoda. Named for its sword-like shape, the Sword Pool is claimed to be the site of King Helü's tomb entrance, where legend holds that three thousand precious swords and numerous treasures were interred with him. The Sword Pool remains sealed to this day to protect the Tiger Hill Pagoda, making it the most mysterious place on the Tiger Hill.

始发生倾斜，也被称为"中国的比萨斜塔"。在虎丘塔的修缮过程中，发现了许多珍贵的文物，其中最著名的是一件秘色瓷莲花碗，被专家认定为国宝级的文物，现为苏州博物馆的镇馆之宝之一。

### 4. 平江路

苏州在1000多年前的宋元时期叫"平江"，平江路的名字就来源于此。平江路是一条历史悠久的古街。南宋时期的苏州城市地图——《平江图》上就有平江路，河街的格局与现在的基本一致。

今天的平江路聚集了丰富的历史古迹和人文景观，被誉为"没有围墙的城市建筑博物馆"。漫步平江路，不仅可以领略"君到姑苏见，人家尽枕河"的古城风貌，品尝苏州老字号的传统美食，欣赏苏绣、苏扇、桃花坞年画等非遗文化，还可以坐在古老的茶楼里，听上一段昆曲，品尝一杯苏州太湖东山产的碧螺春。不少年轻人喜欢穿上汉服，在平江路上边走边拍照，成为一种新时尚。

The Tiger Hill Pagoda is the oldest extant Buddhist pagoda south of the Yangtze River, with over a thousand years of history. The pagoda has seven stories and stands 47.7 meters tall. Due to foundation issues, it began to tilt during the Ming Dynasty, hence called "China's Leaning Tower of Pisa". During the pagoda's restoration, many precious cultural relics were discovered, including an olive-green porcelain lotus bowl, now recognized as a national treasure and a centerpiece of the Suzhou Museum.

### 4. Pingjiang Road

Named "Pingjiang", an alias of Suzhou during the Song and Yuan Dynasties, Pingjiang Road is a historic riverside street. The river and street layout, as depicted on the "Map of Pingjiang" from the Song Dynasty, remains largely unchanged today.

Today's Pingjiang Road is rich in historical relics and cultural landscapes and is known as the "unwalled architectural museum". Along Pingjiang Road, one can appreciate the ancient cityscape characterized by the phrase "Wherever you go in Gusu, rivers follow", taste traditional delicacies from time-honored Suzhou brands, enjoy intangible cultural heritage such as Suzhou embroidery, Suzhou fans, and Taohuawu New Year pictures, sit in an ancient teahouse, listen to the Kunqu Opera, and taste the Biluochun tea from Dongshan on the bank of the Taihu Lake. In recent years, the street has also welcomed the new trend of young people wearing traditional Chinese attire from ancient times.

## 七、非遗文化

### 1. 苏绣

苏绣起源于苏州，是中国四大名绣[①]之一，也是苏州最著名的非物质文化遗产之一。早在春秋时期，吴国就已将刺绣用于服饰。苏绣到了清朝进入了全盛时期，当时皇室的刺绣品几乎都出自苏绣艺人之手。苏绣的最大特色是精细，同一色系会有十五六种不同深浅的丝线。有时为了达到艺术效果，一根丝线最多可以被分成128份。苏绣最著名的是"双面绣"，就是在同一块布的正反两面，同时绣出颜色和内容截然不同的图像，工艺高超令人惊叹。苏绣作品经常作为国礼赠送给外宾，是国际舞台上一抹亮丽的中国符号。

### 2. 昆曲

昆曲起源于苏州昆山一带，至今已有600多年历史，是中国最古老的戏剧形式之一。昆曲的最大特色是"美"和"雅"，无

---

① 中国四大名绣：苏绣、湘绣、蜀绣和粤绣。
The four famous embroideries of China refers to the Su embroidery (in Jiangsu Province), Xiang embroidery (in Hunan Province), Shu embroidery (in Sichuan Province), and Yue embroidery (in Guangdong Province).

## VII. Intangible Cultural Heritage

### 1. Suzhou Embroidery

Originating in Suzhou, Suzhou embroidery is celebrated as one of China's four great traditional embroidery styles and is one of the city's most treasured items of intangible cultural heritage. According to legend, as early as the Spring and Autumn Period, the State of Wu had used embroidery in clothing. Suzhou embroidery entered its golden age during the Qing Dynasty, when silk products embroidered by Suzhou artisans were used by the imperial family. The greatest feature of Suzhou embroidery is its fineness, with one color coming in fifteen or sixteen different shades of silk thread. Sometimes, a single silk thread is divided into 128 parts to achieve certain decorative effects. Suzhou embroidery is most famous for its "double-sided embroidery", where different colors and patterns are embroidered on the front and back of the same piece of silk, a skill that induces amazement. Often presented as diplomatic gifts, Suzhou embroidery has become a dazzling symbol of Chinese culture on the international stage.

### 2. The Kunqu Opera

Originating from the Kunshan area of Suzhou, the Kunqu Opera with a history of over 600 years is one of the oldest forms of Chinese drama. The Kunqu Opera is distinguished by its exquisite beauty and elegance, evident in its language, vocal style, costumes, and performance, all crafted to impart a sense of refined aesthetics and nobility to its audiences. Most Chinese operas have been influenced by the Kunqu Opera. Therefore, it is known as the "ancestor of a hundred operas". Classic works such as *The Peony Pavilion*, *The Palace of Eternal Life*, and *The Peach Blossom Fan* stand

论在语言、唱腔、服饰还是表演方面，都能给人以优美和高雅的感受。中国大部分戏曲都受到过昆曲的影响，昆曲因而被誉为"百戏之祖"。昆曲《牡丹亭》《长生殿》《桃花扇》等，都是中国古代戏曲文学中的不朽之作。2001年，昆曲被联合国教科文组织列为第一批"人类口头和非物质文化遗产代表作"。

as immortal masterpieces in the Chinese operatic repertoire. In 2001, the Kunqu Opera was listed as a "Masterpiece of the Oral and Intangible Heritage of Humanity" by UNESCO.

## 练习二

### 一、判断题

1. 自2500年前建立以来，苏州城的位置从来没有改变过。　☐
2. 被誉为"没有围墙的城市建筑博物馆"的是苏州平江路。　☐
3. 制作碧螺春茶的最佳时间是清明节后。　☐
4. 网师园是中国第一个出口到国外的园林。　☐
5. 位于苏州城东南角的虎丘被称为"吴中第一名胜"。　☐

### 二、思考题

1. 苏州为什么会被称为"人间天堂"？
2. 苏州园林有哪些特色？
3. 苏州为什么要保护古城？

### 三、拓展题

1. 以小组为单位，讨论以苏州为代表的吴文化有哪些特征，并以PPT形式进行汇报。
2. 选择一个你认为苏州最有特色的景点，拍一个小视频。
3. 观看一次昆曲表演，并与自己国家的戏曲做一个比较。

无锡 MUXI

第三章

———

太 / 湖 / 明 / 珠

The Pearl of the Taihu Lake

无锡，简称"锡"，大运河从城中贯穿而过，是一座有着 3000 多年悠久历史的文化名城、工商名城、旅游名城、教育名城。

# 一、城市概况

## 1. 地理环境

无锡位于江苏东南部，地处长江三角洲中段，北面靠着长江，南面是太湖，西边是常州，东边是苏州，地理位置优越。无锡气候温润，地势平坦，水系发达，总面积4627.46平方公里，常住人口749万人。

太湖位于江苏和浙江两省交界处，水域面积2338平方公里，是中国第三大淡水湖。无锡城区紧靠太湖，像是镶嵌在太湖湖畔的一颗明珠，熠熠生辉，早在20世纪初便赢得了"太湖明珠"的美誉。2002年，歌曲《太湖美》被定为无锡的市歌；2020年，"深海技术科学太湖实验室"在无锡正式揭牌成立；为吸引更多人才，无锡还推出了"太湖人才计划"。太湖已经成为无锡的一张城市名片。

# I. Overview

## 1. Geographical Environment

Wuxi is located in the southeast of Jiangsu Province in the middle of the Yangtze River Delta. It borders the Yangtze River to the north, the Taihu Lake to the south, Changzhou to the west, and Suzhou to the east. The city enjoys an excellent location in flat topography, a mild climate, and an extensive water system. It has an area of 4,627.46 square kilometers and a population of 7.49 million.

The Taihu Lake, which sits on the border between Jiangsu Province and Zhejiang Province, is the third largest freshwater lake in China, with a water area of 2,338 square kilometers. The urban area of Wuxi is situated close to the Taihu Lake like a shining pearl by the water, hence the city's nickname in the early 20th century. In 2002, "Beautiful Taihu Lake" was announced as the Song of Wuxi. In 2020, the Taihu Lab of Deepsea Technology was set up in Wuxi. Wuxi also launched a recruitment project named after the Taihu Lake to attract more talented professionals. The Taihu Lake has thus become a "business card" for Wuxi.

## 2. Development

There is no agreement on the origin of the name of Wuxi. According to historical books, Wuxi was once abundant in tin ore, but the mines were exhausted in the Han Dynasty, hence the name "Wuxi", which literally means "no tin". Wuxi was one of the major constituent settlements of the State of Wu. The county of Wuxi was set up in 202 BC, and the name Wuxi has been used ever since.

## 3. Wuxi Today

Wuxi is a major city in the Yangtze River Delta and an important member of the

## 2. 城市变迁

无锡地名的由来有多种说法，没有定论。根据史书记载，无锡的锡山原本富含锡矿，在汉朝开采殆尽，因此得名"无锡"。无锡是吴文化的重要发祥地之一，西汉（公元前202年）正式设置无锡县，名称沿用至今。

## 3. 今日无锡

无锡是长三角地区中心城市之一，上海大都市圈和苏锡常都市圈的重要组成部分。作为长三角一体化的重要节点城市，无锡拥有完善的立体交通网络，公路、铁路、水运、航空四位一体。市内京沪高速铁路、沪宁城际铁路穿城而过，设有无锡站、无锡东站、无锡新区站等6个铁路客运站点，距上海虹桥国际机场仅约半小时高铁车程。无锡硕放国际机场与国内50多个城市通航，还有国际航班直飞新加坡、大阪、首尔、芽庄等。便利的交通条件极大地促进了无锡与周边城市群的联动发展。

无锡是一座务实进取、敢做善为、开放包容的城市，连续4年荣获"中国最具幸福感城市"称号。在加强环境保护的同时，无锡不断推进城市建设。优质的教育、医疗资源，高效安全的公共交通体系，以及良好的生态环境，使无锡成为市民生活水平优越、幸福指数不断提高的宜居城市。

Shanghai and Suzhou-Wuxi-Changzhou metropolitan areas. With the further integration of the Yangtze River Delta, Wuxi has developed a comprehensive transportation network of highways, railways, water transportation, and aviation. The Beijing-Shanghai high-speed railway and the Shanghai-Nanjing intercity railway pass through six railway stations in the city, including Wuxi Station, Wuxi East Station, and Wuxi New Area Station. It takes only about half an hour to go from Shanghai Hongqiao International Airport to Wuxi by high-speed rail. Wuxi Shuofang International Airport offers domestic flights to over 50 cities in China, plus direct flights to Singapore, Osaka, Seoul, and Nha Trang. Convenient transportation has greatly promoted the harmonious development between Wuxi and the surrounding cities.

Wuxi is a pragmatic, proactive, open, and inclusive city recognized as one of "China's happiest cities" for four consecutive years. While strengthening environmental protection measures, Wuxi is actively promoting its urban construction. It is a highly livable city with high-quality education and medical resources, efficient and safe public transportation systems, and a good environment.

## 二、文化印象

从古老的吴文化起源，到近代民族工业与现代乡镇企业的摇篮，无锡作为国家历史文化名城，拥有丰富且独特的历史文化遗产和浓郁的地方文化底蕴。

### 1. 惠山泥人

惠山位于无锡市西郊，这里的黑泥细腻柔软，黏（nián）度较高，可塑性强。惠山泥人就是用惠山黑泥制作的彩色泥塑，也是国家级非物质文化遗产，相传已有400多年的历史。在唐朝，惠山的农民在农闲时用泥土捏一些小玩意儿，后来做泥人的越来越多，"家家善彩塑，户户做泥人"。惠山泥人最具代表性的形象是两个健壮、可爱的孩子"阿福""阿喜"，他们手里捧着象征吉祥如意的鲤鱼、元宝、桃子等物品，能给人们带来平安幸福。

### 2. 宜兴紫砂

宜兴被誉为"中国陶都"。在宜兴出土的陶器可以追溯到7000多年前。"家家捶泥声，户户制陶忙"仍是当今宜兴陶业的真实写照。紫砂壶作为宜兴紫砂制品的代表，始于宋朝，兴盛于明朝，已有600多年的发展历史。紫砂壶的原料是紫砂泥，泥质细腻、透气性强，用来泡茶可以较长时间地保持茶水的味道。而且，紫砂壶用的时间越久，表面会变得越来越光滑、温润、富有光泽。紫砂壶质地独特、造型多样，在使用过程中强调心境平和，体现了中国人追求平衡、和谐的审美观。

## II. Cultural Impressions

From the ancient origin of the Wu culture to a cradle of modern industry and modern township enterprises, Wuxi is rich in historical heritage and boasts unique local cultural flavors.

### 1. Huishan Clay Figurines

Huishan is located in the western suburb of Wuxi. A fine, soft black clay found in Huishan boasts high viscosity and strong plasticity, and can be used to make Huishan clay figurines. With a history of over 400 years, these colored clay sculptures have become a national intangible cultural heritage. In the Tang Dynasty, farmers in Huishan began to make small things out of the black clay for fun. Later, this handicraft became so popular in Huishan that almost every household made colored figurines. The most commonly referenced image in Huishan clay figurines is that of two plump, cute children, Afu (lucky) and Axi (happy). They hold in their arms some auspicious items such as carps, ingots, and peaches, believed to bring people peace and happiness in Chinese culture.

### 2. Yixing Purple Clay Pottery

Ancient pottery unearthed in Yixing, the Ceramic Capital of China, can be traced back more than 7,000 years. Nowadays, many households in Yixing are still busy pounding clay and making pottery. Purple clay teapots, one of the quintessential Yixing purple clay products, have been made for over 600 years, beginning in the Song Dynasty and reaching a peak in the Ming Dynasty. Purple clay is soft and porous, and teapots made from it do a great job of keeping the aroma of tea. These teapots have a unique texture and diverse designs; the longer they are used, the glossier their surfaces will become. A purple clay teapot needs to be handled with care and a peaceful mind, a reflection of the Chinese aesthetic pursuit of balance and harmony.

## 三、教育交流

### 1. 高等教育概况

无锡高等教育资源丰富，目前共有普通高校13所，其中本科院校3所，专科院校10所，在校生超过15万人。以江南大学为代表的综合性、研究型高校，以无锡学院为代表的应用型本科高校，以无锡职业技术学院为代表的职业技能型高职院校共同构成了无锡多层次、多元化、高质量的高等教育体系。

### 2. 高校介绍

江南大学（www.jiangnan.edu.cn）源起1902年创建的三江师范学堂，办学历史悠久，是教育部直属重点大学，国家"211工程"重点建设高校和"双一流"建设高校。学校有18个学院，在校生3.4万余人，其中国际学生300余人。学校有7个博士学位授权点、27个硕士学位授权点、44个本科专业招收国际学生。自1964年招收国际学生以来，已培养研究生、本科生、语言培训生等不同层次的国际学生近万名。

### 3. 特色专业

食品科学与工程、轻工技术与工程是江南大学的两大王牌专业。在2023年"软科世界一流学科排名"中，"食品科学与工程"学科连续五年蝉联世界第一，"纺织科学与工程"学科排名世界第二。学校建有8个国家级科研平台。设计学、控制科学与工程、化学工程与技术也是江南大学的优势学科。

## III. Education and International Exchanges

### 1. Overview of Higher Education

Wuxi boasts a total of 13 higher education institutions (three universities and ten vocational colleges) and over 150,000 students enrolled. A multi-level, diversified, and high-quality higher education system has been formed in Wuxi, with comprehensive research-oriented universities such as Jiangnan University, application-oriented universities like Wuxi University, and skills-oriented vocational colleges represented by Wuxi Institute of Technology.

### 2. Introduction to Universities

Originating from the Sanjiang Normal School in 1902, Jiangnan University (www.jiangnan.edu.cn) has a long history of education. A key university administrated by the Ministry of Education, Jiangnan University is a member of the "211 Project" and a "Double First Class Project". It has 18 schools and over 34,000 students, including over 300 international students. It offers 7 doctoral degree programs, 27 master's degree programs, and 44 undergraduate programs, all of which admit international students. Since 1964, it has educated nearly 10,000 international students of different levels, including postgraduates, undergraduates, and language learners.

### 3. Featured Disciplines

Jiangnan University's top programs include Food Science & Engineering and Light Industry Technology & Engineering. In the 2023 Global Ranking of Academic Subjects by Shanghai Ranking, the university's Food Science & Engineering program was again ranked first worldwide for the fifth consecutive year, and its Textile Science & Engineering program ranked second. The university has eight national research platforms and boasts top programs in Design, Control Science & Engineering, and Chemical Engineering & Technology.

## 四、经济腾飞

### 1. 工商名城

19世纪末，一批民族资本家在无锡开办纱厂、面粉厂等，民族工商业逐步形成并发展迅速，无锡被誉为"中国近代民族工业的发祥地"。目前，高端纺织服装、物联网、集成电路、生物医药等代表性产业蓬勃发展。海澜之家、雅迪电动车都是来自无锡的品牌。2023年，无锡的地区生产总值超过1.5万亿元，在省内排第三名，仅次于苏州和南京。

### 2. 科技创新

无锡正逐渐成为科技创新的前沿阵地。"神威·太湖之光"超级计算机在无锡的国家超级计算无锡中心安装并投入运行，"奋斗者"号万米载人潜水器的关键组件在无锡的中国船舶七〇二所组装。此外，深海技术科学太湖实验室、长三角太阳能光伏技术创新中心，江苏集萃集成电路应用技术创新中心等新型研发机构也集聚在此。这都将推动城市的创新驱动发展，加快实现高水平科技自立自强，努力将无锡打造成"国内一流、具有国际影响力的产业科技创新高地"。

## IV. Economic Takeoff

### 1. Industrial and Commercial City

At the end of the 19th century, a group of Chinese businessmen built yarn and flour mills in Wuxi, thus starting the city's modern industry. Later, Wuxi become known as the birthplace of modern Chinese industry. Wuxi has witnessed the development of many robust industries, such as high-end textiles and clothing, the internet of things, integrated circuits, and biomedicine. Hailan Home and Yadi Electric Vehicles, two well-known brands, are based in Wuxi. In 2023, the city's GDP exceeded 1.5 trillion yuan, ranking third in Jiangsu Province behind Suzhou and Nanjing.

### 2. Technological Innovation

Wuxi is gradually becoming the forefront of technological innovation. The Sunway TaihuLight supercomputer was installed and now operates at the National Supercomputing Center in Wuxi, and the key components of the 10,000-meter manned submersible "Fendouzhe" (Striver) were assembled in Wuxi. Many research institutes have gathered here, such as the Taihu Lab of Deepsea Technology, the Yangtze River Delta Solar Photovoltaic Technology Innovation Center, and the Jiangsu Jicui Integrated Circuit Application Technology Innovation Center. This technology cluster will drive innovation, accelerate technological self-reliance and self-improvement, and transform Wuxi into a first-class industrial and technological innovation highland with global prestige.

## 五、特色美食

### 1. 阳山水蜜桃

无锡阳山镇是中国著名的水蜜桃之乡。由于日照充足和特别的火山灰土壤，阳山出产的水蜜桃的果形更大，香气浓郁，入口即化。阳山水蜜桃已有近百年栽培史，不仅是馈赠亲朋好友的佳品，还远销国外，成为一张散发着甜蜜芬芳的无锡"城市名片"。

### 2. 阳羡茶

宜兴古称"阳羡"，宜兴南部的丘陵山区气候湿润、雨水充沛，是江苏主要茶叶产区。从唐朝起，这里的茶就被选为进献给皇室的贡品。唐朝诗人卢全曾写道："天子未尝阳羡茶，百草不敢先开花。"阳羡茶以绿茶"阳羡雪芽"和红茶"阳羡金毫"最为著名。宜兴现有茶园约7.5万亩，是江苏最大的产茶基地。

### 3. 太湖三白

太湖三白是指太湖的三种河鲜类特产：白鱼、白虾、银鱼。因为都是白色的，故名"太湖三白"。

白鱼肉质细嫩、鲜美，最常见的做法是加入盐、姜、葱等调料清蒸。

白虾呈透明状，煮熟之后会变成温润饱满的白色。简单水煮后，加入小葱、姜片和料酒，就可以勾出白虾清甜鲜美的味道。

银鱼个头不大，大的跟小手指差不多，小的只有牙签粗细，通体细嫩透明、洁白无鳞。银鱼可以和鸡蛋一起炒熟，或者加入笋丝做成银鱼羹。

## V. Specialty Food

### 1. Yangshan Honey Peach

Yangshan Town in Wuxi is renowned as the "Hometown of Honey Peach" in China. Due to abundant sunlight and the unique volcanic ash soil, the peaches are big and juicy with a rich aroma. The honey peaches have been grown in Yangshan for nearly 100 years. They make excellent gifts for friends and are also exported overseas, becoming a sweet, fragrant icon of Wuxi.

### 2. Yangxian Tea

Yixing, formerly "Yangxian", is one of the major tea-producing areas in Jiangsu because of its humid climate and abundant rainfall in its hilly and mountainous areas. Since the Tang Dynasty, the tea produced in Yixing was selected as a tribute to the imperial family, and Lu Tong, a poet in the Tang Dynasty, wrote a poem praising the tea. Yixing is the largest tea production base in Jiangsu Province, with about 500 hectares of tea gardens. Yixing is most famous for its green tea "Snow Sprout" and black tea "Golden Hair".

### 3. The Three Whites of the Taihu Lake

The Taihu Lake abounds with fish and shrimp. "Three Whites" refers to white fish, white shrimp, and whitebait found in the lake.

The white fish is tender and delicious. It is usually steamed with seasonings such as salt, ginger, and scallions.

The white shrimp starts transparent and turns white when cooked. It takes on a sweet, delicious taste after a quick boil with scallion, ginger slices, and rice wine.

Whitebaits are extremely small. The big ones are about the size of a little finger, and the small ones are as thin as a toothpick, and they have delicate, transparent bodies. Whitebait can be stir-fried with eggs or made into a soup with shredded bamboo shoots.

## 六、名胜古迹

无锡是吴文化的重要发源地之一，名胜古迹众多。鼋头渚（Yuántóu Zhǔ）、蠡园（Líyuán）、寄畅园、惠山古镇等，都展现了秀美的江南风光和深厚的历史文化底蕴。

### 1. 南长街

南长街沿古运河而建，以独特的运河水乡风貌著称。保存了上百座老房子，既有粉墙黛瓦的江南民居，又有中西合璧的石库门别墅。其中，明朝建造的清名桥不仅是南长街的标志性建筑，也是大运河的重要组成部分。漫步南长街，游客既能欣赏粉墙黛瓦的江南民居、中西合璧的石库门别墅，还能品尝到各式各样的地道无锡美食。

### 2. 惠山古镇

惠山由九座小山峰组成，最高的也只有300多米，但这里不仅是无锡的"母亲河"梁溪河的源头，而且山脚下的惠山古镇保存了很多明清时期的园林、祠堂、牌坊、古桥和老街，被誉为展现江南地区历史文化的"露天历史博物馆"。古镇的建筑以黑白两色为主，充满了浓郁的水墨风情。天下第二泉、愚公谷、寄畅园等景点吸引了历代文人墨客，留下了许多诗词歌赋和轶事佳话。

## VI. Historical Sites and Scenic Spots

Wuxi, as one of the birthplaces of the Wu culture, is endowed with many scenic spots and historical sites, such as Yuantou Zhu, Liyuan Garden, Jichang Garden, and Huishan Ancient Town. The beautiful landscapes showcase picturesque Jiangnan scenery and rich historical and cultural heritage.

### 1. Nanchang Street

Nanchang Street, built along the ancient canal, is well-known for its unique water town style. Many old houses are well preserved with traditional white walls and black tiles. There are also Shikumen villas that blend Chinese and Western styles. The Qingming Bridge, built in the Ming Dynasty, is a landmark of Nanchang Street and an important component of the Grand Canal. You can enjoy different styles of architecture and taste a variety of authentic local cuisine as you stroll along the street.

### 2. Huishan Ancient Town

The Huishan Hill consists of nine small peaks, the highest of which is just over 300 meters. The hill is the source of the Liangxi River, the mother river of Wuxi, which breathes life into the ancient town at the foot of the mountain. Classical gardens, ancestral temples, memorial archways, ancient bridges, and streets of the Ming and Qing Dynasties have been preserved intactly in the town. It is known as an "open-air historical museum" that shows the history and culture of the Jiangnan region. The buildings are built with black tiles and white walls, resembling works of Chinese ink painting. The spring water, the valleys, and the gardens have attracted a lot of scholars and tourists since ancient times, who have left many poems, songs, and anecdotes behind.

### 3. 鼋头渚

鼋头渚是太湖西北岸的一个半岛，因有巨石突入湖中，就像鼋（一种与龟外形相似，但体型巨大的动物）昂起头浮在水上，"渚"是水中的一小块陆地，因而得名"鼋头渚"。鼋头渚不仅是欣赏太湖景色的最佳地点，还是赏樱、观鸟，游览道教与佛教文化遗址，体验吴越文化的绝佳场所。

### 3. Yuantou Zhu

Yuantou Zhu is a peninsula on the northwest bank of the Taihu Lake. A huge rock protrudes into the lake, looking like a Yuan (a type of large softshell turtle) raising its head out of the water, hence the name "Yuantou Zhu" (a waterside patch like a turtle head). It is an ideal place to enjoy the scenery of the lake, observe birds and cherry blossoms, visit Taoist and Buddhist sites, and experience the local Wuyue culture.

## 七、历史名人

### 1. 徐霞客

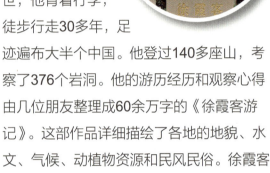

徐霞客（1587—1641）是明朝杰出的地理学家、探险家。从22岁启程到54岁去世，他背着行李，徒步行走30多年，足迹遍布大半个中国。他登过140多座山，考察了376个岩洞。他的游历经历和观察心得由几位朋友整理成60余万字的《徐霞客游记》。这部作品详细描绘了各地的地貌、水文、气候、动植物资源和民风民俗。徐霞客开始旅游的日子——5月19日——也被定为"中国旅游日"。

### 2. 阿炳

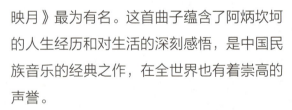

阿炳（1893—1950）是无锡著名的民间音乐家，创作了大量二胡独奏作品。流传至今的几首作品中，《二泉映月》最为有名。这首曲子蕴含了阿炳坎坷的人生经历和对生活的深刻感悟，是中国民族音乐的经典之作，在全世界也有着崇高的声誉。

### 3. 徐悲鸿

徐悲鸿（1895—1953）是杰出的画家和美术教育家，是中国现代美术事业的奠基者之一。他的作品题材广泛，尤其是奔马图最为人称道。他参照西方的透视法，在技法上运用中国水墨的晕染技法，以墨的浓淡表现明暗，使奔马形象生动。

## VII. Historical Figures

### 1. Xu Xiake

Xu Xiake (1587–1641) was an outstanding geographer and explorer in the Ming Dynasty. From the age of 22 to his death at 54, he traveled almost half of China on foot. He visited over 140 mountains and 376 caves. Several of his friends compiled his travel experiences and observations into a travelogue of over 600,000 words entitled *Xu Xiake's Travels*, which provides a detailed description of the landforms, hydrology, climate, flora and fauna, and folk customs of various regions. May 19th, the date on which Xu Xiake started his travels, is designated as China Tourism Day to commemorate Xu's adventures.

### 2. Abing

Abing (1893–1950) was a famous folk musician from Wuxi who created many *erhu* solo works. Among his works that have been passed down to this day, "Erquan Yingyue" (Moon Reflected in the Second Spring) is the most famous. The music tells of Abing's tumultuous life and profound insights. It is a classic work for *erhu*, a Chinese musical instrument with a high reputation worldwide.

### 3. Xu Beihong

Xu Beihong (1895–1953) was an outstanding painter, art educator, and one of the founders of modern Chinese art. His works cover a wide range of themes, and his paintings of galloping horses are highly praised. When creating these paintings, he adopted both Western perspective and the dyeing technique of Chinese ink painting, portraying light and dark with the intensity of ink to depict vivid images of galloping horses.

Xu once said, "No matter how well a painter paints and how great his achievements are, it is only his personal achievement. If art

徐悲鸿曾说："一个画家，他画得再好，成就再大，只不过是他一个人的成就；如果把美术教育发展起来，就能培养出一大批画家，那就是国家的成就。"他积极推动美术教育改革，曾任中央美术学院首任院长，为中国培养了大批美术人才。

### 4. 钱钟书

钱钟书（1910—1998）是中国现代著名学者、作家。他知识渊博，学贯中西，对中国的史学、哲学、文学等有深入研究，对西方学术思想也有深入理解，出版了大量学术著作。钱钟书的小说风格独特。他的作品《围城》是一部长篇讽刺性小说，以20世纪三四十年代的中国为背景，描绘了主人公方鸿渐的人生经历，揭示了人们在婚姻、事业、生活上"城外的人想冲进去，城里的人想逃出来"的心理现象，是中国现代文学的经典之作。

education is developed, it can cultivate many painters, which is the country's achievement." He actively promoted the reform of art education and served as the first president of the Central Academy of Fine Arts, which cultivated a large number of art talents for China.

### 4. Qian Zhongshu

Qian Zhongshu (1910–1998) was a famous modern Chinese scholar and writer proficient in both Chinese and Western studies. He conducted in-depth research on Chinese history, philosophy, and literature, and had a deep understanding of Western academics. He published a large number of academic works, but his most famous work is probably *Fortress Besieged*, a satirical novel set in the 1930s and 1940s. This novel depicts the life of an intellectual Fang Hongjian, and reveals people's inner conflicts regarding their marriages, careers, and lives, demonstrating that those outside want to get in, and those inside want to get out. It is a classic of modern Chinese literature.

### 练习

#### 一、判断题

1. 太湖是中国最大的淡水湖。☐
2. 鼋头渚是太湖东南岸的一个半岛。☐
3. 惠山古镇被称为江南历史文化的"露天历史博物馆"。☐
4. 《围城》是徐悲鸿创作的一部长篇小说。☐

二、思考题

1. 无锡的江南民居有什么建筑特色?

2. 无锡有一个地方叫"鼋头渚",这三个字有什么样的来历?

3. 为什么阳山的水蜜桃非常有名?

三、拓展题

以小组为单位开展一次社会实践,调研无锡南长街的商业业态,并与南长街历史上的商业业态进行比较分析。

# Chapter 4

常州

CHANGZHOU

# 第四章

中 / 华 / 龙 / 城

## The Dragon City of China

常州位于江苏南部，别名"龙城"，是全国唯一被东经 120 度经线穿越城区的城市。它不仅地理位置独特，而且历史悠久。作为连接无锡、南京和镇江的重要纽带，常州也是苏锡常都市圈的关键成员之一，拥有约 530 万人口。

## 一、城市概况

### 1. 地理环境

常州，位于江苏南部、长江三角洲中部，是全国唯一被东经120度经线（"北京时间"基准线）穿越城区的城市。常州东连无锡，西接南京、镇江，南与安徽相邻。

常州四季分明，夏季炎热潮湿，冬季寒冷湿润。常州的地貌以平原为主，同时拥有山丘和平原湖泊。常州东有太湖，北依长江，京杭大运河穿城而过，加上西太湖和长荡湖，形成了河道纵横、湖泊相连、江河相通的江南水乡风貌。

常州交通便捷，有发达的立体交通网络。京沪高铁、沪宁高速、312国道，以及长江常州港等交通枢纽环布城市内外。奔牛国际机场不仅开设了通往韩国、日本、泰国、印度尼西亚等多条国际航线，还有通达北京、香港、台北、广州、深圳、成都、大连等20多个国内主要城市的航线。

## I. Overview

### 1. Geographical Environment

Changzhou is located in the south of Jiangsu Province at the center of the Yangtze River Delta. It is the only city in China to be bisected by the 120-degree east longitude line, on which Beijing Time (UTC+08:00) is based. The city is surrounded by Wuxi to the east, Nanjing and Zhenjiang to the west, and Anhui Province to the south.

The four seasons are clear in Changzhou, with hot, humid summers and cold, wet winters. The terrain is mostly flat, with some hills and lakes. The Taihu Lake to the east, the Yangtze River to the north, and the Beijing-Hangzhou Grand Canal running through the city, along with the West Taihu Lake and the Changdang Lake, form a network of crisscrossing rivers, inter connected lakes, and connected waterways, creating a unique "waterside town" view characteristic of Jiangnan.

An extensive transport network connects Changzhou to several hubs, including the Beijing-Shanghai High-speed Railway, the Shanghai-Nanjing Expressway, the National Highway 312, and the Changzhou Port on the Yangtze River. Benniu International Airport in Changzhou offers international flights to the Republic of Korea, Japan, Thailand, and Indonesia, as well as domestic flights to over 20 Chinese cities including Beijing, Hong Kong, Taipei, Guangzhou, Shenzhen, Chengdu, and Dalian.

### 2. Development

Changzhou has a rich history of early human activities, as proven by the discovery of the "Eosimias sinensis" fossil at the Shuimu Mountain, dating back about 45 million years, 10 million years prior to the hominid fossil found in North Africa.

Changzhou's history dates back over 2,500

## 2. 城市变迁

常州是人类早期活动的区域之一。水母山考古发现的"中华曙猿"化石证明了常州地区在约4500万年前就有古生物的存在，这比北非"人类祖先"的化石记录还要早1000多万年。

常州有2500多年的建城史，可以追溯到公元前547年的春秋时期，当时吴国的季札被封在延陵，这是常州建城的开始。随后，常州经历了多次名称变更，如晋陵、武进等。到了公元589年的隋朝，随着行政制度的调整，常州这一名称正式确立。"龙城"这个别称则来源于民间神话故事"六龙降魔"及清朝乾隆皇帝在天宁寺题写的"龙城象教"匾额。中华人民共和国成立后，常州成为江苏管辖的地级市。

## 3. 今日常州

常州简称"常"，古称毗陵，人口约530万，与苏州、无锡构成了苏锡常都市圈。近年来，常州加强与以色列、德国等国家的合作关系，大力推进制造产业的智能化与绿色化转型，成为长三角地区重要的现代制造业基地。在城市发展和环境保护方面，常州展现出卓越的平衡能力。常州不仅连续获评"全国文明城市""全国优秀旅游城市"和"国家环保模范城市"等多项国家级称号，常州的武进区更是荣获联合国人居环境特别荣誉奖，并成为中国第一个被授予"人居实验城市"称号的地区。常州正以"全国新能源之都"为建设目标，全力推进城市升级转型，在经济发展模式、技术创新等方面进行全面改革。同时，不断深化人文建设，让市民在享受经济发展的同时，也能感受到浓郁的文化氛围和宜居的生活环境。

years, when Ji Zha of the State of Wu was enfeoffed in Yanling in 547 BCE during the Spring and Autumn Period. The city went by numerous names over the course of history, including Jinling and Wujin, before officially being given the name Changzhou in 589 CE during the Sui Dynasty. The title "Dragon City" originates from the folk tale "Six Dragons Subduing Demons" and the plaque "Buddhism in the Dragon City" in the Tianning Temple written by Emperor Qianlong of the Qing Dynasty. After the People's Republic of China was founded, Changzhou was promoted to a prefecture-level city in Jiangsu.

### 3. Changzhou Today

Changzhou, abbreviated as "Chang", historically called Piling, is home to about 5.3 million people. It is part of the Suzhou-Wuxi-Changzhou metropolitan area. In recent years, Changzhou has increased collaboration with nations such as Israel and Germany, promoting intelligent and green manufacturing transformations and establishing itself as a major modern manufacturing center in the Yangtze River Delta. The city excels at balancing urban development and environmental protection, earning several national titles such as "National Civilized City" "National Excellent Tourism City" and "National Environmental Protection Model City". Wujin District has also received the UN-Habitat Scroll of Honor Award and became China's first "Human Habitat Experimental City". Changzhou aspires to be a "National Hub of New Energy" encouraging urban development and comprehensive economic and technological advancements. Concurrently, the city focuses on strengthening cultural construction, allowing inhabitants to benefit from economic progress while also enjoying a rich cultural environment and a high quality of life.

## 二、文化印象

常州作为国家历史文化名城，有着深厚的文化底蕴和独特的地域特色，是中国吴文化与齐梁文化的重要发源地。在历史上，常州不仅名人辈出，在非物质文化遗产方面也表现出色，常州梳篦、留青竹刻、乱针绣等传统技艺传承至今，展现了江南传统工艺的精巧细致。

### 1. 常州梳篦

常州梳篦是一项拥有1600多年历史的传统手工艺，分为篦箕和木梳两个种类。它曾被选为宫廷专用的珍品，而享有"宫梳名篦"的美名。篦箕用天然毛竹、坚固的牛骨和防潮的生漆等材料制成；而木梳则多用质地细腻的黄杨木或硬度适中的石楠木为原料。梳篦不仅实用，能清除头发污垢，促进头部血液循环，还因为精美的设计和工艺，有欣赏和装饰价值。

## II. Cultural Impressions

Changzhou, a historical and cultural city, has a rich legacy and unique regional characteristics. It is an important birthplace of Wu and Qiliang culture. Changzhou has given rise to many notable personalities throughout its history and excelled at preserving intangible cultural heritage. Traditional techniques such as the comb production, bamboo carving, and random stitch embroidery have been passed down through generations, exhibiting the exquisite craftsmanship of traditional Jiangnan crafts.

### 1. Changzhou Combs

The Changzhou combs, a product of traditional craftsmanship dating back over 1,600 years, are classified into two types: combs made of bone and bamboo, and wooden combs. They were once exclusively used at the imperial court and historically referred to as the "Palace Comb". The former is made of natural bamboo, tough water buffalo or yellow cattle bones, and moisture-proof lacquer. Wooden combs, typically constructed of delicate boxwood or moderately durable Briar, are useful for removing particles from hair and increasing blood circulation, as well as being admired for their intricate design and craftsmanship.

### 2. 留青竹刻

留青竹刻被称为"留青"，是因为这种独特的雕刻技术是在竹子表面一层约0.1毫米厚的青皮上进行雕刻。这种工艺起源于唐朝，经过数百年的发展，到了清朝末年已经名声显赫。留青竹刻的成品形式多样，有工艺挂屏、台屏、笔筒和臂搁等，不仅实用，更是赏心悦目。竹刻的题材广泛，有细腻婉约的花草树木、生动活泼的虫鱼鸟兽、意境悠远的山水人物和结构精巧的亭台楼阁等。

### 3. 乱针绣

乱针绣创始于20世纪30年代。它既是一种以针线为工具，用乱针技法制作的"针画"，也是一种融合画理与绣理的刺绣艺术。它模仿绘画的效果，在表现光影、色彩和立体质感上，达到了很高的艺术境界，被称为"中国第五大名绣"。这种绣法采用长短不一、方向交错的针法，看似杂乱无章，其实构图严谨，色彩丰富，将绘画艺术与刺绣工艺融为一体。

## 三、教育交流

常州古时就以"儒风蔚然"著称，意思是常州的儒家文化氛围浓厚、教育兴盛、人才辈出，是东南地区的佼佼者。近现代以来，常州崇文重教的传统不仅没有衰退，反而更加深入人心。

### 2. Liuqing Bamboo Carving

Liuqing bamboo carving got its name from the unique technique of carving on a 0.1-millimeter layer of green bamboo skin. This craft dates back to the Tang Dynasty and became widely recognized by the end of the Qing Dynasty. Liuqing bamboo carvings are available in a variety of styles, such as hanging screens, tabletop screens, pen holders, and tabletop armrests, combining functionality with artistic appeal. Typical patterns include delicate flowers, trees, insects, fish, birds, animals, landscapes, pavilions, and towers, all of which are exquisitely detailed.

### 3. Random Stich Embroidery

Random stitch embroidery, which originated in the 1930s, is created with needlework and random stitch techniques. This embroidery combines the art of painting and stitching techniques, resulting in a high level of artistic expression featuring light, shadow, colour, and three-dimensional texture. The style uses stiches of varied lengths and alternate directions that, while appearing disorganized, are meticulously designed and vividly coloured. This style of embroidery is regarded as the "fifth most famous embroidery style in China".

## III. Education and International Exchanges

Changzhou has long been recognised for its "Confucian scholar style," reflecting in its strong Confucian cultural environment, vibrant education, and an abundant amount of talents, making it one of the outstanding cities in China's southeastern region. This legacy of valuing education lives on today and is deeply etched in the hearts of its people.

## 1. 高等教育概况

常州拥有11所高等院校，其中本科院校3所、专科院校8所，在校生总数8万余人，包含研究生6200余人和国际学生800余人。全市高校教师队伍素质优良，学科专业较为齐全，教学科研水平高，并且致力于国际教育交流。常州有两所国家级现代产业学院和两所"专精特新"产业学院，为国际学生提供了丰富的学习资源和发展机会。

## 2. 高校介绍

常州大学（www.cczu.edu.cn）是常州最早开展本科教育的高校。学校由江苏省人民政府与中国三大能源公司——中国石油天然气集团有限公司、中国石油化工集团有限公司及中国海洋石油集团有限公司联合共建，不仅是一所公办本科院校，还是江苏高水平大学建设高峰计划建设高校，并已通过中国高校来华留学质量认证。石油石化和创新创业是常州大学的办学特色，为学生提供了独特的学术研究与实践平台。学校与30多个国家和地区的60余所大学建立紧密合作关系。为了满足国际学生的多元化需求，学校特别开设4个全英语授课的本科专业，并开放所有本、硕、博层次的专业申请，吸引了来自40多个国家的600多名国际学生在校学习。此外，学校举办的国际文化节、"知行中国"社会实践项目、"中国故事汇"等一系列品牌活动，极大地丰富了国际学生的校园生活，深受广大学生的喜爱。

## 1. Overview of Higher Education

Changzhou has eleven higher education institutions, including three universities and eight vocational colleges. The overall number of students exceeds 80,000, including around 6,200 postgraduate students and more than 800 international students. The city's institutions are known for their superb faculty, diverse range of fields, high-quality teaching and research, and a strong emphasis on international educational exchanges. There are two national-level modern industrial colleges, as well as two "specialized, refined, and innovative" industrial colleges, which provide international students with an abundance of resources and opportunities.

## 2. Introduction to Universities

Changzhou University (www.cczu.edu.cn) is Changzhou's first public university to provide undergraduate programs. The university is a collaborative effort between the Jiangsu Provincial People's Government and three major energy companies (China National Petroleum Corporation, Sinopec, and China National Offshore Oil Corporation). It is an outstanding university under the Jiangsu Summit Plan for High-Level University Construction. The university has passed Higher Education Accreditation for International Students in China. Changzhou University, which specializes in petrochemicals, innovation, and entrepreneurship, offers students a one-of-a-kind academic research and operational platform. The university has formed close collaborations with more than 60 universities in over 30 countries and regions. To meet the needs of international students, the university offers four undergraduate majors taught exclusively in English, and applications are accepted for all undergraduate, postgraduate, and doctorate programs, attracting over 600 international students from more than

### 3. 特色专业

常州大学的化学工程与工艺、石油工程、计算机科学与技术、国际经济与贸易四个一流专业深受国际学生喜爱，是学校的特色优势专业。这些专业通过跨学科协作，成功研发了一系列创新技术与装备，包括苯酚烷基化清洁催化技术、危化品气瓶动态监管公共平台，以及高效回收油气成套技术及装置等60余项成果。这些研究成果不仅展现了学校的学术研究与技术创新实力，还广泛应用于中国众多大型石油石化企业中，产生了显著的社会、经济和生态效益。

## 四、经济腾飞

常州是江苏省内经济发达城市之一。20世纪七八十年代，常州经历了快速的工业化进程，这一时期的"工业一条龙"发展模式和乡镇企业"苏南模式"掀起全国"中小城市学常州"的热潮，使常州成为闻名全国的"工业明星城市"。至今，常州仍然保持着强劲的工业基础和创新活力，智能制造装备、新能源、新型碳材料构成了常州经济腾飞的三大产业集群。2023年，常州实现了历史性跨越，成为GDP万亿之城，同时，还位列中国百强城市排行榜全国第21位、江苏第4位，标志着常州的经济规模和综合实力达到了一个新的高度。

40 countries. Furthermore, the university arranges a variety of well-received activities, including the International Cultural Festival, Understanding China, and China Story Show, which considerably enrich the life on campus for international students.

### 3. Featured Disciplines

Changzhou University boasts four first-class majors: Chemical Engineering and Technology, Petroleum Engineering, Computer Science and Technology, and International Economics and Trade. These majors are highly sought after by international students because of their unique characteristics. They have encouraged the development of novel technologies and equipment through interdisciplinary collaboration. Key examples include Phenol Alkylation Clean Catalytic technology, a public platform for dynamic monitoring of hazardous chemical gas cylinders, and over 60 accomplishments in efficient oil and gas recovery technology and equipment. These achievements illustrate the university's academic and technological strengths and have practical implications for many large petroleum and petrochemical industries in China, resulting in considerable social, economic, and environmental benefits.

## IV. Economic Takeoff

Changzhou is one of the most economically developed cities in Jiangsu Province. In the 1970s and 1980s, the city underwent rapid industrialization, driven by the "industrial one-stop" development model and the "Sunan model" of township enterprises. These initiatives sparked a nationwide trend of "small and medium-sized cities learning from Changzhou", establishing it as a renowned "industrial star city" within China. Today, Changzhou continues to boast a robust industrial foundation and

### 1. 智能制造装备产业

1912年，常州厚生机器厂创立，成为中国最早生产内燃机的3家企业之一；1920年，震华电机制造厂创立，开创了中国电机制造先河。经过百年发展，前者成为常州第一家上市公司——常柴股份有限公司，在内燃机领域持续创新；后者则演变为江苏华电戚墅堰发电有限公司，在电力生产领域发挥着重要作用。当前，常州的智能制造装备产业及其产品已处于国内领先地位，多次荣获中国工业大奖及制造业单项冠军，这些荣誉在全国地级市中位居第一。此外，常州的智能制造装备产业集群被纳入中国首批战略性新兴产业集群，标志着常州在国家战略层面的产业布局中占有重要位置。

innovative vitality. It has developed three major industrial clusters—intelligent manufacturing equipment, new energy, and new carbon materials—that have become pivotal for its economic growth. In 2023, Changzhou achieved a historic milestone by having its GDP exceed one trillion yuan. Additionally, it ranked 21st in the national ranking of China's top 100 cities and fourth within Jiangsu Province, reflecting its significant economic scale and comprehensive strength.

### 1. Intelligent Manufacturing Equipment Industry

Changzhou's journey in the intelligent manufacturing equipment industry began in 1912 with the establishment of the Housheng Machinery Factory, one of China's earliest enterprises to produce internal combustion engines. In 1920, Zhenhua Electric Motor Manufacturing Factory was founded, pioneering the electric motor manufacturing industry in China. Over the past century, these pioneering companies have evolved significantly. Housheng Machinery Factory became Changchai Co., Ltd., the first listed company in Changzhou, renowned for continuous innovation in internal combustion engines. Zhenhua Electric Motor Manufacturing Factory transformed into Jiangsu Huadian Qishuyan Power Generation Co., Ltd., a key player in power production. Today, Changzhou's intelligent manufacturing equipment industry and its products take the leading position in the nation, earning numerous Chinese industrial awards and winning manufacturing industry championships—achievements that place Changzhou first among prefecture-level cities in China. Furthermore, the city's intelligent manufacturing equipment industry cluster has been recognized as one of China's first strategic emerging industry clusters, underscoring

## 2. 新能源产业

1958年，常州变压器厂成立，标志着常州新能源产业的萌芽。20世纪80年代，常州的电线电缆产业悄然兴起。进入21世纪，光伏产业全面起步，开启了从无到有的飞跃。2010年，波士顿电池制造中心在常州落户，进一步推动了动力电池的本土生产。至此，常州新能源产业从无到有，形成了"发电、存储、输送、应用"的新能源产业闭环，产业集聚度列全国第三。2013年，常州成功自主研发了三代核电AP1000壳内电缆，填补了国际核电领域的重大技术空白。常州溧阳市的动力电池产业集群和新北区的新能源汽车电气设备产业集群，均获得国家认可，入选国家中小企业特色产业集群。

Changzhou's vital role in the national strategic industrial layout.

## 2. New Energy Industry

The origins of Changzhou's new energy industry can be traced back to 1958 with the establishment of the Changzhou Transformer Factory. The 1980s saw the rise of the wire and cable industry, which laid the groundwork for future advancements. The 21st century marked a significant turning point with the rapid development of the photovoltaic industry, transforming Changzhou's energy landscape. In 2010, the Boston Battery Manufacturing Center set up operations in Changzhou, accelerating the local production of power batteries and solidifying the city's role in the new energy sector. By this time, Changzhou had established a comprehensive new energy industry, forming a closed-loop system encompassing power generation, storage, transportation, and application. The city now boasts the third-largest industry agglomeration scale in China. A major milestone was achieved in 2013 when Changzhou independently developed the third-generation nuclear power AP1000 in-shell cables, filling a significant technological gap in the international nuclear power field. The city's contributions have been recognized at the national level, with the power battery industry cluster in Liyang City and the new energy vehicle electrical equipment industry cluster in Xinbei District being designated as national characteristic industrial clusters for small and medium-sized enterprises.

## 3. New Carbon Material Industry

Since 2008, Changzhou has strategically developed its new carbon material industry, focusing on two major industrial clusters: graphene and carbon fiber composite materials. The city has achieved significant milestones

### 3. 新型碳材料产业

2008年起，常州开始布局新型碳材料产业，精心打造了石墨烯和碳基纤维复合材料两大产业集聚区。目前，石墨烯产业和高端碳纤维领域取得了显著成果，不仅规模化生产能力领跑全国，碳纤维复合织物市场占有率也位居全国第一。值得一提的是，常州自主设计的第一条百吨级高性能碳纤维生产线打破了国外技术垄断。常州新型碳材料产业集群入围国家先进制造业集群。

当前，常州通过培育和发展先进制造业集群，持续推进现代化产业体系转型升级，努力将自身打造成为引领长三角，在全国领先，并具有国际影响力的"新能源之都"。

## 五、特色美食

"走遍神州，吃在常州。"常州菜融汇了南北菜系的精华，鲜、香、醇、润、咸中带着微甜，令人回味无穷。历史悠久的"老字号"餐馆如德泰恒、府前楼、兴隆园等，传承着一代代经典的味道。地方特色小吃如银丝面、大麻糕等让人念念不忘。此外，溧阳白茶、金坛雀舌等江南名茶清新淡雅，都是茶中上品。

### 1. 经典小吃

银丝面强调的是面条的质地和汤底的鲜美。制作时，将大量蛋清加入面粉中，能使面条颜色洁白如雪，而且增加了面条的弹性和爽滑的口感；用黄鳝骨、猪骨、鸡等长时间慢炖出的汤底浓郁鲜美；用小锅现炒浇头保证了食材的新鲜。以上三者——面的制作、汤的熬制、浇头的搭配缺一不可。

in both fields. Changzhou's graphene industry and high-end carbon fiber sector not only lead in production capacity within China but also dominate the market share for carbon fiber composite fabrics nationally. A noteworthy achievement is the independently designed first 100-ton high-performance carbon fiber production line, which has successfully broken the overseas technological monopoly. Changzhou's new carbon material industry cluster has been recognized as a part of the National Advanced Manufacturing Industry Cluster, reflecting its importance and innovation.

Currently, Changzhou is actively nurturing and developing advanced manufacturing clusters, and continuously driving the transformation and upgrading of its modern industrial systems. The city aims to establish itself as a leading "new energy hub" in the Yangtze River Delta, setting benchmarks both nationally and internationally.

## V. Specialty Food

"Enjoy a taste of all China in Changzhou" aptly describes the city's rich culinary heritage. Changzhou cuisine uniquely blends the essences of northern and southern Chinese cuisines, characterized by fresh, fragrant, mellow, moist, and salty with slightly sweet flavors that leave an unforgettable aftertaste. Changzhou boasts a number of long-standing, "time-honored" restaurants such as Detaiheng, Fuqianlou, and Xinglongyuan. These establishments have faithfully passed down their classic flavors through generations, offering a taste of tradition and authenticity. The city is also renowned for its local specialty snacks. Silver thread noodles and sesame cakes are among the most famous, leaving a lasting impression on those who sample them.

大麻糕是有咸、甜两种风味的椭圆形烧饼。用精白面粉、芝麻、糖、盐等原料，从和面开始，到包馅，再到最后的烘烤，每一步都需要精确的技巧和经验。成品外皮金黄酥脆，内里绵软，香脆甜鲜。

## 2. 传统名菜

砂锅鱼头选用天目湖的鳙<sub>yōng</sub>鱼头，洗净后煎至金黄色，放到砂锅里，加入天目湖水，并添加8种佐料，用小火炖3小时以上，直到汤变成乳白色，鱼肉白中带着红。这道菜营养丰富，吃起来鲜美、没有腥味，鱼肉肥嫩不腻。

In addition to its food, Changzhou is famous for its top-quality Jiangnan teas. Liyang white tea and Jintan "sparrow tongue" tea are two notable varieties, both known for their fresh and elegant flavors. These teas are highly regarded and add to the city's rich gastronomic reputation.

### 1. Classic Snacks

Silver thread noodles are renowned for their unique texture and delicious soup base. Achieving their snow-white appearance and smooth, elastic texture involves incorporating a significant amount of egg white into the flour. This not only enhances their visual appeal but also provides a delightful mouthfeel. The soup base, essential to the dish, is made by slowly simmering eel bones, pig bones, chicken, and other ingredients for an extended period. This slow cooking process extracts the maximum flavor, resulting in a rich and delicious broth that perfectly complements the noodles. To ensure the ingredients' freshness, a small pot is used for stir-frying and topping the noodles. This method preserves the vibrant flavors and textures of the toppings, enhancing the overall taste. The meticulous preparation of the noodles, the careful boiling of the soup, and the precise combination of ingredients are all crucial to achieving the perfect bowl of silver thread noodles.

The sesame cake is an oval-shaped baked cake that comes in both salty and sweet flavors. Made with refined flour, sesame seeds, sugar, and salt, every step from kneading the dough to filling and baking demands precise skills and experience. The finished product features a golden, crispy exterior, a soft interior, and a fragrant, sweet taste.

### 2. Traditional Dishes

Claypot braised fishhead is typically made with carp heads from the Tianmu Lake. The crap heads are washed thoroughly, and

### 3. 江南名茶

常州以溧阳白茶和金坛雀舌茶在江南地区享有盛名。这两种茶选材讲究，只采嫩芽和刚长出的一片嫩叶，再经过杀青、冷却、定型和干燥等一系列工序制作而成。溧阳白茶外形细长扁平，绿中带着黄色；冲泡后，茶水鹅黄清澈、香气芬芳、口感鲜爽而且回味甘甜。金坛雀舌茶外形扁平，像小鸟的舌头，颜色鲜绿润泽；泡开后茶水鲜绿明亮，口感清爽。

## 六、名胜古迹

常州是中国著名的旅游城市之一，以天宁禅寺、茅山道教景区、春秋淹城等景观为代表。

### 1. 天宁禅寺

天宁禅寺始建于唐朝，距今已有1350多年的历史，是中国佛教音乐梵呗的发源地之一。天宁禅寺因其雄伟的建筑、高大庄严的佛像、历史上的许多高僧以及广为人知的法会活动，被誉为"东南第一丛林"①。清朝

---

① "丛林"是佛教寺院的一种代称。僧人在寺庙中一起居住、研究佛法，智慧和善行聚集在寺庙之中，就好像树木聚在一起成了丛林。所以将僧人居住的寺庙称为"丛林"。

The term "jungle" is used metaphorically to refer to a Buddhist temple. Here, monks live and study the Dharma collectively, and it's a place where wisdom and good conduct converge, similar to how trees come together to create a jungle. Hence, the temple where monks dwell is poetically called a "jungle".

---

fried until golden brown, placed in a clay pot filled with water from the Tianmu Lake, and seasoned with a combination of eight spices. The fishhead is simmered on low heat for over three hours until the broth turns milky white and the fish meat becomes white with a hint of red. This dish is nutritious, delicious, free of any fishy smell, tender, and not greasy.

### 3. Renowned Jiangnan Teas

Changzhou is renowned in the Jiangnan region for its Liyang white tea and Jintan "sparrow tongue" tea. These teas require careful selection, using only tender buds and newly grown leaves, which are processed by withering, cooling, shaping, and drying. Liyang white tea has a slender and flat appearance with a green-yellow hue. When brewed, it produces a clear yellow tea with a fragrant aroma, refreshing taste, and sweet aftertaste. Jintan "sparrow tongue" tea resembles the tongue of a sparrow with its flat shape and bright, moist green color. After brewing, the tea turns bright green and offers a refreshing taste.

## VI. Historical Sites and Scenic Spots

Changzhou is one of China's famous tourist cities, featuring attractions such as the Tianning Temple, the Maoshan Taoist Scenic Area, and the ancient site of Yancheng in the Spring and Autumn Period.

### 1. The Tianning Temple

The Tianning Temple, originally built during the Tang Dynasty, has a history stretching back over 1,350 years. It is one of the birthplaces of Fanbei, Chinese Buddhist music. Known as the "Number One Temple in the Southeast"[1], it is renowned for its magnificent architecture, towering and solemn Buddha statues, prominent monks, and well-known Buddhist activities. Emperor Qianlong of the Qing Dynasty visited three times to light incense and worship the

乾隆皇帝曾三次到这里点香拜佛，并亲手题写了"龙城象教"的匾额，这是对天宁禅寺特殊地位的高度认可。寺内的天宁宝塔总高153.79米，不仅是寺内的标志性建筑，也是目前全球最高的佛塔。

## 2. 茅山道教

金坛茅山是"三茅真君"修行的地方，也是中国道教分支——上清派的发源地，被列为中国道教的"第一福地，第八洞天"。传说，在西汉时期，来自陕西咸阳的茅盈和他的两个兄弟，先后来到茅山，开始了采集草药、炼制丹药、救死扶伤的生活。他们在这里静心修炼，最终成为神仙，被后人尊称为"三茅真君"。为了纪念他们的贡献，后人在这里建造了道观，供奉他们。公元492年，著名的道士陶弘景在茅山将儒家、道教和佛教的思想融合，创建了上清派中最有影响力的分支——茅山宗。这一宗派注重通过身心修养，达到长寿的目标。

Buddha, bestowing the temple with a plaque inscribed "Buddhism in the Dragon City", highlighting its special status. The Tianning Pagoda within the temple stands at 153.79 meters, making it not only a landmark but also the tallest Buddhist pagoda in the world.

## 2. Maoshan Taoism

The Maoshan Mountain in Jintan holds significance as the practice site of "Sanmao Zhenjun" (the Three True Lords of Maoshan) and the birthplace of the Shangqing School, a prominent branch of Chinese Taoism. It is revered as the "first blessed place and eighth heavenly cave" of Chinese Taoism. Legend has it that during the Western Han Dynasty, Mao Ying and his two brothers from Xianyang Shaanxi Province settled in Maoshan, engaging in activities like herb collection, pill refining, and healing. Through meditation and practice, they attained immortality and were called "Sanmao Zhenjun" by later generations. Taoist temples were constructed in their honor. In 492 AD, the renowned Taoist Tao Hongjing established the Maoshan Sect, a significant branch of the Shangqing School, blending Confucian, Taoist, and Buddhist ideologies. This sect focuses on achieving longevity through physical and mental cultivation.

### 3. 春秋淹城

淹城是中国目前保存最完整的春秋晚期的地面城池遗址，有2900年左右的历史。遗址"三城三河"[①]的结构十分罕见，为研究中国乃至世界城市规划发展的连续性和多样性提供了重要的实物资料。在遗址的考古发掘中发现的一系列重要文物，不仅展示了当时的工艺技术，还反映了春秋时期的生活风貌。其中，部分出土文物如独木舟、三轮青铜盘，以及青铜钩鑃（diào）等被列为国家一级文物。2009年，淹城荣获联合国LivCom环境可持续发展项目金奖。

## 七、历史名人

常州自古人才辈出，到了近现代更是人才济济，涌现出了"常州三杰"、赵元任、周有光以及华罗庚等多位杰出人物。

### 1. 常州三杰

"常州三杰"是指瞿秋白、张太雷、恽代英三位中国共产党的早期领导人，他们都出生在常州，对革命事业作出了巨大贡献。瞿秋白在中国共产党的理论建设、文化和教育工作方面有着重要影响，还是中国革命文

---

[①] "三城三河"结构指三条城垣（yuán）和三条护城河相互套叠的结构。

The "three cities and three rivers" structure refers to a unique layout where 3 city walls and 3 moats are nested within each other.

### 3. Yancheng Spring and Autumn Park

Yancheng stands as a remarkable testament to the late Spring and Autumn Period, boasting the most well-preserved ground city ruins in China with a history spanning approximately 2,900 years. The layout of the "three cities and three rivers" site is exceptionally rare, offering invaluable insights into urban planning and development for China and the world. Archaeological excavations at the site have unearthed a plethora of significant cultural relics, showcasing the craftsmanship and lifestyle of the period. Among these treasures are canoes, three-wheeled bronze plates, and bronze hooks, recognized as national first-class cultural relics. In recognition of its historical and cultural significance, Yancheng was awarded the United Nations LivCom Award for Environmental Sustainable Development Project Gold Award in 2009.

### VII. Historical Figures

Since ancient times, Changzhou has been full of talented people, and their number has increased in modern times. Many outstanding figures have emerged, such as "The Three Heroes of Changzhou", Zhao Yuanren, Zhou Youguang, and Hua Luogeng.

### 1. The Three Heroes of Changzhou

Qu Qiubai, Zhang Tailei, and Yun Daiying, known as "The Three Heroes of Changzhou", were three early leaders of the Communist Party of China (CPC). They were born in Changzhou and made great contributions to the revolution. Qu Qiubai had a significant influence on the construction, culture, and education of the CPC and was also one of the quintessential founders of Chinese revolutionary literature. Zhang Tailei was among the founders of the Communist Youth League of China and one of the main leaders of the Guangzhou Uprising.

学事业的重要奠基人之一。张太雷是中国共产主义青年团创始人之一，也是广州起义的主要领导人之一。恽代英是中国共产党早期青年运动领导人之一，先后参与领导五卅运动、南昌起义和广州起义。这三位杰出的革命家因为共同的出生地和在早期革命发挥了重要作用，被称为"常州三杰"。

### 2. 赵元任

赵元任在语言学领域有着开创性的贡献，被公认为"中国现代语言学之父"。他同时还是音乐家、作曲家，对中国音乐的研究也有着重要贡献。赵元任精通英、法、德等外语。他运用自己对语言的深刻理解，翻译了《爱丽丝梦游仙境》，力求在译文中保留原文的幽默与奇幻色彩，同时使中文读者能顺畅地阅读。他还进行了深入的方言调查研究，其语言学代表作有《现代吴语的研究》等。他的音乐代表作《教我如何不想她》旋律优美，成为中国近代音乐史上的经典之作。

### 3. 周有光

周有光是著名的语言学家、文字改革家，参加制订了汉语拼音方案，被誉为"中国汉语拼音之父"。他的工作极大促进了中文的现代化和国际化，对中国文化的普及和国际交流产生了深远影响。

Yun Daiying was one of the leaders of the early youth movement of the CPC and was credited with taking a leading role in the May 30th Movement, Nanchang Uprising, and Guangzhou Uprising. These three outstanding revolutionaries, "The Three Heroes of Changzhou" who share a common birthplace, are honored for their significance in the early revolution.

### 2. Zhao Yuanren

Zhao Yuanren made groundbreaking contributions in the field of linguistics and is recognized as the "father of Modern Chinese Linguistics". He was also a musician and composer, making significant contributions to the study of Chinese music. Zhao Yuanren was proficient in English, French, German, and several other foreign languages. He used his profound understanding of languages to translate *Alice's Adventures in Wonderland* into Chinese, striving to retain the humour and fantasy of the original text in the translation and giving Chinese readers the opportunity to read and enjoy the novel in their native language. He also conducted in-depth dialect investigation and research, with representative works in linguistics such as *A Study of Modern Wu Dialect*. His musical masterpiece "How Can I Stop Missing Her" has a beautiful melody and has become a classic in the history of modern Chinese music.

### 3. Zhou Youguang

Zhou Youguang was a famous linguist and script reformer who participated in the formulation of the Chinese Pinyin scheme and is known as the "father of Chinese Pinyin". His work has greatly promoted the modernization and internationalization of Chinese language and has had a significant impact on the popularization of Chinese culture and international exchanges.

### 4. 华罗庚

华罗庚是国际知名的数学家。他解决了高斯完整三角和的估计难题，给出了更精确的估计；他对华林问题和塔里问题进行改进并提出了新的方法和思路；他还善于将抽象的数论方法应用到其他数学分支乃至实际问题中。"华氏定理""华氏不等式"等以他命名的数学研究成果提供了重要的理论工具和证明技巧，至今仍是相关研究领域的基石。

## 八、生态保护

作为中国生态文明建设示范区的常州在生态文明建设和乡村振兴方面不断努力。溧阳市桂林村、金坛区仙姑村等村落通过经济发展、空间环境提升、文化传承等综合发展策略，探索个性化的乡村建设之路。这些乡村注重生态修复和环境保护，通过植树造林、水体治理等措施恢复自然生态；还积极发展绿色经济，如生态农业和乡村旅游等，为村民创造了新的就业机会；同时，通过改善基础设施、美化环境、提升居住条件等，提高了当地居民的生活质量。

文化传承也是乡村建设中的重要一环，通过保护传统建筑、举办文化节庆活动、传承手工艺和非物质文化遗产，这些乡村不仅传承了地域文化，增强了文化自信，还促进了文化旅游的融合发展。

常州在生态文明建设和乡村振兴方面的探索，向外界展现了如何在尊重自然、传承文化的基础上，实现乡村振兴与现代化建设的和谐统一，为全国提供了可持续发展和乡村振兴的宝贵经验。

### 4. Hua Luogeng

Hua Luogeng (Hua Loo-Keng) was an internationally renowned mathematician. He solved the estimation problem of Gaussian complete trigonometric sums and provided more accurate estimates. He made improvements to Waring's and Tower of Hanoi problems and proposed new methods and ideas. He was also adept at applying abstract number theory methods to other branches of mathematics and even practical problems. The mathematical research achievements named after him, such as Hua's Theorem and Hua's Inequation, provide important theoretical tools and proof techniques, and are still the cornerstone of related research fields to this day.

## VIII. Ecological Protection

Changzhou serves as a model city for China's ecological civilization construction as it is constantly making advancements in ecological conservation strategies and rural revitalization. This is evidenced by comprehensive development strategies such as economic development, spatial environment improvement, and cultural inheritance. Villages such as Guilin Village in Liyang City and Xiangu Village in Jintan District are exploring personalized rural construction paths. These rural areas focus on ecological restoration and environmental protection through measures such as afforestation and water management, thereby facilitating the emergence of environmentally friendly economic ventures such as ecological agriculture and rural tourism. This in turn creates employment opportunities for rural inhabitants while improving infrastructure, beautifying the environment, as well as enhancing the living conditions and quality of life for the local residents.

Cultural inheritance is also an important part of rural construction. By protecting traditional architecture, organizing cultural festivals, and inheriting handicrafts and intangible cultural heritage, regional culture is inherited, cultural confidence is enhanced, and the integrated development of cultural tourism is promoted.

Changzhou's exploration in ecological civilization and rural revitalization has demonstrated to the world how to harmoniously unify rural revitalization with modernization rooted in nature conservation and cultural inheritance. This approach has provided valuable experience nationwide for sustainable development and rural revitalization.

## 练习

### 一、判断题

1. 常州的第一个城市名称叫晋陵。☐

2. 常州梳篦有600年历史。☐

3. 溧阳白茶、金坛雀舌、苏州碧螺春都是江南名茶。☐

4. 天宁宝塔是世界最高的佛塔。☐

5. 赵元任被誉为"中国汉语拼音之父"。☐

### 二、思考题

1. 为什么说常州是人类最早生活的区域之一？

2. 为什么把常州称为中国"工业明星城市"？

3. 常州的新能源产业集群发展现状怎么样？

### 三、拓展题

以小组为单位，组织开展寻访常州活动，结合在常州的吃、住、行等日常生活，感受常州的经济、文化、社会等发展成果。以"印象常州"为主题，用短视频、PPT或撰写心得体会的形式，交流展示大家对常州的印象。

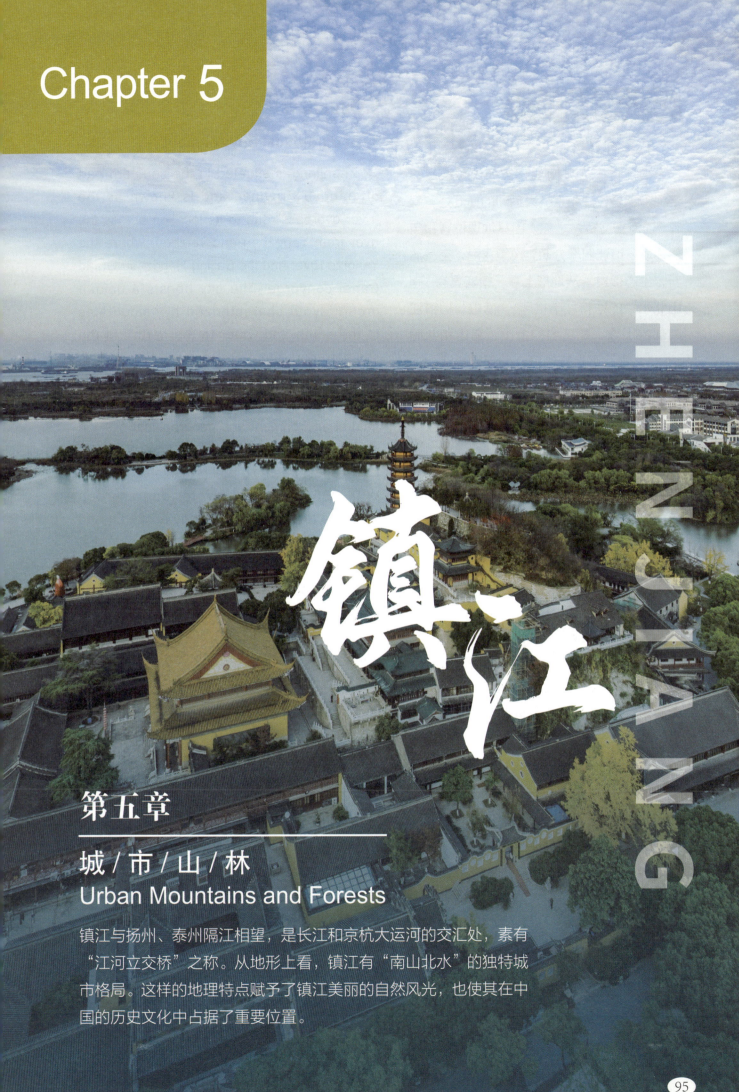

# Chapter 5

镇江

ZHENJIANG

第五章

城 / 市 / 山 / 林
Urban Mountains and Forests

镇江与扬州、泰州隔江相望，是长江和京杭大运河的交汇处，素有"江河立交桥"之称。从地形上看，镇江有"南山北水"的独特城市格局。这样的地理特点赋予了镇江美丽的自然风光，也使其在中国的历史文化中占据了重要位置。

# 一、城市概况

## 1. 地理环境

镇江位于江苏南部，与扬州和泰州隔江相望，是长江和京杭大运河的交汇处，素有"江河立交桥"之称。因其地理位置和自然环境，镇江四季分明，风景秀丽，空气清新，生态优良。从地形上看，镇江具有"南山北水"的独特城市格局。"南山"指镇江南部的山脉，如著名的金山、焦山和北固山；"北水"则指穿越镇江北部的长江。全市有235座山峰，63条河流，城区绿化覆盖率达42.3%，素有"大江风貌、城市山林"之称。因水资源丰富，全市鱼类品种超过90种，其中，刀鱼、鲥鱼、鳗鱼、河豚尤为著名。这片水域还是白鳍豚、中华鲟等中国国家重点保护的珍稀水生动物的栖息地。总而言之，镇江是名副其实的国家生态文明先行示范区。

## 2. 城市变迁

镇江有文字记载的历史超过3000年，文化底蕴丰厚，人文遗产丰富，曾是江苏的省会。镇江古时候先后使用过"谷阳""京口"等名字，自北宋以后，"镇江"一名沿用至今。作为吴文化的重要发源地之一，镇江在中华文化史上有着重要的地位，是中国许多重要古典文学著作的诞生地，《文心雕龙》《昭明文选》《梦溪笔谈》等均在此写成。镇江不仅是文人竞相歌颂的地方，由于其独特的战略位置，自古以来一直是兵家必争之地。

## I. Overview

### 1. Geographical Environment

Zhenjiang is situated in the southern part of Jiangsu Province and is known as the "river overpass" due to its location across the river from Yangzhou and Taizhou, where the Yangtze River and the Beijing-Hangzhou Grand Canal converge. The city boasts a unique urban layout characterized by "mountains to the south and water to the north": in the southern part, there are renowned mountains like Jinshan, Jiaoshan, and Beigu, while to the north, the Yangtze River flows. Zhenjiang's natural environment and geographical position contribute to its distinct seasons, beautiful landscapes, fresh air, and remarkable ecology. With 235 peaks, 63 rivers, and a green coverage rate of 42.3%, the city is often hailed as "urban mountains and forests over the great river". Its abundant water resources support diverse fish species, including saury, reeves shad, eel, and pufferfish. Zhenjiang's waters serve as a sanctuary for rare aquatic animals under national key protection in China, such as the white-sided dolphin and the Chinese sturgeon. Zhenjiang is an example of a national ecological civilization pilot demonstration zone.

### 2. Development

With a written history stretching back 3,000 years, Zhenjiang boasts a rich cultural heritage and was once the capital of Jiangsu Province. Formerly called "Guyang" and "Jingkou", Zhenjiang has been known by its current name since the Northern Song Dynasty. As a significant birthplace of the Wu culture, Zhenjiang holds a prominent position in China's cultural history and has inspired numerous classical literary works. The city is not only famous for attracting scholars and poets but also for its historical significance as an often fought-over region due to its strategic location.

由于地处长江和京杭大运河的交汇处，19世纪末至20世纪初，镇江因水运便利，迅速从一个传统的内河港口发展成新兴的航运和贸易重要节点。这一时期，镇江吸引了许多国内外商人投资设厂，许多著名的轮船公司都在镇江建造码头，促进了货物的快速周转与运输，推动了城市经济持续发展。

### 3. 今日镇江

镇江现在的交通网络十分发达，水路、公路和铁路全面发展，是国家认定的综合性交通枢纽。从镇江驾车前往南京市区只要45分钟，乘坐高铁仅需20分钟。长途旅行同样便捷，乘坐高铁到上海只需1小时，到北京最快也控制在4小时以内。虽然镇江目前没有机场，但离南京禄口机场和常州奔牛机场都只有60公里左右，至扬州泰州机场约70公里，乘车前往都只需1小时左右。

近年来，镇江明确树立了"创新创业福地、山水花园名城"的城市新形象。在努力保护自然生态的同时，确保城市生活品质，提升居民生活质量。镇江在保持制造业、轻工业、航运业等传统支柱产业优势的基础上，引导产业升级转型，大力发展航空航天和新能源等新兴产业。目前，镇江已经与澳大利亚、德国、巴西、法国、日本等国的16个城市建立了友好关系，国际交流合作的范围和深度都不断扩大和深化。

Zhenjiang experienced rapid development in the late 19th and early 20th centuries as it was transformed from a traditional inland port to an important hub for shipping and trade. Situated at the confluence of the Yangtze River and the Beijing-Hangzhou Grand Canal, the city's convenient water transportation attracted domestic and foreign investors. As a result, numerous factories were established, and renowned steamship companies constructed piers in the city. These contributed to the efficient turnover and transportation of goods, and led to the economic growth of the city.

### 3. Zhenjiang Today

Zhenjiang is renowned for its well-developed transportation network, which includes waterways, highways, and railways, and it is effectively a transportation hub. The city's strategic location allows convenient access to Nanjing, which is only 45 minutes away by car or 20 minutes by high-speed train. In addition, it offers easy connectivity to more distant destinations. It takes an hour to travel from Zhenjiang to Shanghai and a maximum of 4 hours to Beijing by high-speed train. Although the city currently lacks an airport, Nanjing Lukou Airport, Changzhou Benniu Airport, and Yangzhou Taizhou Airport are all accessible within an hour's drive.

Zhenjiang has emerged as a thriving center for innovation and entrepreneurship, and at the same time, it is famous for its beautiful gardens. The city places great importance on preserving its natural environment while striving to improve the quality of life for its residents. In addition to its traditional industries, such as manufacturing, light industry, and shipping, it actively promotes the growth and transformation of aerospace and new energy sectors. Zhenjiang has also fostered friendly relationships with 16 cities globally, including those in Australia, Germany, Brazil, France, and Japan.

## 二、文化印象

### 1. 名人字画

自古以来，山清水秀的自然风光吸引了无数文人墨客在镇江游览山水，创作了大量诗词佳作，并留下了许多珍贵的书法作品。王羲之、颜真卿、苏轼、米芾等名家都在这里留下了珍贵的书法作品。其中，收藏在焦山的《瘗鹤铭》被称为中国书法的"大字之祖"，是中国书法发展史上的重要里程碑。北宋时期，书法名家米芾因喜爱镇江的自然风光，在此生活了40年之久，并开创了独特的"米氏云山"画风，成为众人敬佩的书画大师。到了18世纪，一批画家聚集在镇江，致力于"实景山水"画的创作，他们传承了中国传统山水画的精髓，并更注重写实，形成了著名的"京江画派"。

### 2. 大众篆刻

镇江篆刻历史悠久，焦山西麓保存的80方摩崖石刻和焦山碑林中近500方历经数千年的碑刻，为镇江篆刻艺术的发展奠定了坚实的基础。在此基础上，镇江篆刻逐渐孕育出独具一格的"镇江印派"。该印派最大的贡献是将篆刻艺术推广到民间，使其更加贴近生活，易于学习，极大地促进了篆刻艺术在镇江的普及和繁荣。近年来，镇江设立了500多个篆刻艺术推广示范点和相关社团，

## II. Cultural Impressions

### 1. Calligraphy and Painting

Since ancient times, the beautiful natural scenery of Zhenjiang has attracted numerous scholars and calligraphers including Wang Xizhi, Yan Zhenqing, Su Shi, and Mi Fu, who left a wealth of poetry and calligraphy masterpieces. The "Yi Crane Inscription" in Jiaoshan, considered the "ancestor of big-character calligraphy", marks a significant milestone in the evolution of Chinese calligraphy. During the Northern Song Dynasty, Mi Fu, a celebrated calligrapher living in Zhenjiang for four decades, developed a distinctive painting style known as "Mi's cloudy mountain" and earned widespread admiration for his mastery of calligraphy and painting. In the 18th century, Zhenjiang became a hub for painters dedicated to creating realistic landscape paintings. This led to the establishment of the renowned "Jingjiang School", which emphasized realism while preserving the essence of traditional Chinese landscape painting.

### 2. Seal Engraving

Zhenjiang boasts a rich history in seal engraving. There are 80 cliff stone carvings preserved at the west foot of the Jiaoshan Mountain and nearly 500 inscriptions in the Jiaoshan Stele Forest dating back thousands of years. These ancient artifacts have laid a strong foundation for the evolution of the seal engraving art of Zhenjiang and led to the emergence of the distinctive "Zhenjiang School" of seal engraving. This school has played a crucial role in making seal engraving more accessible to the public, bridging the gap between art and everyday life, and fostering the widespread popularity and success of seal engraving in the city. In recent years, Zhenjiang has taken significant steps to promote the art

创立了全国第一个篆刻艺术推广协会，连续成功举办了十届大众篆刻艺术培训，累计参与培训人数超过3000名。为了适应数字化的需求，镇江还建立了大众篆刻网站，自主研发数字篆刻技术及设备，开通了大众篆刻公交专线。篆刻成了一项市民喜爱的文化活动，也成为镇江的重要文化名片。

### 3. 赛珍珠

诺贝尔文学奖和普利策奖获得者赛珍珠（1892—1973）在中国生活了近40年。她在镇江度过了童年和部分青少年时期，这对她的成长和日后的文学创作产生了深远的影响，镇江被她亲切地称为"中国故乡"。赛珍珠热爱中国传统文化，虽然她一生都用英文写作，但作品几乎全部是中国题材，尤其是那些对中国社会和人民生活的描写，无不透露出她早年在镇江的生活痕迹。她在镇江的故居保存完好，保留了她生前居住时的原貌。镇江人民还在她的故居旁建立了赛珍珠纪念馆，陈列了与她相关的书籍、个人物品和影音资料，吸引了无数市民和国际访客前来参观。

of seal engraving by establishing over 500 demonstration sites and associations, including the country's first association dedicated to promoting the seal engraving art. It has also organized ten consecutive public seal engraving art training sessions, which attracted over 3,000 participants. To keep up with the digital era, the city has embraced digital technology by launching a public seal engraving website and creating digital tools for seal engraving. It has even gone so far as to introduce a public seal engraving bus line. The citizens of Zhenjiang welcome these cultural activities, which have been a prominent cultural symbol of the city.

### 3. Pearl S. Buck

Pearl S. Buck (1892–1973), winner of both the Nobel Prize for Literature and the Pulitzer Prize, lived in China for nearly four decades. She spent her childhood and part of her teenage years in Zhenjiang, a place she affectionately referred to as her "hometown in China" that had greatly influenced her life and literary works. Despite writing exclusively in English, Buck had a deep appreciation for traditional Chinese culture, and her works are centered on Chinese themes, particularly Chinese society and the lives of the Chinese people, reflecting her early experiences in Zhenjiang. Her former residence in Zhenjiang has been well preserved to maintain its original state. In the Pearl S. Buck Memorial Hall adjacent to her former residence, Buck's books, personal belongings, and audio-visual materials are displayed, attracting numerous domestic and international tourists.

## 三、教育交流

### 1. 高等教育概况

镇江目前有9所高校，在校学生超过12万人，其中包括约2万名研究生，约3000名学历留学生。这些高校学科门类齐全、教学质量高、师资队伍强大，国际交流频繁，为国际学生提供了丰富的学习资源和发展机会。市内交通便利，生活设施完善，学习氛围良好，是一个适合求学、居住的城市。在学习之余，学生还可以深入体验镇江丰富的历史文化和自然风景。

### 2. 高校介绍

江苏大学和江苏科技大学是镇江两所办学历史最为悠久、办学实力最强、社会影响力最大的两所高校。

#### 1）江苏大学

江苏大学（www.ujs.edu.cn）是一所以工科为主，工农结合为特色的综合性大学，是中国最早确定的88所重点大学之一。学校非常重视来华留学教育，是中国首批通过来华留学生高等教育质量认证的21所高校之一，也是以优秀等级通过再认证的高校之一。学校与全球64个国家和地区的242所高校及科研机构建立了长期合作关系。面向国际学生，学校开设了18个全英文授课的本科专业。江苏大学的国际学生来自111个国家和地区，规模维持在2300人左右，这一数字在江苏省内位居前列。学校精心打造了一系列品牌文化活动，如国际文化节、丝路梅花讲坛、"感知中国""知行中国""中外青年看江苏"等，深受国际学生欢迎。

江苏大学第十四届国际文化节开幕式
OPENING CEREMONY OF JIANGSU UNIVERSITY 14TH INTERNATIONAL CULTURE FESTIVAL

## III. Education and International Exchanges

### 1. Overview of Higher Education

Zhenjiang is home to nine colleges and universities with a student population of over 120,000, including 20,000 graduate students and about 3,000 international students. These educational institutions offer a wide range of disciplines and have highly qualified faculty members. International students have access to abundant learning resources and development opportunities with frequent international exchanges. Zhenjiang provides convenient transportation, excellent living facilities, and an excellent study environment, so it is an ideal city for studying and living. Additionally, students can immerse themselves in Zhenjiang's rich history, culture, and natural beauty to enhance their overall experience.

### 2. Introduction to Universities

Jiangsu University and Jiangsu University of Science and Technology, two universities in Zhenjiang, are celebrated for their historical significance, academic excellence, and profound impact on society.

### 1) Jiangsu University

Jiangsu University (www.ujs.edu.cn), a comprehensive university known for its strengths in industry and agriculture, ranks among China's 88 prestigious universities. The university places significant emphasis on providing high-quality education to international students, and is one of the first 21 universities in China to receive accreditation for excellence in higher education for international students. Additionally, it has successfully undergone re-accreditation with outstanding results. Jiangsu University has developed extensive partnerships with 242 universities and research institutions in 64 countries and regions. For international students, the university offers 18

## 2）江苏科技大学

江苏科技大学（www.just.edu.cn）是一所以"船舶、海洋、蚕桑"为特色的行业特色型大学，享有"造船工程师摇篮"的美誉。作为江苏唯一一所以船舶与海洋工程装备产业为王牌专业的大学，学校在该领域内享有显著的专业优势和深厚的教学科研基础。学校与澳大利亚、加拿大、俄罗斯、美国、英国、法国等多个国家广泛开展交流合作，现有学历留学生700人左右。为了让国际学生更好地了解中国，学校举办了"美丽乡村行""蚕桑基地行"等丰富多彩的社会实践活动，受到了国际学生们的喜爱。

### 3. 特色专业

江苏大学的农业工程学科和江苏科技大学的船舶与海洋工程专业共同构成了镇江地区高等教育的两大亮点。

undergraduate programs taught in English. With a student population of about 2,300 from 111 countries and regions, Jiangsu University boasts one of the largest international student populations in Jiangsu Province. The university organizes various cultural events, including the International Cultural Festival, the Silk Road Plum Blossom Forum, "Experiencing China", "Global Young Leaders Fellowship", and "Chinese and Foreigners' Perception of Jiangsu", all of which are highly popular among international students.

## 2) Jiangsu University of Science and Technology

Jiangsu University of Science and Technology (www.just.edu.cn), a specialized university known for its focus on shipbuilding, ocean engineering, and sericulture, enjoys the title "cradle of shipbuilding engineers". It is the only university in Jiangsu Province to offer Naval Architecture & Ocean Engineering as its flagship program, for it boasts a strong academic foundation and professional advantages in this field. Thanks to its collaborative programs with countries including Australia, Canada, Russia, the United States, the United Kingdom, and France, the university has an international student population of about 700. The university organizes cultural activities such as the "Beautiful Countryside Tour" and "Sericulture Base Tour" to help the international students understand China.

## 3. Featured Disciplines

The Agricultural Engineering program at Jiangsu University and the Naval Architecture & Ocean Engineering major at Jiangsu University of Science and Technology are two prominent higher-education disciplines in Zhenjiang.

With a rich history in agricultural engineering, Jiangsu University educated China's first group

江苏大学的农业工程学科历史悠久，培养了中国第一批农机领域的本科生、研究生乃至博士后研究人员。该学科在农业机械方面也取得了显著成就，开发出无人驾驶联合收割机、蔬菜移栽机、葡萄采摘机器人等26种高端智能装备，为提升农业生产效率，推动农业现代化进程做出了重要贡献。

江苏科技大学的船舶与海洋工程专业在深海装备研发领域发挥着关键作用，参与了超深水半潜式钻井平台、"蛟龙号"载人潜水器等多个尖端科研项目。该专业还积极推动船舶制造业的技术革新，如开发的数字化设计与制造系统、高效焊接装备及船舶企业管理软件等，在各大船舶企业中广泛应用，有效提升了行业的技术水平与管理效率。

## 四、经济腾飞

镇江不仅自然条件优越，而且地处上海经济圈和南京都市圈交汇区域，在经济发展上受到两大经济圈的辐射带动，有很强的区位优势。近年来，镇江经济发展稳定。根据最新统计数据，2023年镇江的地区生产总值为5264.07亿元，同比增长6.3%，在江苏省内位居前十。总体而言，镇江传统产业与新兴产业并驾齐驱：化工产业、装备制造、造纸、建材、电力、眼镜制造等传统产业基础牢固；新材料、新能源、生物医药等新兴产业稳步增长；新兴的航空航天产业发展速度尤为引人注目。

of students specializing in agricultural machinery, including undergraduates, postgraduates, and postdoctoral researchers. The discipline has achieved significant milestones in developing 26 kinds of advanced intelligent equipment, such as unmanned combine harvesters, vegetable transplanting machines, and grape-picking robots, and plays a crucial role in enhancing agricultural productivity and promoting agrarian modernization.

The Naval Architecture & Ocean Engineering program at Jiangsu University of Science and Technology is instrumental in advancing research and development for deep-sea equipment, and contributes to cutting-edge scientific research projects like the ultra-deepwater semi-submersible drilling platform and the Jiaolong manned submersible. Additionally, the program is dedicated to driving technological innovation within the shipbuilding sector by implementing digital design and manufacturing systems, efficient welding equipment, and shipbuilding enterprise management software. Major shipbuilding companies have widely adopted these advancements, which help to improve industry standards and operational efficiency.

## IV. Economic Takeoff

Zhenjiang benefits from excellent natural conditions and significant economic growth driven by two major economic hubs — Shanghai's economic circle and Nanjing's metropolitan area. The city has achieved stable economic development in recent years, with a projected GDP of 526.407 billion yuan in 2023, marking a 6.3% increase from the previous year and securing a position in the top 10 cities in Jiangsu Province. Zhenjiang's economy is characterized by a balanced mix of traditional industries like chemical

## 1. 化工产业与装备制造产业

化工产业是镇江的支柱产业之一，拥有坚实的产业基础和强大的企业集群。其中，规模较大、技术先进的化工企业包括索普化工、镇江奇美化工、壳牌（镇江）公司等。其中，索普化工作为镇江化工领域的领头羊，规模与影响力尤为显著。公司年收入约80亿元，不仅彰显了其在行业内的领先地位，也推动了地方经济发展。作为醋酸生产领域的佼佼者，索普化工的醋酸产能全国第一，世界第三，充分展现了其在该领域的实力和影响力。

装备制造产业也是镇江不可或缺的支柱力量，涵盖电气装备、汽车及零部件制造、船舶海工装备等多个细分产业。主要企业有大全集团、现代重工（中国）电气、北汽蓝谷麦格纳汽车、沃得农业机械、沃得重工、镇江船厂、中船动力、蓝波船舶、现代造船等，共同推进产业升级与技术创新。

manufacturing, equipment production, paper making, construction materials, power generation, and glass manufacturing, alongside the steady expansion of emerging sectors such as new materials, renewable energy, and biotechnology, with notable progress in the aerospace industry.

## 1. Chemical Industry and Equipment Manufacturing Industry

The chemical industry, boasting a strong foundation and a group of enterprises, is a pillar industry of Zhenjiang. Notable among these are large and technologically advanced enterprises such as SOPO Chemicals, Zhenjiang Chimei Chemicals, and Shell (Zhenjiang) Company. Sopo stands out in the chemical industry of Zhenjiang. With significant scale, influence, and annual revenue of approximately 8 billion yuan, SOPO takes up a leading role and contributes to local economic growth. As a leader in the acetic acid production field, SOPO ranks first in national and third in global fully demonstrating its strength and influence in this area.

The equipment manufacturing sector plays a crucial role in Zhenjiang's economy. It encompasses various sub-industries like electrical equipment, automotive and parts manufacturing, and marine engineering equipment. Key players in this sector include Daqo Group, Hyundai Heavy Industries (China) Electrics, BAIC Blue Valley Magna Automobile, World Agricultural Machinery, World Heavy Industry, Zhenjiang Shipyard, China Shipbuilding Power, Blue Wave Shipbuilding, and Hyundai Shipbuilding. Together, these enterprises work towards driving industrial advancement and fostering technological innovation.

### 2. 新能源产业

近年来，镇江在绿色新能源领域的步伐明显加快，大力推动太阳能光伏发电、动力电池制造、氢能技术等关键产业。镇江计划通过技术创新与政策引导，发展清洁低碳能源，基本形成清洁、低碳、高效的能源供应体系。

### 3. 眼镜产业

镇江的丹阳是全国最大的镜片生产基地，有1600多家眼镜相关企业，近5万名从业人员，组成了庞大的眼镜生产网络。丹阳每年生产镜片四亿多副，不仅占据了国内市场总量的75%，还占全球总量的一半，被誉为"中国眼镜之都"。

## 五、特色美食

### 1. 镇江三怪

镇江三怪指香醋、肴（当地人读xiāo）肉和锅盖面，是镇江最有代表性的三种特产。之所以说它们"怪"，是因为第一，"香醋摆不坏"。镇江香醋酸而不涩、香而微甜，而且放的时间越久，味道就越浓郁，可以长期保存。第二，"肴肉不当菜"。与其他肉制品不同，肴肉通常被当作冷菜或零食，配上香醋风味更好。第三，"面锅里面煮锅盖"。这是一种特殊的煮面方法。煮面的时候将一只小木锅盖放在锅里一起煮。这样做可以使汤面不浑浊，而且面条更容易熟透。镇江三怪中的每一"怪"都有古老而独特的文化故事，为镇江的饮食文化增添了丰富的色彩。

### 2. New Energy Industry

In recent years, significant advancements have been made in Zhenjiang's green new energy sector, which focuses on promoting key industries such as solar photovoltaic power generation, power battery manufacturing, and hydrogen energy technology. The city aims to achieve clean and low-carbon energy production through technological innovation and policy guidance, ultimately establishing a clean, low-carbon, and efficient energy supply system.

### 3. Eyewear Industry

Danyang, located in Zhenjiang, is the primary hub for lens production in China. A vast network for producing eyeglasses, in which 1,600 businesses employ nearly 50,000 workers, has been established. Over 400 million pairs of eyeglasses are produced annually in Danyang, accounting for 75% of the national production volume and half of the global market. Thanks to its significant contribution to the eyeglasses industry, Danyang has earned the title of "the eyewear capital of China".

## V. Specialty Food

### 1. Three Unique Delicacies of Zhenjiang

Zhenjiang is renowned for its three most famous delicacies: balsamic vinegar, crystal pork, and pot cover noodles. These three delicacies are considered unique for various reasons. Zhenjiang balsamic vinegar has a sour yet mild taste, a pleasant aroma, and a touch of sweetness. As it ages, the flavor intensifies, making it ideal to be left on a shelf and "forgotten" about for a few years. Crystal pork is typically not served as a main dish in Zhenjiang but rather enjoyed cold or as a snack, often paired with balsamic vinegar to enhance its flavor. In the traditional method of cooking pot cover noodles, a small wooden cover is put inside the pot, so that the broth is

### 2. 扬中河豚

河豚，又叫"气泡鱼"，广泛分布于沿海地带，长江入海口区域尤为丰富。镇江扬中市的河豚及其烹饪方法最为出名。每年3月至5月，特别是清明节前，扬中的河豚最为鲜嫩，被誉为"百鱼之王"，与鲥鱼、刀鱼并称"长江三鲜"。河豚的传统烹饪方法是红烧或白汁，配上竹笋和扬中的特产蔬菜秧草，这样的搭配使得汤汁黏稠浓郁，不油腻，口感层次丰富。河豚含有天然毒素，因此制作过程相当严格，但一旦品尝过，就会有"一朝食得河豚肉，终生不念天下鱼"的感叹。

### 3. 东乡羊肉

东乡羊肉是镇江的一道传统美食，因盛产羊肉的地区位于镇江的东部，被称为"东乡"，东乡羊肉由此得名。东乡羊肉的肉质细嫩，不膻不腻，鲜美无比，而且营养丰富，有滋养身体、温补中气、增强体质的功效。

clear and the noodles are evenly cooked. Each of these iconic Zhenjiang delicacies is steeped in cultural significance, adding to the city's rich culinary heritage.

## 2. Yangzhong Pufferfish

Pufferfish, also called "bubble fish", can be found in coastal areas, especially the Yangtze River estuary area. Yangzhong, a part of Zhenjiang, is renowned for its pufferfish and cooking techniques. From March to May, particularly before the Qingming Festival, Yangzhong pufferfish is considered freshest and most tender, therefore called "king of 100 fish". It is known as one of the "three fresh fish of the Yangtze River", alongside reeves shad and saury. Pufferfish is traditionally braised or cooked in a white sauce with bamboo shoots and Yangzhong's specialty vegetable seedlings to create a dense and rich soup that is full of flavor and not the least greasy. Pufferfish contain natural toxins, so its cooking must be done carefully. However, it leaves a lasting impression once tasted: "Once you eat pufferfish, other fishes will never again cross your mind."

## 3. Dongxiang Lamb

Zhenjiang is renowned for its Dongxiang lamb, a cherished local delicacy. The name "Dongxiang" originates from the eastern part of Zhenjiang, where high-quality lamb is produced. This tender and flavorful lamb is delicious and highly nutritious, well-known for its ability to nourish the body and improve overall physical well-being.

## 六、名胜古迹

作为拥有3000余年历史的文化名城，镇江有许多引人入胜的历史遗迹和自然风光。尤其是由金山、焦山和北固山共同构成的镇江三山风景名胜区，是镇江标志性的自然景观。

### 1. 金山

金山位于镇江西北，原来是长江中的一个岛屿，有"江心一朵美芙蓉"的美誉。1903年左右，随着长江北移而与陆地连成一片。金山上建有中国佛教名寺——金山寺（又名江天禅寺），是中国四大名寺之一。金山更因《白蛇传》中"水漫金山"的传说、梁红玉擂鼓战金山的壮举以及苏东坡妙高台赏月舞剑的逸事而闻名。

### 2. 焦山

焦山是一座被长江水环绕的山，山上树木茂盛，就像飘浮在长江中的翡翠，所以也被称为"江中浮玉"。焦山原名"樵山"（qiáo），因纪念曾经隐居在山中的东汉隐士焦光而改名为"焦山"并沿用至今。定慧寺、碑林和摩崖石刻是焦山最著名的三个景点。定慧寺是一座拥有悠久历史的佛教寺院，起源可以追溯到东汉时期，历史上多次更名、重建。在寺庙天王殿前的东侧，有一座御碑亭，亭子里有一块御碑，刻着清朝乾隆皇帝第一次南巡时作的《游焦山歌》。乾隆皇帝一生6

## VI. Historical Sites and Scenic Spots

As a renowned cultural city with a rich history spanning over 3,000 years, Zhenjiang has several fascinating historical sites and natural landscapes. One of the most popular attractions is the Zhenjiang Three Mountains Scenic Area, the city's most famous area of natural beauty encompassing the mountains of Jinshan, Jiaoshan, and Beigu.

### 1. The Jinshan Mountain

Situated in the northwest of Zhenjiang, Jinshan was originally an island in the Yangtze River. Around 1903, the river shifted northward, and Jinshan became connected to the mainland. Jinshan is home to the renowned Chinese Buddhist temple, the Jinshan Temple, also known as "the temple of river and sky", one of China's four famous temples. It is also associated with various legends, such as the story of "Jinshan Flood" from *The Legend of the White Snake*, Liang Hongyu's heroic act of beating drums and fighting on Jinshan, and Su Dongpo's moon gazing and sword dancing.

### 2. The Jiaoshan Mountain

Jiaoshan is a mountain surrounded by the Yangtze River. Its luxuriant trees resemble green jade, hence its nickname "jade floating in the river". Originally known as "Qiaoshan", it was later renamed "Jiaoshan" in tribute to Jiao Guang, a hermit of the Eastern Han Dynasty who lived in seclusion on the mountain. There are three attractions on the mountain: the Dinghui Temple, the Forest of Steles, and the Cliff Carvings. The Dinghui Temple, a Buddhist temple with a long history dating back to the Eastern Han Dynasty, has seen numerous renovations and name changes over the years. In front of the temple stands the Heavenly King's Palace, which houses a royal tablet pavilion engraved with the "Song of the

次南巡，5次都到了焦山，显示了他对焦山和定慧寺的偏爱和重视。碑林内收藏着历代书法碑刻400多块，是江南第一大碑林。这些碑刻都镶嵌在回廊和亭阁中，令人流连忘返。摩崖石刻在焦山西麓的峭壁上，这些石刻跨越多个朝代，自六朝以来，唐、宋、明清乃至近代，诸多历史名人的题诗、题词被镌（juàn）刻在此，形成了一条壮观的天然卷轴。碑林和摩崖石刻一起构成了"江南第一碑林"。

### 3. 北固山

　　北固山北临长江，高55.2米，长约200米。因山壁陡峭，易守难攻，所以得名"北固"。山中最为出名的景点是甘露寺和北固楼。甘露寺建于东吴甘露年间，与三国时期吴国的历史传说紧密相连。如《三国演义》中"刘备招亲"的故事就发生在此。北固楼是北固山上的一座楼阁，六朝时，梁武帝萧衍（yǎn）登上此楼远眺，被壮丽的景色所感动，挥笔题下"天下江山第一楼"。

Tour in the Jiaoshan Mountain" composed by Emperor Qianlong during his southern journey. The emperor's frequent visits to Jiaoshan and the Dinghui Temple during his southern tours underscore his deep affection and regard for the area. The Forest of Steles south of the Yangtze River, with over 400 calligraphy inscriptions on steles in cloisters and pavilions, is the largest in the area. The Cliff Carvings at the western base of Jiaoshan are a stunning sight and date back to the Six Dynasties, the Tang, Song, Ming, Qing Dynasties, and even modern times, featuring poems and inscriptions by renowned historical figures. Together, the Forest of Steles and the Cliff Carvings form the "No.1 stele forest in Jiangnan".

### 3. The Beigu Mountain

　　The Beigu Mountain sits just south of the Yangtze River, with a height of 55.2 meters and a length of about 200 meters. Its name "Beigu" (formidable against the north) derives from its steep and easily defensible terrain. Among the notable attractions on the mountain are the Ganlu Temple and the Beigu Tower. The Ganlu Temple, constructed during the Ganlu period of the Kingdom of Wu, holds significant historical connections to the Three Kingdoms era. In *Romance of the Three Kingdoms*, it is in this place that Liu Bei married a princess of Wu. Additionally, the Beigu Tower, a pavilion on the Beigu Mountain, was visited by Xiao Yan, Emperor Wu of Liang during the Southern Dynasties. Overwhelmed by the breathtaking scenery, the emperor wrote "the No.1 tower of the world's rivers and mountains".

# 七、乡村振兴

习近平总书记强调："要提升乡村产业发展水平、乡村建设水平、乡村治理水平。"这一战略的目的是全面振兴乡村，激活乡村经济，增加农民的收入，共筑美好生活。通过多年的努力，镇江的许多乡村在苏南地区脱颖而出，其中，句容茅山镇丁庄村和白兔镇就以显著的发展成效成为当地乡村振兴的杰出代表。

句容市茅山镇丁庄村在茅山北侧，在现代科技和先进种植技术的帮助下，村民专注于葡萄种植，建成了万亩葡萄示范园，为市场提供了高品质的"丁庄葡萄"。近年来，丁庄大力发展观光、休闲、旅游和水果采摘活动，举办葡萄旅游节，将传统农业与现代旅游相结合，推动了乡村旅游的蓬勃发展，提升了"丁庄葡萄"品牌的市场影响力和产品附加值。丁庄因此被评为"全国一村一品示范村"、江苏省省级生态示范村、江苏省科普示范村。

# VII. Rural Revitalization

CPC General Secretary Xi Jinping has stressed the importance of improving rural development, construction, and governance. This strategy aims to revitalize the rural areas, stimulate the rural economy, improve farmers' income, and create a better quality of life. Zhenjiang has witnessed the remarkable development of several rural settlements. Dingzhuang Village of Maoshan Town and Baitu Town, both in Jurong, are examples of successful rural revitalization in southern Jiangsu Province.

Dingzhuang Village, located on the north side of the Maoshan Mountain in Maoshan Town, Jurong, has embraced modern technology and advanced planting techniques to specialize in grape cultivation. Village residents have established a grape-growing demonstration farm spanning hundreds of hectares that caters to the market's demand for high-quality Dingzhuang grapes. After much effort, Dingzhuang has emerged as a hub for grape production and has gained recognition for its exceptional produce. In recent years, the village has diversified its offerings to include sightseeing, leisure, tourism, and fruit-picking activities. Grape tourism festivals that blend traditional agriculture with contemporary tourism trends are held for the growth of rural tourism and for the marketing of the Dingzhuang grapes. As a result, Dingzhuang Village has been honored as a National "One Village, One Product" Demonstration Village, an Ecological Demonstration Village in Jiangsu Province, and a Science Popularization Demonstration Village in Jiangsu Province.

Baitu Town, also in Jurong, is well-known for growing top-quality strawberries and serves as a major source of high-quality strawberries in Jiangsu Province. Since the 1980s, Baitu

白兔镇同样位于句容，因出产优质草莓而出名，其草莓产品在市场上供不应求，是江苏省内优质草莓的主要来源地。自20世纪80年代起，白兔镇率先引入国外优良草莓品种进行规模化种植。近年来，为了进一步提升竞争力，白兔镇和江苏省农业科学院共同成立了白兔草莓研究院，在示范园中开展草莓新品种的研发、种植技术的试验与推广，以及面向农户的田间指导示范与技术培训等工作。白兔镇不仅培育出多个有机草莓品种，还广泛分享种植技术，白兔镇也赢得了"中国草莓之乡"的美誉。

Town has been at the forefront of introducing foreign strawberry varieties for large-scale cultivation. In recent years, Baitu Town and Jiangsu Academy of Agricultural Sciences have joined forces to establish the Baitu Strawberry Research Institute to boost its competitiveness. The institute focuses on developing new strawberry varieties, testing and promoting planting techniques, providing field guidance, and training farmers in the demonstration gardens. The town has produced a variety of organic strawberries and shared its planting technique widely, thus earning the title of "China's strawberry town".

## 练习

### 一、判断题

1. 镇江从地形上看具有"南水北山"的独特城市形态。　☐
2. 镇江是国家级水路、公路和铁路交通枢纽。　☐
3. 现今典藏于金山的《瘗鹤铭》被称为中国"大字之祖"。　☐
4. "工中有农，以工强农"是江苏科技大学的特色。　☐
5. 焦山被誉为"江中浮玉"。　☐

### 二、思考题

1. 江苏大学的特色学科是什么？对社会发展有何贡献？
2. 香醋、肴肉和锅盖面为何被称为镇江"三怪"？
3. 镇江的新能源产业包括哪些？

### 三、拓展题

实地探访茅山镇丁庄村和白兔镇，访谈当地农民和科技人员，并通过视频介绍科技是如何在乡村振兴中发挥实际作用的。

YANGZHOU

扬州

第六章

淮 / 左 / 名 / 都

An Important City to the East of the Huaihe River

扬州是一座既古老又现代的城市，承载着悠久的历史，融合了南北的风俗习惯，坚守着千年的文化传承，处处体现着开放与包容。扬州是多元的，这里有雄伟壮阔的大江大河，也有如诗如画的水边人家；曾经经历过盐商云集的热闹繁华，也拥有深宅大院的宁静恬淡。

## 一、城市概况

### 1. 地理环境

扬州在江苏中部，因其位于淮河下游东侧，被称为"淮左名都"。扬州地处长江和京杭大运河两条著名水脉的交汇处。扬州地势平坦、河流众多、四季分明、气候温和。因为自然环境秀美和居住环境舒适，扬州被评为联合国人居奖城市、中国首批优秀旅游城市、中国国家园林城市，是中国最美丽宜居的城市之一。

### 2. 城市变迁

"扬州"这个名字最早出现在《尚书·禹贡》（公元前500年）。历史上扬州先后有过"广陵""江都""维扬"等名称。公元前486年，吴王夫差下令开凿邗沟，并筑造了邗城。邗城就是今日扬州的雏形。由于地处京杭大运河交通线的中枢位置，历史上的扬州数度繁荣，尤其在两汉、隋唐、清朝达到顶峰。

### 3. 今日扬州

扬州是与大运河同生共长的城市，大运河塑造了扬州独特的城市气质。今天的扬州虽然历经城市的变迁，但深厚的历史文脉从未中断。作为中国百强城市之一，扬州不仅经济实力雄厚，更拥有丰富的文化遗产和旅游资源。扬州在中国最具活力的"长三角"经济圈内，是上海经济圈和南京都市圈的节点城市，是"一带一路"、长江经济带、大运河文化带、长三角区域一体化等战略叠加融合实施城市。截至2023年底，扬州共有常住人口458.5万人。

扬州交通系统发达便捷。高速公路网络四通八达，连接全国各地；拥有扬州站、扬州东站、高邮站等6个铁路客运站，共有开往北京、上海、广州等国内主要城市近200

## I. Overview

### 1. Geographical Environment

Yangzhou is located in the middle of Jiangsu Province, on the east bank of the lower reaches of the Huaihe River, at the intersection of the Yangtze River and the Beijing-Hangzhou Grand Canal. It has flat terrain, numerous rivers, four distinct seasons and a mild climate. Because of its beautiful natural environment and comfortable living environment, Yangzhou has been awarded the United Nations Habitat Award City, China's Outstanding Tourist City, China's Garden City, etc. Praised as "an important city to the east of the Huaihe River", Yangzhou is one of the most beautiful and livable cities in China.

### 2. Development

The name "Yangzhou" first appeared in *The Book of History* (500 BC). In old days, there were other names like "Guangling", "Jiangdu", and "Weiyang". In 486 BC, the King of Wu ordered the excavation of a ditch and the construction of a city nearby, which was the original site of today's Yangzhou. Due to its location at the center of the Beijing-Hangzhou Grand Canal, Yangzhou prospered several times in history, and reached its peak in the Han, Sui, Tang and Qing Dynasties.

### 3. Yangzhou Today

Yangzhou grows together with the Grand Canal, and the Grand Canal has shaped Yangzhou's unique urban temperament. Although Yangzhou has gone through many changes, its historical legacy has never been compromised. As one of the top 100 cities in China, Yangzhou is not only strong in economic development, but also in culture and tourism. In the Yangtze River Delta economic circle, which is the most dynamic in China, Yangzhou is an important node of Shanghai economic circle

个班次；扬州泰州国际机场已开通国内外航线64条，其中国际（地区）航线14条。扬州已与全球15个国家23个城市结为友好城市。

## 二、文化印象

### 1. 历史文化名城

由于其独特的地理位置，扬州几乎经历了通史般的繁荣和全面的文化兴盛。作为中国首批24座历史文化名城之一，扬州涌现出了一大批极具地方特色的文化形态。扬州八怪、扬州戏曲、扬州工艺、扬派盆景、淮扬菜系等，独树一帜，异彩纷呈。同时，扬州还拥有古琴、漆器、玉雕、雕版印刷、扬剧、扬州评话、扬州清曲、扬州弹词等一大批非物质文化遗产。此外，瘦西湖是中国湖上园林的杰出代表，个园是中国四大名园之一，何园则被誉为"中国晚清第一名园"。

and Nanjing metropolitan circle, and a strategic spot for the integration of the Belt and Road Initiative, the Yangtze River Economic Belt, the Grand Canal Cultural Belt and the Yangtze River Delta. By the end of 2023, Yangzhou had a permanent population of 4.585 million.

Yangzhou has a developed and convenient transportation system. A network of expressways leads to all parts of the country. It has six railway passenger stations, including Yangzhou Station, Yangzhou East Station and Gaoyou Station, with nearly 200 trains bound for Beijing, Shanghai, Guangzhou and other major cities in China. Yangzhou Taizhou International Airport has opened 64 routes, including 14 international (regional) routes. Yangzhou has 23 sister cities in 15 countries around the world.

## II. Cultural Impressions

### 1. Famous Historical and Cultural City

Due to its unique geographical location, Yangzhou has experienced all-round cultural prosperity in its entire history. As one of the first 24 famous historical and cultural cities in China, Yangzhou boasts a large number of cultural forms with local characteristics. The Eight Eccentric Painters and Calligraphers of Yangzhou, Yangzhou opera, Yangzhou handicraft, Yang bonsai, Huaiyang cuisine, etc., are unique and colorful. At the same time, Yangzhou also a large collection of intangible cultural heritage, such as Guqin, lacquer ware, jade carving, carved printing, Yangzhou opera, Yangzhou Pinghua (musical storytelling), Yangzhou Qingqu (folk music), and Yangzhou Tanci (musical storytelling). In addition, the Slender West Lake is an outstanding representative of lake gardens in China, the Half Bamboo Garden is one of the four famous gardens in China, and the He Garden is known as the "No.1 garden in the late Qing Dynasty".

### 2. 生态旅游城市

扬州是生态环境优美的旅游胜地，尤以春天最为迷人。"故人西辞黄鹤去，烟花三月下扬州""天下三分明月夜，二分无赖是扬州"，古诗中不乏对扬州明媚春光的赞颂。据史书记载，清朝乾隆皇帝曾经6次顺着京杭大运河探访江南，每次都必到扬州。直到今天，扬州仍是最有名气的旅游城市之一，吸引大批国内外游客慕名前来。2023年，扬州被央视评为中国"十大旅游向往之城"。

### 3. 世界美食之都

扬州的饮食文化和历史文明一样悠久，闻名世界的淮扬菜就在这里形成。2019年，扬州入选联合国教科文组织评选的"世界美食之都"。扬州美食已经成为扬州走向世界、世界认识扬州的金色名片。扬州的饮食文化是美味的，更是休闲的。走在扬州的大街小巷，品尝地道的淮扬美食，更能感受到这座城市由美食文化营造的慢生活的节奏和舒适悠闲的氛围。

## 三、教育交流

### 1. 高等教育概况

扬州目前共有8所高校，其中本科院校2所，专科院校6所，总计在校学生数量超过12万人，其中国际学生近3000人。扬州凭

## 2. Ecological Tourism

Yangzhou is a tourist destination with beautiful environment, especially in spring. "My old friend departs from the Yellow Crane Tower; in the mist and flowers of spring, he goes down to Yangzhou." "The clear moon over the world, two thirds shine on Yangzhou", there is no shortage of ancient poetry praising Yangzhou's wonderful spring. According to historical records, Emperor Qianlong of the Qing Dynasty visited Jiangnan six times along the Beijing-Hangzhou Grand Canal, and he always went to Yangzhou. Until today, Yangzhou is still one of the most famous tourist cities, attracting a large number of domestic and foreign tourists. In 2023, Yangzhou was listed as one of China's "Top Ten Tourist Cities" by CCTV.

## 3. City of Gastronomy

Food in Yangzhou has as long a history as the city itself, and Yangzhou is the birthplace of the world-famous Huaiyang cuisine. In 2019, Yangzhou was named a "City of Gastronomy" by UNESCO. Yangzhou cuisine has become a famous icon for Yangzhou to reach out to the world and for the world to know Yangzhou. Yangzhou's food is delicious and casual. Walking in the streets of Yangzhou, tasting the authentic Huaiyang cuisine, you can feel the slow pace of life and the comfortable and leisurely atmosphere created by the city's food culture.

## III. Education and International Exchanges

### 1. Overview of Higher Education

There are 8 universities in Yangzhou, including 2 undergraduate colleges and 6 vocational colleges, with a total of over

借深厚的历史沉淀、丰富的人文内涵以及优质的教育资源，吸引着众多中外学子前来求学深造。

## 2. 高校介绍

扬州大学（www.yzu.edu.cn）是江苏省属重点综合性大学，2023年成为"双省部共建高校"。其办学历史可以追溯至1902年，是中国率先进行合并办学的高校。扬州大学拥有多个校区，学科门类齐全，涵盖农学、理学、工学、医学、法学等多个领域，是全国首批博士、硕士学位授权单位。

扬州大学具有招收国际学生的资格，其中本科招生专业10个，硕士招生专业56个，博士招生专业32个。目前在校国际学生2400余人，规模总量位居江苏省第二位，生源地覆盖全球80多个国家。

## 3. 特色专业

扬州大学拥有国家级特色专业六个：农学、动物医学、化学、数学与应用数学、水利水电工程、汉语言文学，均面向国际学生进行招生。

120,000 students, including nearly 3,000 international students. Thanks to its profound historical and cultural legacy and rich educational resources, Yangzhou attracts a lot of Chinese and foreign students.

### 2. Introduction to Universities

Yangzhou University (www.yzu.edu.cn) is a key comprehensive university in Jiangsu Province, a university jointly built by Jiangsu Province and the Ministry of Education. Its origin can be traced back to 1902, and it is the first university in China to experience a merge. Yangzhou University has multiple campuses and a complete range of disciplines, covering agronomy, science, engineering, medicine, law and other fields. It is one of the first institutions in China to confer doctor's and master's degrees.

Yangzhou University is qualified to recruit international students in its 10 undergraduate programs, 56 master programs and 32 doctoral programs. At present, the university enrolls more than 2,400 international students from more than 80 countries, ranking second in Jiangsu Province.

### 3. Featured Disciplines

Yangzhou University has six state-level programs: agronomy, veterinary medicine, chemistry, mathematics and applied mathematics, water conservancy and hydropower engineering,

## 四、经济腾飞

### 1. 文化旅游

旅游业是扬州经济产业的重要组成部分。扬州现有国家A级旅游景区57家，总量位居全省第一。2023年，扬州旅游接待总人次达1.0321亿，首次突破1亿，创历史新高。扬州举办了一系列富有城市特色的文化旅游活动，如"烟花三月"国际经贸旅游节、世界运河城市论坛、扬州鉴真半程马拉松、中国早茶文化节等，以推动城市旅游经济的发展，促进文化和旅游深度融合，提升城市形象与知名度。

### 2. 现代农业

扬州是著名的"鱼米之乡"，是全国重要的商品粮基地和水禽水产主产区，拥有众多国家级、省级农业龙头企业。扬州的农产品有较强的地域特征，高邮鸭、宝应荷藕、扬州鹅、仪征市茶叶等一批名优特色农产品享誉海内外。

## 五、特色美食

### 1. 淮扬菜系

扬州是中国传统四大菜系之一淮扬菜的发源地之一。淮扬菜常被选入国宴招待各国领导人。淮扬菜以严格优质的选材、精湛细致的刀工、典雅讲究的摆盘、南北适宜的口味，深受食客的喜爱。其代表性菜品有蟹粉狮子头、文思豆腐、三套鸭等。

and Chinese language and literature, all of which are open to international students.

## IV. Economic Takeoff

### 1. Cultural Tourism

Tourism is an important part of Yangzhou's economy. The number of national A-level tourist attractions in Yangzhou, 57, ranks first in the province. In 2023, the total number of tourist arrivals in Yangzhou reached 103.21 million, surpassing 100 million for the first time and reaching a record high. Yangzhou has hosted a series of cultural tourism activities with urban characteristics, such as the Yangzhou "Flowery March" International Economy, Trade and Tourism Festival, World Canal Cities Forum, Yangzhou Jianzhen Half Marathon and China Morning Tea Culture Festival, in order to promote the development of tourism, help to integrate culture with tourism, and expand the influence of the city.

### 2. Modern Agriculture

Yangzhou, a famous "land of fish and rice", is an important production base of grains, poultry and aquatic products, and has a lot of leading agricultural enterprises in the national and provincial level. There are strong regional characteristics to Yangzhou's agricultural products, such as Gaoyou duck, Baoying lotus root, Yangzhou goose, Yizheng tea, etc., which are well-known at home and abroad.

## V. Specialty Food

### 1. The Huaiyang Cuisine

Yangzhou is one of the birthplaces of the Huaiyang cuisine, one of the four traditional Chinese culinary styles. The Huaiyang cuisine is often selected for state banquets, where world leaders are entertained, and is popular among gourmets for its strict selection of high-quality materials, exquisite and meticulous knife work, elegant dish setting, and good taste for

### 2. 早茶文化

在清朝，扬州的盐商在吃早饭时常常要喝茶，逐渐发展成扬州独特的早茶文化。"早上皮包水"，扬州人的一天是从喝早茶开始的。喝早茶，在扬州既是一种世代相传的生活习惯，也是一种惬意休闲的生活方式。"饮茶如筵"，一餐早茶就是一桌完整的筵席，从凉菜到热炒，再到各式点心、主食、水果、佐料小碟，一应俱全。

### 3. 扬州炒饭

"扬州炒饭炒遍全球"，只要有华人的地方，几乎都能见到它的踪影，普及程度使其几乎成为蛋炒饭的代名词。扬州炒饭的主要食材有米饭、火腿、鸡蛋、虾仁等，烹饪过程中要求翻炒均匀、米饭颗粒分明、软硬有度，配料丰富多样、口感鲜嫩滑爽、香糯可口。

## 六、名胜古迹

### 1. 瘦西湖

扬州在隋唐时期是南北水运交通的重要枢纽，大量商人在此聚集，并开始修建私家园林。到清朝康乾盛世，瘦西湖经过精心规划和建设，成为其中最著名的园林之一。因为其湖面形状狭长，人们把它命名为"瘦西湖"，虽然不如杭州西湖面积大，但是修长秀气，有一种"清瘦"之美。

people from north and south. Representative dishes include pork balls with crab sauce, Wensi tofu, three-nested duck and so on.

## 2. Morning Tea Culture

In the Qing Dynasty, salt merchants often drank tea at breakfast, and this habit gradually developed into Yangzhou's unique morning tea culture. "Water in the morning", Yangzhou people start their day with morning tea. Drinking morning tea in Yangzhou is not only a habit passed down from generation to generation, but also a comfortable and casual way of life. "Drinking tea is like enjoying a feast", a breakfast tea is served on a table, from cold dishes to hot stir-fried dishes, and then to all kinds of dim sum, staple food, fruit, seasoning, etc.

## 3. Yangzhou Fried Rice

"Yangzhou fried rice overwhelms the world." There is Yangzhou fried rice as long as there are Chinese people present. It is so popular that it almost becomes synonymous with egg fried rice. The main ingredients of Yangzhou fried rice include rice, ham, eggs, shrimps, etc. In the cooking process, the grains of rice are stirred evenly to become clear and suitably soft, while the ingredients are rich and diverse to offer a fresh, smooth, fragrant and delicious taste.

## VI. Historical Sites and Scenic Spots

### 1. The Slender West Lake

In the Sui and Tang Dynasties, Yangzhou was an important hub of water transportation between the north and the south, where a large number of merchants gathered and began to build private gardens. By the Qing Dynasty, the Slender West Lake had been carefully planned and built as one of the most famous gardens in the city. Because of its long and narrow shape,

## 2. 个园

　　个园是清代盐商的私家园林，在明代"寿芝园"的基础上几次增建而成，是中国四大名园之一。园中有大量的竹子，所以取"竹"字的一半，名为"个园"。个园的一大特色，是运用不同的石头和假山造型，创造出模仿春夏秋冬四季景色的"四季假山"。

## 3. 文昌阁

　　文昌阁又叫"魁星楼"。在古代，人们认为魁星决定考生的命运，考生们会参拜文昌阁，希望可以金榜题名。扬州文昌阁始建于明朝，高3层24米，是当时扬州府学（官方教育机构）的重要标志，现在是扬州的地标性建筑之一。城市的规模不断扩大，新的商业区不断涌现。但文昌阁始终是扬州人心目中的市中心，因为它见证了这座城市的古老与繁华，也亲历了这座城市的现代与发展。

people named it "Slender West Lake". Although not as large as the West Lake in Hangzhou, it is slender and elegant, exuding a "thin" beauty.

## 2. The Geyuan Garden

Originally the private garden of salt merchants in the Qing Dynasty, built several times on the basis of the Shouzhi Garden in the Ming Dynasty, the Geyuan Garden is one of the four most famous gardens in China. Its Chinese name 个 is actually half of 竹 (bamboo), because there are a lot of bamboos in the garden. A notable feature of the garden is the use of different stones and rockeries to create a "rockery of four seasons" that mimics the scenery in spring, summer, autumn and winter.

## 3. Wenchang Pavilion

Wenchang Pavilion is also called the Tower of the Literary Star. In ancient times, people believed that the Literary Star was the patron god of scholars. In order to pass the imperial examinations, scholars would visit the pavilion, hoping to be named on the golden list. Wenchang Pavilion, at a height of 24 meters in three floors, was built in the Ming Dynasty as a symbol of the official educational institution of Yangzhou (Fuxue). It is now one of the landmarks in Yangzhou. The city is growing in size and new business districts are springing up, but the pavilion has always been the center of Yangzhou in people's minds, because it has witnessed the history and the modern development of the city.

## VII. Ecological Protection

Yangzhou is located at the confluence of the Yangtze River and the Grand Canal. Water gives it life and beauty. Yangzhou's ecological protection, first of all, is to restore the water ecology.

### 1. Protection of the Yangtze River

A number of measures have been taken to

## 七、生态保护

扬州地处长江和大运河交汇处，依水而建，因水而美。生态保护，首先是要修复水生态。

### 1. 长江保护

扬州采取了多项措施改善长江的水质。比如，采用码头岸电（岸上供电）系统替代船上的柴油发电机，减少浓烟和柴油的污染。关闭了长江岸边的多个化工企业。此外，作为国家南水北调东线工程的"源头"城市，扬州坚持源头治理，有效保护和修复长江生态环境和源头水质，保证持续输送一江清水北上。

### 2. 江淮生态大走廊

扬州境内共有长江岸线80多公里、大运河140多公里，连同沿运河的宝应湖、高邮湖、邵伯湖，形成了一纵一横两条生态廊道，这"一纵"就是1800平方公里的江淮生态大走廊。扬州通过源头治理、保护生物多样性、恢复水体环境等措施，努力提升区域生态环境质量。

### 3. 生态宜居名城

扬州坚持绿色发展，积极打造美丽宜居的生态旅游城市。因为自然环境优美、居住环境舒适，扬州先后获得联合国人居奖城市、中国首批优秀旅游城市、中国国家园林城市等称号，还曾3次在联合国气候变化大会上展示生态文明建设的成果。

improve the water quality of the Yangtze River. For example, the use of shore power system (drawing electric power directly from the land) to replace diesel generators on board helps to achieve "zero fuel consumption" and reduce carbon emissions. Chemical companies along the banks of the Yangtze River have been shut down. In addition, as the "source" city of the eastern route of the National South-to-North Water Diversion Project, Yangzhou adheres to the source control protocols, effectively protects the ecological environment and source water quality of the Yangtze River, and ensures the continuous transmission of clean water northward.

### 2. Jianghuai Ecological Corridor

In Yangzhou, the waterfront length of the Yangtze River amounts to more than 80 kilometers and that of the Grand Canal, over 140 kilometers. Together with the Baoying Lake, the Gaoyou Lake and the Shaobo Lake along the canal, two ecological corridors are created in the vertical and horizontal directions, and the vertical one is the 1,800-square-kilometer of Jianghuai ecological corridor. Yangzhou strives to improve the quality of regional ecological environment through measures such as source control, biodiversity protection and water environment restoration.

### 3. Ecologically Livable City

Yangzhou adheres to green development and seeks to become a beautiful and livable city of eco-tourism. Because of its beautiful natural environment and comfortable living environment, Yangzhou has won the title of United Nations Habitat Award City, China's first Outstanding Tourism City, China's National Garden City, etc., and has been invited to showcase its achievements in ecological construction at the United Nations Climate Change Conference three times.

## 八、诗词扬州

### 1. 二十四桥明月夜

"二十四桥明月夜，玉人何处教吹箫？"是唐代诗人杜牧的诗句，用来表达自己离开扬州后对好友的思念。诗中写道，深秋的扬州依然绿水青山、草木葱茏，二十四桥月夜仍然乐声悠扬，表达了作者对过往扬州生活的深情怀念。

### 2. 二分无赖是扬州

"天下三分明月夜，二分无赖是扬州。"出自唐代徐凝的《忆扬州》。意思是说，天下明月的光华有三分，扬州就占去了两分。诗人用夸张的手法，表达了扬州的美丽和繁华，是天下月色最美的地方，绚烂夺目。

### 3. 故人西辞黄鹤楼

"故人西辞黄鹤楼，烟花三月下扬州。"是唐代著名诗人李白的诗句。"下扬州"指沿着长江走水路顺流而下，后也指顺着运河南下。由于扬州便捷的地理位置，繁华的城市经济，无数文人从北方坐船到扬州游览。在相当长的时间里，"下扬州"一度成为风尚。直到今天，扬州仍是中国著名的旅游城市，每年吸引着大批中外游客。

## VIII. Poetry about Yangzhou

### 1. Twenty-four Bridges Steeped in the Moonlight

"Twenty-four bridges steeped in the moonlight, where is the handsome man teaching girls to play bamboo flutes?" It was written by Du Mu, a Tang Dynasty poet, to express his longing for his good friend after he left Yangzhou. In the poem, Yangzhou in late autumn is still green and lush, and the moonlight on the 24 bridges is still melodious; it expresses the author's deep nostalgia for the past life in Yangzhou.

### 2. Two Thirds Shine on Yangzhou

"The clear moon over the world, two thirds shine on Yangzhou." This line comes from Xu Ning's "Recalling Yangzhou" in the Tang Dynasty. It means that Yangzhou takes up two thirds of the clear moon that shines on the world. Exaggeration is employed to highlight the beauty and prosperity of Yangzhou, which is the most beautiful place in the dazzling moonlight.

### 3. My Old Friends Departs from the Yellow Crane Tower

"My old friend departs from the Yellow Crane Tower; in the mist and flowers of spring, he goes down to Yangzhou." It's a poem written by Li Bai, a famous poet in the Tang Dynasty. "Go down to Yangzhou" refers to the waterway along the Yangtze River downstream, and later also to the canal down the south. Due to Yangzhou's convenient geographical location and prosperous economy, countless literati traveled to Yangzhou by boat from the north. For a long time, "go down to Yangzhou" became a fashion. Until today, Yangzhou is still a famous tourist city in China, attracting a large number of tourists from home and abroad every year.

## 练 习

### 一、判断题

1. 扬州是淮扬菜的唯一发源地。 ☐

2. 扬州地处长江和京杭运河的交叉处。 ☐

3. 扬州位于江苏省的中部、淮河的上游。 ☐

4. 农学、动物医学、化学等是扬州大学的特色专业。 ☐

### 二、思考题

1. 为什么说烟花三月"下"扬州，而不是"上"扬州？

2. 淮扬菜有什么特点？和其他的中国菜系有什么不同？

3. 扬州瘦西湖作为湖上园林的杰出代表，有什么特点？

### 三、拓展题

1. 尝试做一次扬州炒饭，并拍摄一个小视频。

2. 以小组为单位，找一找其他描写扬州的诗句，做一个"诗词扬州"报告。

# Chapter 7

南通

第七章

中／国／近／代／第／一／城
The First City of Modern China

南通，简称"通"，是中国近代民族工业发祥地之一，并在文化、
科教等领域拥有多个"第一"，因此被称为"中国近代第一城"。

## 一、城市概况

### 1. 地理环境

南通位于江苏省东南部，南临长江，东濒黄海，经崇启大桥与上海跨江相连，是江苏唯一同时拥有沿江沿海深水岸线的城市。由于南通拥有宝贵的海岸线和长江航道，紧挨着长江入海口，在长江三角洲城市群中具有独特的位置优势，素有"江海门户"之称。

南通形状像一个半岛，三面被水包围，除了南面长江边上的狼山一带是山丘以外，其余都是平原。地势平坦，河、江、海贯通全市，交织成网。全市最高点是军山，高108.5米。南通四季分明，气候温和，年平均气温15℃左右。

### 2. 城市变迁

6500年前，随着长江的沙土慢慢堆积，陆地逐渐由西向东、从北向南渐渐扩大，其中，海安是最早形成的陆地，随后是如皋。5000多年前，这两地就有人类生活居住，在海安发现的新石器时代青墩遗址，是江淮东北原始文化的重要代表。南北朝时期，长江口附近泥沙堆积，形成了海上沙洲，被称为"胡逗洲"。后周时期（958年），南通在胡逗洲上建城，称"通州"。由于三面环水，偏远且交通不便，南通是出了名的"难通"，导致当地人的思想和经济发展受到了限制。

## I. Overview

### 1. Geographical Environment

Nantong is located in the southeast of Jiangsu Province, facing the Yangtze River to the south and the Yellow Sea to the east. Connected to Shanghai via the Chongqi Bridge across the river, Nantong is the only city in Jiangsu that has both riverside and seaside deep-water shorelines. With its valuable waterways in the Yangtze River and its adjacency to the estuary into the sea, Nantong enjoys a unique locational advantage in the Yangtze River Delta city cluster and is known as the "gateway to the river and the sea".

Nantong is shaped like a peninsula, surrounded by water on three sides, and with the exception of the hills along the Yangtze River to the south, the city features flat terrain. A number of rivers, such as the Yangtze River, run through the city in a network of waterways before finally joining the sea. The highest point in the city is Junshan, at an elevation of 108.5 meters. Nantong has distinct seasons and a mild climate, with an average annual temperature of about 15°C.

### 2. Development

6,500 years ago, as the silt of the Yangtze River slowly accumulated in this area, the land gradually expanded from west to east, and from north to south. Hai'an was the first to form, followed by Rugao. Then, 5,000 years ago, these two places already had human habitation. The Neolithic Qingdun site, discovered in Hai'an, is an important representative of the primitive culture of northeastern Jianghuai region. During the Southern and Northern Dynasties, the accumulation of silt near the mouth of the Yangtze River formed an offshore sandbank, known as "Hudou Island". In the later Zhou period (958 AD), the town of Nantong was

1984年5月，南通成为中国首批对外开放的14个沿海城市之一，这一举措为南通的对外交流和经济发展开启了新篇章。经过40余年的发展，南通由"难通"变为"好通"，成为一个现代、开放、宜居的美丽城市。

### 3. 今日南通

近年来，南通坚持生态优先、绿色发展，取得了显著成效。南通连续5次被评为"国家卫生城市"，2019年被评为"全国水生态文明城市"，2022年被命名为"国家生态文明建设示范区"，2023年获生态环境部通报表扬，成为江苏唯一获得表扬的地级市。

南通将打造8条过江通道，逐渐形成"八龙过江"的交通格局，这既是南通全方位融入苏南、对接上海、推进高质量发展的基础性工程，也是打通南通"南不通"的战略措施。目前，苏通长江公路大桥、崇启大桥、沪苏通长江公铁大桥都已建成通车，已经开工建设的3条过江通道正在加紧建设。

built on Hudou Island, then called "Tongzhou". Surrounded by water on three sides, it was rather remote and hardly had any forms of transportation; thus, Nantong was famously "difficult to pass" and the local development was limited.

In May 1984, Nantong became one of the first group of 14 coastal cities in China to open up to the outside world. This move opened a new chapter for Nantong's international exchange and economic development. After more than 40 years of development, Nantong has transformed from "difficult to pass" to "easy to pass", becoming a modern, open, livable and beautiful city.

### 3. Nantong Today

In recent years, Nantong has focused on ecological protection and green development and achieved remarkable results. The city was named a "National Clean City" for five consecutive times, a "National Water Ecological City" in 2019, a "National Ecological Construction Demonstration Zone" in 2022, and was the only prefecture-level city in Jiangsu Province to be commended by the Ministry of Ecology and Environment in 2023.

8 river-crossing channels like "Eight Dragons Crossing the River" will be completed in Nantong. This is both an infrastructure project for Nantong to fully integrate into southern Jiangsu, connect with Shanghai, promote its high-quality development, and a strategic measure to solve the "difficult to pass" situation in Nantong. At present, the Subei-Nantong Yangtze River Highway Bridge, Chongqi Bridge, and Shanghai-Suzhou-Nantong Yangtze River Railway Bridge have all been completed and have opened to traffic. Furthermore, the construction of three river-crossing channels is being accelerated.

## 二、文化印象

### 1. 博物馆之城

1905年，著名实业家张謇（jiǎn）在南通创办了南通博物苑，这是中国人独立创办的第一座公共博物馆，以"设为痒序学校以教，多识鸟兽草木之名"为宗旨，融合中国古代园林特点与近代博物馆理念，是一座"园馆一体"的综合性博物馆。

南通作为中国博物馆的发祥地，已经实现了"县县有博物馆"，形成了主体多元、类型丰富的现代博物馆体系。截至2023年底，南通已建成31家备案博物馆，包括21家国有博物馆，如南通博物苑、中国珠算博物馆、审计博物馆、中华慈善博物馆、南通城市博物馆等；另有10家非国有博物馆，如南通蓝印花布博物馆、南通风筝博物馆、南通通作家具博物馆等。这些博物馆集历史底蕴与时代风貌于一体，是市民和游客走近历史、了解南通、感受科学魅力、接受文化熏陶，以及休闲旅游的理想场所。

## II. Cultural Impressions

### 1. City of Museums

In 1905, the famous industrialist Zhang Jian founded the Nantong Museum in Nantong. This was the first public museum to be established by the Chinese independently, and its purpose was to "create a school to teach people the names of birds, beasts, plants, and trees". It combines the characteristics of ancient Chinese gardens with modern museum concepts, so it is called "garden and museum as one".

In Nantong, the birthplace of Chinese museums, every county has a museum, and these museums feature a rich variety of themes and types. As of the end of 2023, there were 31 registered museums in Nantong, including 21 state-owned museums, such as the Nantong Museum, the Chinese Abacus Museum, the Audit Museum, the Chinese Charity Museum, the Nantong City Museum, etc., and 10 non-state-owned museums, such as the Nantong Blue Print Textiles Museum, the Nantong Kites Museum, the Nantong Traditional Furniture Museum, etc. These museums tell about the vicissitudes of time, and are ideal places for people to learn about the local history, understand the city of Nantong, experience the beauty of science and culture, and enjoy a leisurely tour.

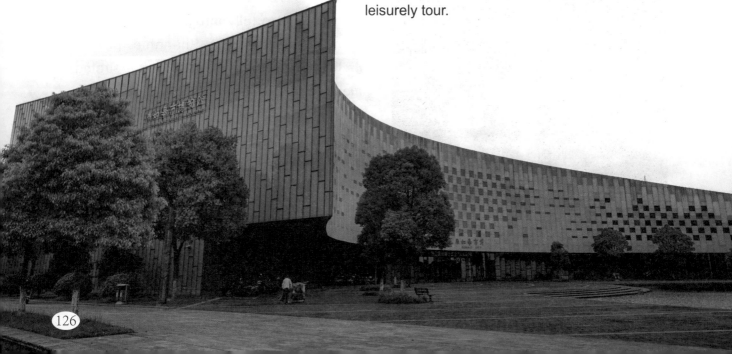

## 2. 非物质文化遗产

非物质文化遗产（以下简称非遗）作为文化资源的重要组成部分，在南通文化中占有重要地位。南通现有1个项目被联合国教科文组织列入《人类非物质文化遗产代表作名录》，还有12项国家级非遗项目，53项省级项目。

南通仿真绣、南通蓝印花布印染技艺、梅庵派古琴技术、风筝制作技艺（南通板鹞风筝）、童子戏等，这些都是南通人民日常生活和精神世界的生动体现，记录着南通从古至今的变迁故事，也传承着一代代南通人独特的文化和智慧。

## 三、教育交流

### 1. 高等教育概况

南通在高等教育方面展现出了一定的潜力和竞争优势，其扎实的办学实力培养了大量高素质的应用型和技术技能型人才，为地方经济建设和社会发展作出了积极的贡献。南通有3所本科院校（南通大学及其二级学院杏林学院、南通理工学院）、5所职业教育类专科学校（南通职业大学、江苏工程职业技术学院、江苏航运职业技术学院、南通科技职业学院、江苏商贸职业学院）。这些院校在纺织技术和航运管理等专业领域具备独特优势和鲜明特色，为行业输送了大量专业化人才。

## 2. Intangible Cultural Heritage

Intangible cultural heritage represents an important part of cultural resources and occupies an important position in the culture of Nantong. Nantong currently has 1 item included in the Representative List of the Intangible Cultural Heritage of Humanity by UNESCO, as well as 12 national-level items and 53 provincial-level items.

Nantong's true-to-life embroidery, blue print textiles, Mei'an School's Guqin techniques, kite-making skills (Nantong whistle kite), child plays, etc., are all vivid manifestations of the daily life and wisdom of the people of Nantong and reflect Nantong's changes from ancient times to the present.

## III. Education and International Exchanges

### 1. Overview of Higher Education

Nantong boasts a certain level of potential and competitive advantages in higher education, and a large number of talented people in applied and technical fields have been educated in the city to contribute to the local economic construction and social development. There are 3 undergraduate institutions (Nantong University and its secondary college Xinglin College, Nantong Institute of Technology) and 5 vocational colleges (Nantong Vocational University, Jiangsu Engineering Vocational and Technical College, Jiangsu Shipping Vocational and Technical College, Nantong Science and Technology Vocational College, and Jiangsu Business Vocational College) in Nantong. They all have unique advantages and distinctive features in professional fields such as textile technology and shipping management, and have trained a large number of professional talents.

## 2. 高校介绍

南通大学（www.ntu.edu.cn）建于1912年，是江苏省人民政府和中国交通运输部共建的综合性大学、"江苏高水平大学建设高峰计划"建设高校。学校设有26个学院、1个独立学院（杏林学院）、1家直属大型综合三级甲等医院（南通大学附属医院）和国际教育学院、继续教育学院。临床医学、工程学、药理学与毒理学、计算机科学等9个学科进入ESI学科全球排名前1%。学校提供的专业涵盖文理工医，本、硕、博学生共计4万余人，其中国际学生1300多人。

学校高度重视来华留学教育，是中国政府奖学金院校。学校致力于国际交流与合作，与澳大利亚、美国、意大利等国家和港澳台地区的140余所高校和科研院所开展合作办学与科研、师生交流、师资培训等项目。

## 2. Introduction to Universities

Nantong University (www.ntu.edu.cn), established in 1912, is a comprehensive university jointly built by the People's Government of Jiangsu Province and the Ministry of Transport of China. It is one of the universities under the Peak Plan of Jiangsu High-level University Construction. It has 26 colleges, 1 independent college (Xinglin College), and 1 directly affiliated comprehensive hospital (Affiliated Hospital of Nantong University), as well as the School of International Education, and the School of Continuing Education. 9 disciplines, including Clinical Medicine, Engineering, Pharmacology & Toxicology, and Computer Science are listed in the top 1% of ESI global ranking. The university offers a wide range of disciplines covering humanities, sciences, engineering, and medicine, with a total enrollment of over 40,000 students, including more than 1,300 international students.

The university attaches great importance to the international student education in China and it is one of the institutions eligible for the Chinese Government Scholarship. The university is committed to international exchanges and cooperation, and has established partnerships with over 140 universities and research institutes in countries such as Australia, the United States, and Italy, as well as regions like Hong Kong, Macao and Taiwan regions, for joint programs, research, faculty and student exchanges, and faculty training.

## 四、经济腾飞

南通的经济发展稳健。改革开放初期，南通成为中国首批14个对外开放的沿海城市之一；2020年，南通全市生产总值突破万亿元，成为江苏第4座"万亿之城"；2023年，南通首次跻身全国城市经济前20强。纺织业、建筑业和船舶海工是南通的支柱性产业。近年来，南通努力打造船舶海工和高端纺织国家级产业集群，共筑"一带一路"绿色产业链。

### 1. 纺织之乡

1895年，近代实业家张謇开始筹办大生纱厂，奠定了南通纺织业发展的基础。南通作为中国近代纺织工业的摇篮，不仅有中国第一家纺织厂，也创办了中国第一所纺织高等院校。经过上百年的变革与发展，南通已形成产业门类齐全、龙头企业集聚的高端纺织产业集群，是世界三大家纺中心之一，家纺市场规模世界第三、中国第一，有"世界家纺看中国、中国家纺看南通"的美誉。其中，中国叠石桥国际家纺城占有全球家纺市场近6成份额。

## IV. Economic Takeoff

Nantong's economic development is robust. As mentioned earlier, at the beginning of the reform and opening-up, Nantong became one of the first group of 14 coastal cities in China to open up to the outside world. In 2020, Nantong's GDP exceeded one trillion yuan, turning the city into the fourth "trillion city" in Jiangsu Province. In 2023, Nantong entered the top 20 of the economically strongest cities in China for the first time. Textiles, construction, and shipbuilding and offshore engineering are the pillar industries of Nantong. In recent years, Nantong has been striving to build a national-level industrial cluster of shipbuilding and offshore engineering and high-end textiles, and has jointly built a green industrial chain for the Belt and Road Initiative.

### 1. Home of Textile Industry

In 1895, the Chinese industrialist Zhang Jian founded Dasheng Cotton Mill, which laid the foundation for the development of Nantong's textile industry. As the cradle of the modern textile industry in China, Nantong boasts the first textile factory in China and the first textile college in China. After more than a hundred years of development, a high-end textile cluster with a complete range of industries and a number of leading enterprises has been created in Nantong. Now, recognized as one of the three centers of home textiles in the world, Nantong is the largest production base of home textiles in China and the third largest in the world. People say, "The world looks to China for home textiles, and to Nantong for China's home textiles." The China Dieshiqiao International Home Textiles City in Nantong accounts for nearly 60% of the global market in home textiles.

### 2. 建筑之乡

1988年，南通承建的拉萨饭店为江苏省获得了第一个全国建筑工程质量最高荣誉"中国建设工程鲁班奖"。此后，"南通铁军"屡创佳绩。2005年，南通仅用两年时间高质量完成了阿联酋迪拜双塔工程，荣获首届境外工程鲁班奖。截至2023年12月，南通已获得鲁班奖124个，数量居全国地级市之首。全市5000多家建筑企业中，6家建筑企业入选"全球最大250家国际承包商"，25家企业拥有特级资质。近年来，南通以建筑架起与世界沟通的桥梁，深入参与"一带一路"共建国家和地区的建设，包括俄罗斯、新加坡、东南亚、中东、非洲等，不仅助力当地的经济发展、改善人民生活条件，还在文化交流方面发挥了积极作用。

### 3. 造船重镇

优越的地理环境使南通成为船舶海工制造的首选之地，其船舶制造、海工装备产业约占全国的十分之一和四分之一。一系列大国重器，如国内首制20000TEU超大型集装箱船、世界首制4000车位LNG双燃料汽车运输船、亚洲最大的重型自航绞吸式挖泥船"天鲲号"、中国首制极地探险邮轮等，都从南通启航。2022年10月，南通牵头泰州、扬州的海工装备和高技术船舶先进制造业集群，成功入选全国先进制造业集群，全力打造世界级船舶海工先进制造业集群。

当前，南通正加快跨江融合、向海发展，努力建设"一枢纽五城市"，奋力打造具有江海特色的现代化产业体系。

## 2. Home of Construction

In 1988, the Lhasa Hotel constructed in Nantong won Jiangsu Province's first-ever national construction quality award, the Lu Ban Prize for Construction Engineering in China. Since then, the "Nantong Construction Army" has achieved remarkable success. In 2005, construction teams from Nantong completed the twin towers in Dubai, UAE, in just two years with high quality, which won the first Lu Ban Prize for overseas projects. As of December 2023, construction companies from Nantong won 124 Lu Ban Prizes, a national No.1 among prefecture-level cities. There are more than 5,000 construction companies in Nantong, and six among them have been included in the "Top 250 International Contractors in the World" and 25 possess top-tier qualifications. In recent years, construction has been used as a bridge for Nantong to communicate with the world, as construction companies from the city are involved in the Belt and Road Initiative projects in Russia, Singapore, Southeast Asia, Middle East, and Africa. While boosting local economic development and improving people's living conditions, construction has played an active role in cultural exchange.

## 3. Town of Shipbuilding

The superb geographical environment has made Nantong a top choice for shipbuilding and offshore engineering & manufacturing, and Nantong's shipbuilding and offshore equipment industry account for about one-tenth and one-quarter of the national markets respectively. A series of large made-in-China vessels, such as the first made-in-China 20,000 TEU ultra-large container ship, the world's first LNG dual fuel car carrier with 4,000 parking spots, Asia's largest heavy self-propelled dredger "Tian Kun", and China's first polar exploration cruise ship, have all set sail from Nantong. In

## 五、特色美食

### 1. 江鲜和海鲜

南通菜被称为"新派江海菜"，以江鲜和海鲜闻名。"长江四鲜"河豚、刀鱼、鲥鱼和鮰(huí)鱼，肉质细腻、味道鲜美；海鲜品种较多，其中文蛤(gé)被誉为"天下第一鲜"，自古就是朝廷贡品。还有梭子蟹、竹蛏(chēng)、鲳鱼、扇贝、带鱼等各类海鲜，不仅丰富了本地人的餐桌，也吸引了众多国内外的美食爱好者。

### 2. 传统点心

南通的传统名点也体现出了江海特色。蟹黄养汤烧卖、金钱萝卜饼、芙蓉藿香(huòxiāng)饺、林梓潮糕、通派火饺、缸爿(pán)等仍然广受欢迎。它们是游客携带回家的独特伴手礼，通过精湛的手工制作，传承着古老的烘焙技艺。

October 2022, Nantong took the lead in the advanced manufacturing cluster of offshore equipment and high-tech ships with Taizhou and Yangzhou, and was successfully selected as a national advanced manufacturing cluster. Today, Nantong aims to build a world-class advanced manufacturing cluster of ships and offshore engineering.

At present, Nantong is accelerating the integration across the river and development towards the sea, embracing "one hub and five cities", and building a modern industrial system with local characteristics.

## V. Specialty Food

### 1. River Delicacies and Seafood

Nantong cuisine is famous for its river delicacies and seafood. The "Four Fresh Delicacies of the Yangtze River", including pufferfish, saury, reeves shad, and catfish, feature delicate meat and a delicious taste. Among the various seafood of Nantong, the clam is known as "the world's No.1 delicious food", and was sent to the imperial court as a tribute in ancient times. Other seafood such as swimming crabs, razor clams, pomfret, scallops, and ribbon fish not only enrich the local dining table but also attract many domestic and foreign gourmets.

### 2. Traditional Dim Sum

The traditional snacks of Nantong also reflect the characteristics of the river and the sea. Crab roe soup dumplings, radish cakes, hibiscus dumplings, Lin Zi cakes, Nantong-style fire dumplings, and cylinder-shaped pastries are widely popular. These distinctive local snacks inherit ancient baking skills through exquisite hand-making and are unique souvenirs for tourists to take home.

## 六、名胜古迹

### 1. 濠河风景名胜区

濠河环绕南通老城区，形如葫芦，被誉为"江城翡翠项链"，是中国仅存的4条古护城河之一，拥有千余年历史。濠河全长10公里，最宽处达215米，最窄处仅有10米。沿岸分布着30多处文物古迹、近代文化教育商业遗迹，其中包括天宁寺、中国珠算博物馆、南通博物苑等著名景点。

### 2. 狼山国家森林公园

狼山国家森林公园位于南通老城区往南约6公里的长江边，由狼山、军山、剑山、马鞍山、黄泥山5座山以及周边地区组成，有"近水可看长江，江上可揽五山"的地理优势。公园的森林覆盖率80.83%以上，各类植物1220余种。公园内的狼山相传曾经有白狼居住而得名，原本在长江之中，北宋时期与陆地相连，是全国佛教八小名山之首。

## VI. Historical Sites and Scenic Spots

### 1. Haohe Scenic Area

The Haohe River, running around the old urban area of Nantong in the shape of a gourd, is known as the "Emerald Necklace of the River City". It is one of the four remaining ancient moats in China and has a history of more than a thousand years. The river is 10 kilometers long, with the greatest width at 215 meters and the narrowest point at only 10 meters. There are more than 30 cultural relics and modern cultural, educational, and commercial sites along the riverbank, including famous attractions such as the Tianning Temple, the China Abacus Museum, and the Nantong Museum.

### 2. The Langshan National Forest Park

Located about 6 kilometers south of the old urban area of Nantong along the Yangtze River, the Langshan National Forest Park consists of the five mountains of Langshan, Junshan, Jianshan, Ma'anshan, and Huangnishan, as well as other surrounding areas. It offers a view of the Yangtze River and overlooks the five mountains. The park has a forest coverage of 80.83% and a variety of 1,220 types of plants. Langshan in the park is said to have been named for the white wolves that once lived there. Originally an island in the Yangtze River, it was connected to the land during the Northern Song Dynasty. Longshan is the first among the "eight minor famous mountains of Buddhism" in China.

In the park, there are cultural relics such as the Langshan Guangjiao Zen Temple, the Zhiyun Tower, the Tomb of Luo Binwang, the Reclining Buddha on Jianshan, and the Memorial Hall of Jianzhen, as well as natural and cultural landscapes such as the Riverside Park and the Nantong Botanical Garden, which attract tourists and Buddhists.

公园里有狼山广教禅寺、支云塔、骆宾王墓、剑山卧佛、鉴真纪念馆等文化古迹，还有滨江公园、南通植物园等自然与人文景观，吸引了无数游客和佛教信徒。

## 七、历史名人

张謇（1853—1926），字季直，江苏南通人，是清末状元，也是中国近代著名的实业家和教育家。他在南通深耕细作，实现了"一个人、一座城"的伟业。

张謇创办了20多家企业。1895年，他创办了大生纱厂，将"棉铁主义"作为"实业救国"的良方，使南通成为当时中国民族资本主义工业的重要据点之一。

张謇还被誉为"近代中国师范教育第一人"，一生创办了370多所学校，包括中国第一所师范学校、第一所纺织学校、第一所盲哑学校等。他为中国近代民族工业的兴起和教育事业的发展作出了巨大贡献。

除了办学，他还创建了中国第一所公共博物馆（南通博物苑）、第一所气象台（军山气象台）。他希望能"使地方无不士、不农、不工、不商之人"，普及教育、提高百姓的谋生技能。

毛泽东曾说："轻工业不能忘记海门的张謇。"习近平总书记则称赞他是"中国民营企业家的先贤和楷模"。

## VII. Historical Figures

Zhang Jian (1853–1926), styled Jizhi, was a native of Nantong, Jiangsu Province. He was the No.1 Scholar in the late Qing Dynasty and a renowned industrialist and educator in modern China. He dedicated himself to developing Nantong, for which he was praised as "one person for one city".

Zhang Jian founded over 20 enterprises. In 1895, he founded the Dasheng Cotton Mill in Nantong because he held "cotton and iron" as a remedy for "industrial salvation". As a result, Nantong became one of the important strongholds of China's national capitalist industry at the time.

Zhang Jian is also known as "the father of modern Chinese normal education". In his lifetime, he founded more than 370 schools, including the first normal school, the first textile school, and the first school for the deaf and mute in China. He made significant contributions to the rise of modern Chinese national industry and the development of Chinese education.

In addition to establishing schools, he also founded the first public museum in China (the Nantong Museum) and the first meteorological station (the Junshan Meteorological Station). He hoped that through the promotion of education and the improvement of people's skills, there would be no one in the local area uneducated in agriculture, industry, and commerce.

"In talking about light industry, we must not forget Zhangjian from Haimen." Mao Zedong once said. President Xi Jinping has praised him as "a pioneer and model of China's private entrepreneurs."

## 练习

### 一、判断题

1. 南通东濒东海，南临长江。　□

2. 狼山列全国佛教八小名山之首。　□

3. 纺织业和旅游业是南通最具标志性的支柱产业。　□

4. 南通是世界第二大家纺中心。　□

5. 濠河是一条古代护城河。　□

### 二、思考题

1. 南通为什么被称为"中国近代第一城"？

2. 南通为什么被称为"建筑之乡"？

3. 以南通为例，请谈谈你对中国的城市经济和城市文化的看法。

### 三、拓展题

1. 拍一个小视频，介绍你最喜欢的南通景点。

2. 做一个PPT，介绍你认为最有特色的南通美食。

3. 邀请你的朋友一起参观南通的博物馆，做一个以"南通博物馆"为主题的小组汇报。

# Chapter 8

XUZHOU

徐州

# 第八章

## 楚 / 韵 / 汉 / 风
### Strategic Place of Chu and Han

徐州素有"彭祖故国、项羽故都、刘邦故里"之称。尤其是"两汉文化看徐州"这句话，在中国更是广为人知。古时候的徐州，金戈铁马、英雄辈出，是兵家必争之地；今天的徐州，依然承载着历史的沧桑与厚重，却焕发出新时代的勃勃生机。

## 一、城市概况

### 1. 地理环境

徐州位于江苏西北部，恰好处于苏（江苏）、鲁（山东）、豫（yù）（河南）、皖（wǎn）（安徽）四省交界地带，拥有得天独厚的地理优势。这座城市虽以平原为主，但市内山丘连绵起伏，植被茂密，河流纵横交错，湖沼、水库星罗棋布，依山傍水、环境宜人，享有"一城青山半城湖"的美誉。

作为华东地区重要的门户城市，徐州交通便利，素有"五省通衢"之称。这里不仅是陇海、京沪两大铁路干线的交会处，而且黄河故道斜穿城市东西，京杭大运河纵贯南北。值得一提的是，4条高铁在徐州形成6个方向的"米字型"枢纽，乘高铁到北京、上海、西安、杭州等城市仅需3个小时。徐州观音国际机场已经开通了直飞日本、韩国、泰国、中国香港、中国台湾等30多条航线。徐州已形成了一个完善、快捷的水陆空三位一体的交通运输系统，有力地支持了地方发展和对外交流。

## I. Overview

### 1. Geographical Environment

Xuzhou is located in the northwest of Jiangsu Province, at the junction of Jiangsu, Shandong, Henan, and Anhui Provinces, hence its unique geographical advantage. Although the city is primarily flatland, it features undulating hills, dense vegetation, crisscrossing rivers, numerous lakes, and reservoirs. The city is surrounded by mountains and waters, and its pleasant environment is reputed as "a city of green hills, half a city of lakes".

As an important gateway city in East China, Xuzhou boasts convenient transportation and is known as "the thoroughfare of five provinces". It is not only the intersection of the Longhai and Beijing-Shanghai railway lines, but also the old course of the Yellow River from east to west, and the Beijing-Hangzhou Grand Canal runs from north to south. Notably, four high-speed railways form a "Union Jack" hub in Xuzhou, connecting it in six directions. Trips to cities such as Beijing, Shanghai, Xi'an, and Hangzhou take only three hours on high-speed trains. Xuzhou Guanyin International Airport has opened more than 30 direct flights to Japan, the Republic of Korea, Thailand, China's Hong Kong and Taiwan regions, and other destinations. A comprehensive, high-speed, water-land-air three-dimensional transportation system has been established in Xuzhou and provides strong support for local development and external exchanges.

### 2. Development

Xuzhou, known as "Pengcheng" in ancient times, was historically one of the nine states of China, with over 5,000 years of civilization and more than 2,600 years of urban development. After Qin Shihuang unified China, Pengcheng County was established here in 242 BC. In

## 2. 城市变迁

徐州，古时候叫"彭城"，历史上是华夏九州之一，有5000多年的文明史和2600多年的建城史。秦始皇统一中国后，公元前242年在这里设立彭城县。公元前206年，项羽建立西楚王国，在彭城设立都城。西汉时期，汉武帝在全国设十三州部监察区，其中有徐州刺史部。东汉末年，曹操将徐州刺史部迁到彭城，彭城从此开始叫"徐州"。中华人民共和国成立后，徐州市成为江苏省管辖的地级市之一。

## 3. 今日徐州

徐州拥有国家老工业基地和资源型城市双重身份，曾经长期依赖煤炭资源驱动经济发展，面临传统产业规模有限、设备老化、技术管理滞后等问题。如今，徐州正积极致力于经济与生态协调发展，着重围绕老工业基地全面振兴和淮海经济区中心城市建设的战略目标，全力推进产业、城市、生态、社会四大转型，逐步探索一条具有徐州特色的振兴转型之路。

206 BC, Xiang Yu founded the Western Chu Kingdom and set up the capital in Pengcheng. During the Western Han Dynasty, Emperor Wu set up thirteen inspectorate regions nationwide, including the Xuzhou Inspectorate. At the end of the Eastern Han Dynasty, Cao Cao moved the Xuzhou Inspectorate to Pengcheng, which then began to be called Xuzhou. After the founding of the People's Republic of China, Xuzhou became a prefecture-level city under the jurisdiction of Jiangsu Province.

### 3. Xuzhou Today

Xuzhou holds dual identities as an old industrial base and a resource-based city. It once relied heavily on coal resources to drive economic development, and faced challenges such as limited scale of traditional industries, outdated equipment, and lagging technology and management. Today, Xuzhou is committed to coordinated economic and ecological development, and focuses on the comprehensive revitalization of the old industrial base and the strategic goal of building the central city of the Huaihai Economic Zone. It is vigorously promoting the transformations in its industry, city, ecology, and society, gradually exploring a path of revitalization and transformation with Xuzhou characteristics.

In recent years, Xuzhou has achieved significant results in ecological environment construction and won titles such as National Environmental Protection Model City and National Ecological Garden City. It has repeatedly won the title of National Civilized City and, for its outstanding achievements in "improving the living environment of the people", it has successfully won the United Nations Habitat Award. From "a city of coal dust, half a city of mud" to "a city of green hills, half a city of lakes", Xuzhou is now focusing on the goal of "building a high-level two-way opening up

近年来，徐州的生态环境建设也取得了明显成效，先后荣获国家环保模范城市、国家生态园林城市等称号，蝉联全国文明城市，更因其在"改善民众生活环境方面做出的突出成就"，成功摘得联合国人居奖殊荣。从"一城煤灰半城土"到"一城青山半城湖"，徐州正聚焦"建设高水平双向开放高地"目标，坚持"生态优先、绿色发展"战略，全力打造陆海内外联动、东西双向互济的全面开放新格局。

## 二、文化印象

### 1. 彭祖文化

彭祖文化与徐州紧密相连。彭祖是中国历史上卓越的养生学家，著有《彭祖经》。早在尧舜时期，彭祖在徐州地区建立了大彭氏国，从此以后，彭祖文化便深根于此，成为徐州城市历史脉络中不可或缺的一部分，并影响了整个淮海地区的文化发展。

彭祖养生注重精神与物质的结合。他身为国君，却生活朴素，唯独讲究烹饪和美食。他烧得一手好菜，最擅长的是雉羹（野<sup>zhì gēng</sup>鸡汤），连尧帝都赞不绝口，夸这汤为"天下第一羹"。彭祖善于选择有营养的食材，搭配使用恰当的器皿，熬制出最鲜美的菜肴，对徐州的饮食文化影响深远。

platform", adhering to the strategy of "ecology first, green development", and striving to create a new pattern of comprehensive opening up with land-sea and east-west interactions.

## II. Cultural Impressions

### 1. The Legend of Peng Zu

The legend of Peng Zu is closely linked with Xuzhou. Peng Zu was a mythical figure in health preservation and the fabled author of *Peng Zu's Classic*. As early as the time of Yao and Shun, Peng Zu established the Great Peng Kingdom in the Xuzhou region. Since then, the legend of Peng Zu has taken root and, as an integral part of Xuzhou's historical context, has influenced the cultural development of the entire Huaihai region.

Peng Zu's health preservation focused on the combination of the spiritual and the material. Although he was a ruler, he lived a simple life, only being particular about cooking and gourmet food. He was excellent at cooking, especially famous for his pheasant soup, which even Emperor Yao praised as "the best soup in the world". Skilled in selecting nutritious ingredients and using appropriate utensils to cook the most delicious dishes, Peng Zu has been a great influence on Xuzhou's culinary culture.

## 2. 两汉文化

徐州，是项羽称霸西楚时的都城，是汉朝开国皇帝刘邦的故乡。可以说，徐州是两汉文化的发源地。两汉时期的400多年里，徐州共有13位楚王和5个彭城王，因此也留下了大量汉朝墓群。汉墓中出土的彩绘兵马俑，生动地再现了2000多年前的宏伟军阵，展现了汉代发达的军事、繁荣的经济和高超的手工技艺。

徐州还是中国汉画像石的集中出土地。汉画像石的题材丰富，不仅反映先民的日常生活，如车马出行、农耕织作等场景，也有神话传说、神话图腾，如伏羲、女娲、麒麟和九尾狐等，形象栩栩如生，展示了汉代匠人的精深技艺和超凡想象力，可以说是汉代社会的一个缩影。

## 三、教育交流

### 1. 高等教育概况

徐州共有19所高等院校，其中有6所本科教育层次院校，包括矿业学科世界领先的中国矿业大学、文化底蕴深厚的江苏师范大学以及专业领域内知名的徐州医科大学等。这些院校不仅为国内学生提供涵盖多个学科领域的本科以上学历教育，同时也向国际学生敞开大门。

## 2. Culture of the Han Dynasty

Xuzhou was the capital of the Western Chu Kingdom under the rule of Xiang Yu and was the hometown of Liu Bang, the founding emperor of the Han Dynasty. It can be said that Xuzhou is the birthplace of the culture of the Han Dynasty. During the over 400 years of the Han Dynasty, 13 Chu kings and 5 Pengcheng kings were enfeoffed in Xuzhou, who left behind a large number of Han tombs. The colorful terracotta warriors unearthed from these tombs vividly recreate the grand military formations of over 2,000 years ago, showcasing the advanced military level, prosperous economy, and superb craftsmanship of the Han Dynasty.

Xuzhou is also an important site of Han stone carvings, which depict the daily life of the ancient people, such as traveling in carriage and on horseback, farming, and weaving, as well as myths and legends, like Fuxi, Nüwa, Qilin, and the nine-tailed fox. These images on the stone carvings are so vivid and lifelike, displaying the exquisite skills and extraordinary imagination of the Han Dynasty craftsmen, that they can be considered a microcosm of the Han society.

## III. Education and International Exchanges

### 1. Overview of Higher Education

There are 19 higher education institutions in Xuzhou, among which 6 universities offer undergraduate education, including China University of Mining and Technology, a leading university in Mining disciplines, Jiangsu Normal University with its deep cultural heritage, and Xuzhou Medical University, renowned in the field of medicine. These institutions provide domestic education across multiple disciplines for the undergraduate degree and above, and are open to international students.

## 2. 高校介绍

### 1）中国矿业大学

中国矿业大学（www.cumt.edu.cn）成立于1909年，是一所直属于教育部的国家重点大学，同时也是国家"双一流"建设高校。学校有强大的学科建设基础，设有21个一级学科博士点，5个专业学位博士点，36个一级学科硕士点，20个专业学位硕士点，涵盖了74个本科专业。学校在校全日制普通本科生2.36万余人，各类博士、硕士研究生1.33万余人。学校与近百所国外高校建立了紧密的伙伴关系，是联合国教科文组织"国际矿业工程教育能力中心"在中国的唯一旗舰高校。此外，学校还在澳大利亚格里菲斯大学设立了"旅游孔子学院"，进一步推动文化交流。学校还因在国际化人才培养方面的杰出表现，被授予全国首批"高层次国际化人才培养创新实践基地"称号。自1954年起，学校开始招收国际学生，至今已接收来自86个国家和地区的国际学生来校学习。

### 2）江苏师范大学

江苏师范大学（www.jsnu.edu.cn）创建于1952年，是江苏高水平大学建设高校。学校现有60个本科招生专业，2个博士学位授权点，32个一级学科硕士点，20个硕士专业学位点，1个服务国家特殊需求博士人才培养项目，1个博士后科研流动站。学校有2个学科入榜2022"软科世界一流学科排名"。

作为全国首批"有资格接收外国留学生的高校"，学校先后接收76个国家和地区的国际学生来校学习。学校还牵头成立了全国中俄合作办学高校联盟和江苏—俄罗斯高校合作联盟，同时加入了江苏—英国高水平大学联盟、金砖国家大学联盟、中国—中东欧国家高校联合会等多个国际学术合作平台。此外，学校与大迈阿密亚裔商务联盟合作，共建迈阿密商务孔子学院。

## 2. Introduction to Universities

### 1) China University of Mining and Technology

Established in 1909, China University of Mining and Technology (CUMT, www.cumt.edu.cn) is a national key university directly under the Ministry of Education and a "Double First-Class" construction university. Boasting a strong foundation in its disciplinary construction, the university has 21 first-level discipline doctoral programs, 5 professional doctoral programs, 36 first-level discipline master programs, and 20 professional master programs, covering 74 undergraduate majors. The university has more than 23,600 full-time undergraduate students and over 13,300 doctor's and master's students. CUMT has established close partnerships with nearly 100 foreign universities and is the only flagship university in China for the UNESCO International Centre of Excellence on Mining Engineering Education. Additionally, the university has established a Confucius Institute at Griffith University in Australia, which helps to promote cultural exchanges. CUMT was honored as one of the first "High-level International Education Innovation Practice Bases in China" for its outstanding performance in educating international students. Since 1954, the university has enrolled international students from 86 countries and regions.

### 2) Jiangsu Normal University

Founded in 1952, Jiangsu Normal University (www.jsnu.edu.cn) is a high-level university in Jiangsu Province. The university offers 60 undergraduate programs, two doctoral programs, 32 first-level discipline master programs, 20 professional master programs, one doctoral program serving special national needs, and one postdoctoral research station. Two of its disciplines were listed in the 2022 Shanghai Ranking's "Global Top of Academic Subjects".

## 3. 特色学科

中国矿业大学作为一所有着鲜明学科特色的高水平高校，在全球学术领域表现卓越。学校的工程学、地球科学、材料科学、化学、数学、环境与生态学、计算机科学、社会科学总论、物理学9个学科领域进入ESI全球排名前1%，其中，工程学和地球科学2个学科领域更是达到了全球前1‰的顶尖水平。学校的矿物资源与开采工程学科在2023年的国际排名位列第17位。形成了矿业工程与安全科学、遥感测绘与环境、地质学与地质工程、土木建筑与力学、机械电气与控制、计算机与信息、管理与经济、化工与材料等国内优势学科领域。

江苏师范大学拥有8个省优势学科和10个省重点学科，化学、工程学、材料科学、数学、社会科学总论、计算机科学、植物与动物科学、农业科学8个学科进入ESI排名前1%。2002年，3个学科入榜"软科世界一流学科排名"，14个学科入榜"软科中国最好学科排名"。学校获批的江苏高校优势学科

As one of the first universities in China qualified to accept international students, the university has received students from 76 countries and regions. It takes the lead in establishing the China-Russia Cooperative Education Alliance and the Jiangsu-Russia Higher Education Cooperation Alliance, and it has joined multiple international academic cooperation platforms such as the Jiangsu-UK High-Level University Alliance, BRICS University League, and China-CEEC Higher Education Institutions Consortium. Additionally, in cooperation with the Greater Miami Asian Business Alliance, the university has established the Miami Business Confucius Institute.

### 3. Featured Disciplines

China University of Mining and Technology (CUMT), as a high-level university with distinct disciplinary features, performs excellently in the global academic field. Nine disciplines at CUMT, including Engineering, Earth Sciences, Materials Science, Chemistry, Mathematics, Environment and Ecology, Computer Science, Social Sciences, and Physics, rank in the top 1% globally according to the Essential Science Indicators (ESI). Among them, Engineering and Earth Sciences rank in the top 0.1% globally. The discipline of Mineral Resources and Mining Engineering ranked 17th internationally in 2023. CUMT has developed disciplinary strengths in Mining Engineering and Safety Science, Remote Sensing and Surveying, Geology and Geological Engineering, Civil Engineering and Mechanics, Mechanical and Electrical Engineering and Control, Computer and Information, Management and Economics, and Chemical Engineering and Materials.

包括中国语言文学、生物学、统计学、光学工程、教育学、区域新型城镇化发展等。

## 四、经济腾飞

徐州兼具国家资源型城市和老工业基地的双重角色，产业经济长久以来以重工业为主导，存在产品层次低、企业管理效率不高、环境污染较严重等问题。近年来，徐州积极推动传统产业的优化升级转型，大力发展现代服务业、推进技术创新，徐州的经济呈现出多元化、高端化的发展趋势，不仅提升了自身经济的质量与效益，也为中国老工业基地的复兴提供了宝贵的经验。

### 1. 工程机械

工程机械产业经过数十年的发展壮大，已成为徐州最具影响力和竞争力的产业。徐州也赢得了中国机械工业联合会认定的"中国工程机械之都"美誉。徐州现有1000多家相关企业，是全国最大的工程机械制造和研发基地。全国工程机械龙头企业徐工集团是全国行业内第一个千亿企业，连续三年位列全球工程机械前三。卡特彼勒（徐州）是全球最大的卡特彼勒超大挖掘机生产基地。此外，徐州还吸引了美驰车桥、利勃海尔、蒂森克虏伯等外资企业，培育了海伦哲、巴特重工、世通重工等本土企业。徐州还是全国最大的工程机械租赁、物流业和配件基地。

Jiangsu Normal University has eight provincially advantageous disciplines and ten provincial key disciplines. Eight disciplines — Chemistry, Engineering, Materials Science, Mathematics, Social Sciences, Computer Science, Plant and Animal Science, and Agricultural Sciences — rank in the top 1% of ESI. In 2002, three disciplines were listed in Shanghai Ranking's "Global Top of Academic Subjects", and fourteen disciplines were listed in Shanghai Ranking's "Best Chinese Subjects". The advantageous disciplines at Jiangsu Normal University approved by Jiangsu Province include Chinese Language and Literature, Biology, Statistics, Optical Engineering, Education, and Regional New Urbanization Development, etc.

## IV. Economic Takeoff

Xuzhou plays a dual role as a resource-based city and an old industrial base. Historically, it was predominated by heavy industries and faced challenges such as low-level products, inefficient management, and significant environmental pollution. In recent years, Xuzhou has actively promoted the optimization and upgrading of traditional industries, vigorously developed modern service industries, and advanced technological innovation. Xuzhou's economy is showing a trend of diversification and high-end development, not only enhancing its own economic quality and efficiency but also providing valuable experience for the revitalization of China's old industrial bases.

### 1. Construction Machinery

After decades of development and growth, the construction machinery industry has become Xuzhou's most influential and competitive industry. Xuzhou has been recognized by the China Machinery Industry Federation as the "Capital of China's Construction Machinery". The city now hosts over 1,000 related

## 2. 新型能源

徐州是传统煤矿开采和煤电工业基地。徐州煤矿和煤电企业积极响应国家"双碳"目标[1]，大力推进绿色转型。徐州通过建设淮海大数据产业园、光伏发电站等，构建"火电+供热+大数据+光伏"的循环经济模式；创新新能源开发利用模式，重点围绕光伏发电、风力发电、废弃矿井储能、氢能产业链、地热利用和综合能源服务等项目，推动能源结构向绿色低碳转变；同时，积极扩大布局可再生能源业务，大力发展新型能源产业、高端服务业，徐州绿色低碳能源产业将迎来更加广阔的发展空间。

---

[1] 中国提出，二氧化碳排放力争于 2030 年达到峰值，努力争取 2060 年前实现碳中和，被称作碳达峰、碳中和目标，简称"双碳"目标或"3060"双碳目标。

China has proposed to strive for peak carbon dioxide emissions by 2030 and achieve carbon neutrality before 2060, known as the "dual carbon" target or "3060" dual carbon target.

enterprises and is the largest construction machinery manufacturing and R&D base in the country. Xuzhou Construction Machinery Group (XCMG), a national industry leader, is the first enterprise in the industry to achieve an annual output value of 100 billion RMB and has ranked among the top three global construction machinery manufacturers for three consecutive years. Caterpillar (Xuzhou) is the world's largest production base for Caterpillar's super large excavators. Additionally, Xuzhou has attracted foreign-invested enterprises such as Meritor, Liebherr, and ThyssenKrupp, and has cultivated local enterprises like Handler, BUT Heavy Machinery, and Shitong Heavy Machinery. Xuzhou is also the country's largest base for the mechanical equipment leasing, logistics, and product accessories.

## 2. New Energy

Xuzhou is a traditional industrial base in coal mining and coal power. The local coal mining and coal power enterprises have responded to the national "dual carbon"* goals and have been actively promoting green transformation. Xuzhou is building a recycling economy model of "thermal power + heating + big data + photovoltaic" by constructing the Huaihai Big Data Industrial Park and photovoltaic power stations. The city is innovating new energy development and utilization models, focusing on projects such as photovoltaic power generation, wind power, abandoned mine storage, hydrogen energy industry chain, geothermal utilization, and comprehensive energy services, in the hopes of driving the energy structure towards green and low-carbon transformation. As the renewable energy business lines are expanding, and the new energy industry and high-end service industry are being developed, the green and low-carbon energy industry in Xuzhou is expected to have even broader development prospects.

## 五、特色美食

### 1. 经典小吃

徐州的地方小吃种类丰富。其中"饦<sup>①</sup>汤"尤为知名。这道菜原名"雉羹"，相传由养生大师彭祖所创，距今已有4000余年的历史。饦汤的选材讲究，原料主要包括母鸡和甲鱼，搭配麦子等谷物，不仅味道醇厚，香气扑鼻，而且营养丰富。

烙馍（徐州方言发音luǒ mō）是徐州的传统面食，可以卷肉、卷菜、卷酱料，但是烙馍卷馓子是经典搭配，在薄薄的烙馍里卷上一小把馓子（sǎn），外面软，里面脆，令人百吃不厌。

此外，香而不腻的把子肉、鲜辣爽口的鳝鱼辣汤、外焦里嫩的水煎包、酥脆可口的八股油条，以及甜品中的羊角蜜、蜜三刀、蜂糕，每一样都是独具特色的地方小吃。

### 2. 传统名菜

羊方藏鱼被称为"中国第一名菜"，由彭祖所创。将鱼放在切开的大块羊肉中炖煮，羊肉酥烂味香，鱼肉鲜嫩可口，汤浓色白。据说汉字"鲜"正是来源于这道菜。

---

① 饦，是一个合成汉字，音sha（啥）。在字典中没有，来源不详，但已经被广泛接受和运用。It is a synthetic Chinese character, pronounced "sha", which does not appear in dictionaries and its origin is uncertain. But it has been widely accepted and used.

# V. Specialty Food

## 1. Classic Snacks

Xuzhou boasts a rich variety of local snacks. The pheasant soup, said to have been created by the legendary figure Peng Zu over 4,000 years ago, is probably the most famous. The soup is actually made from carefully selected ingredients that include chicken, soft-shelled turtle, and flour. It is not only rich in flavor and aroma but also highly nutritious.

Luomo, a traditional baked flatbread, is a characteristic pastry of Xuzhou. It can be used to wrap meat, vegetables, or sauces. A classic combination is Luomo wrapping a handful of crispy fried dough sticks. The outer layer is soft while the inside remains crispy — an irresistibly delicious snack.

Additionally, there are many unique local snacks such as the fragrant braised pork, the spicy and refreshing eel soup, the crispy pan-fried buns, the crunchy eight-strand deep-fried dough sticks, and desserts like sheep-horn honey cakes, honey buns with three cuts and sesame, and honeycomb cakes.

## 2. Traditional Dishes

Sheep cubes stewed with fish, said to have been created by Peng Zu, is known as "China's No.1 dish". It is made by stewing fish inside large pieces of cut-open lamb, resulting in tender lamb and flavorful fish in a rich and white broth. It is said that the Chinese character for "fresh" originated from this dish.

The nourishing duck is believed to have originated from Qin Shihuang's time. This therapeutic dish is made of old male ducks and dried lily flowers. Duck meat is known for its nourishing properties, while dried lily flowers are beneficial for calming the mind, boosting brain health, and promoting mental clarity.

养心鸭子据传源自秦始皇时期，是一道有食疗作用的菜肴。选用老雄鸭为主要材料，配以金针菜制作而成。鸭子能滋补强身，金针菜则能够养心安神、健脑益智。

在徐州，"万物皆可地锅"。地锅本身已有1000多年的历史，而今天我们熟悉的地锅形式则起源于微山湖地区，也有300余年的历史。过去，人们在自家小院里架上铁锅，放入各种食材，沿着锅边贴上面饼。大家围炉而坐，席地而吃，因此称为"地锅"。地锅菜中最著名的是地锅鸡。预热铁锅后，将鸡块放入，加上佐料熬成浓汤，锅边贴满面饼，面饼吸收汤汁后柔韧十足，鲜味浓厚。

此外，徐州还有许多名菜，"霸王别姬""糖醋四孔鲤鱼""龙门鱼""东坡回赠肉"等等，每一道都独具特色，别有风味。

### 3. 彭祖伏羊节

"伏羊"是入伏以后的羊肉。三伏天吃羊肉的习俗起源于彭祖，形成于汉代并流传至今。自古以来，民间流传着"入伏一碗羊肉汤，不用神仙开药方"的说法，在此基础上发展起来的中国彭祖伏羊节是徐州人民的夏季美食狂欢，它使徐州成为享誉全国的"中国伏羊美食之乡"。

In Xuzhou, "everything can be cooked in a ground pot." Cooking in a ground pot has a history of over 1,000 years, and the form we know today originated in the Weishan Lake area about 300 years ago. People would set up an iron pot in their courtyard, add various ingredients, and place dough along the edge of the pot. Then, everyone would sit around and eat. The most famous dish made in this form is chicken. After the iron pot is heated, chicken pieces are put in the pot along with spices to make a rich broth, and dough is stuck to the edges to absorb the flavors — all these make a chewy, flavorful dish.

Besides these, famous dishes of Xuzhou include broiled chicken cutlets with turtle, sweet and sour four-nostril carp, dragon gate fish, and Dongpo braised pork. Each dish has its own unique flavor and characteristics.

### 3. Peng Zu's Summer Lamb Festival

"Summer lamb" refers to lamb eaten in the hottest days of summer. The custom of eating lamb during this period originated from the legend of Peng Zu, took shape in the Han Dynasty, and has been passed down through generations. There is an old saying, "A bowl of lamb soup in the dog days saves you from needing a divine doctor's prescription." Based on this tradition, Peng Zu's Summer Lamb Festival has become a summer culinary celebration for the people of Xuzhou, and the city has gained the nationwide reputation of "China's Capital of Summer Lamb Delicacies".

## VI. Historical Sites and Scenic Spots

### 1. The Yunlong Lake and the Yunlong Mountain

The Yunlong Lake, located in the southern part of Xuzhou, is one of the city's iconic attractions. In 2016, it was named a national

## 六、名胜古迹

### 1. 云龙湖、云龙山旅游景区

云龙湖位于徐州市区南部，是徐州标志性景点之一，2016年被授予国家5A级旅游景区，是一个休闲度假的好去处。云龙山紧邻云龙湖，山有九节，像一条蜿蜒的巨龙，由此得名。不仅自然风光迷人，山上丰富的文化遗迹更是引人入胜，北魏大石佛，唐宋摩崖石刻，宋明清时期的放鹤亭、招鹤亭、饮鹤泉、张山人旧居、兴化禅寺，大士岩等，每一处都见证了云龙山深厚的历史文化底蕴。

### 2. 龟山汉墓

龟山汉墓是西汉第六代楚襄王刘注的夫妻合葬墓，也是中国现存规模最大、保存最完整的汉代崖洞墓。该墓巧妙地利用地形，几乎将整个山体掏空，开凿出超过700平方米的庞大空间。墓内共有15间主次分明、配套齐全的墓室，包括起居室、会客室、马厩和厨房，宛如一座地下宫殿。因其构造精妙，还有许多未解之谜，龟山汉墓被称为"东方金字塔"。

5A-level tourist attraction. It is an excellent destination for leisure and vacation. The Yunlong Mountain, adjacent to the Yunlong Lake, has nine peaks resembling a giant dragon, hence the name. The mountain not only offers stunning natural scenery but also boasts rich cultural relics, including the Grand Buddha of the Northern Wei Dynasty, cliff carvings of the Tang and Song Dynasties, and structures from the Song, Ming and Qing Dynasties such as the Crane Pavilion, the Crane Tower, the Crane Spring, Hermit Zhang's Former Residence, the Xinghua Temple and the Dashi Rock. Each site reflects the deep historical and cultural heritage of the Yunlong Mountain.

### 2. The Han Tomb of Guishan

The Han Tomb of Guishan is the joint tomb of Liu Zhu, the sixth King of Chu of the Western Han Dynasty, and his wife. It is the largest and best-preserved mountain tomb from the Han Dynasty in China. The tomb features an ingenious use of the terrain, as the entire Guishan Mountain is almost hollowed out to create an expansive space of over 700 square meters. Inside the tomb there are 15 chambers that are clearly divided and well-equipped, including living rooms, guest rooms, stables and kitchens, all resembling an underground palace. Due to its intricate construction and many unsolved mysteries, the Han Tomb of Guishan is often referred to as the "Oriental Pyramid".

### 3. Hubushan Historical and Cultural Neighborhood

The Hubushan Historical and Cultural Neighborhood, located in the center of Xuzhou's old city, is a well-preserved complex of ancient buildings. Over 400 houses from the Ming and Qing Dynasties are built along the mountain, arranged in an orderly manner. Most of the houses are traditional courtyard homes

### 3. 户部山历史文化街区

户部山历史文化街区位于徐州老城区中心，是一处保存完好的古建筑群。400多间明清时期的房屋依山而建，错落有致地分布在户部山上。房屋多为传统的四合院，既有北方建筑的规整划一，又有南方民居的曲折秀美。"一座户部山，半部徐州史。"漫步其间，仿佛穿越回400多年前，感受徐州城辉煌灿烂的过往。

戏马台位于户部山最高处。公元前206年，项羽灭秦后，自立为西楚霸王，定都彭城，并在山顶建了一座高台，用于观看将士操练。楚汉战争虽然最终以项羽失败告终，但他的壮志豪情仍吸引了许多文人墨客，谢灵运、苏轼、文天祥、辛弃疾、方孝孺等都在戏马台留下了许多佳作。

除此之外，北魏时期的彭祖楼见证了城市的兴衰更迭；唐朝燕子楼以名媛关盼盼的凄美故事而闻名遐迩；宋朝黄楼为纪念成功治理黄河水患而修筑。还有苏轼亲自命名的快哉亭，宋朝文庙古建筑群，清朝的古民居回龙窝，徐州古城墙，以及花园饭店、钟鼓楼、老东门等地标性建筑，经历了百年风雨，承载了漫长久远的历史沧桑，述说着徐州的古往今昔。

which combine the orderly layout of northern architecture with the winding beauty of southern residences. "One Hubushan, half the history of Xuzhou." Strolling through the neighborhood, one feels like traveling back over 400 years to experience the glorious past of Xuzhou.

Ximatai (horse racing platform) is situated at the highest point of the Hubushan Mountain. In 206 BC, after Xiang Yu defeated the Qin Dynasty, he proclaimed himself King of Western Chu and made Pengcheng his capital. He built a high platform on the mountain to watch his soldiers drill. Although Xiang Yu ultimately lost the war with Han, his heroic spirit continues to inspire many scholars and poets, including Xie Lingyun, Su Shi, Wen Tianxiang, Xin Qiji, and Fang Xiaoru, who left numerous literary works on Ximatai.

Besides these, other notable sites include the Peng Zu Tower from the Northern Wei Dynasty, which witnessed the city's rise and fall; the Swallow Tower from the Tang Dynasty, famous for the tragic story of the noblewoman Guan Panpan; and the Yellow Tower from the Song Dynasty, built to commemorate the successful control of the Yellow River floods. There are also the Pleasant Pavilion named by Su Shi himself, the ancient Confucius Temple from the Song Dynasty, the Huilongwo ancient residences from the Qing Dynasty, the ancient city walls of Xuzhou, as well as landmarks like the Garden Hotel, the Bell and Drum Tower, and the Old East Gate. Having endured centuries of history, these sites carry the profound historical heritage of Xuzhou and record the city's ancient and modern tales.

## VII. Historical Figures

"Nine emperors came from Xuzhou." Throughout the Chinese history, many influential leaders emerged in Xuzhou, a place of strategic importance. According to historical

## 七、历史名人

"九朝帝王徐州籍"，徐州作为兵家必争之地，孕育了许多有重要影响的领袖人物，中国历史上有九位皇帝的籍贯可以追溯到徐州，包括汉高祖刘邦、东吴孙权等，他们或出生于此，或在此兴起，还有许多著名人物，在不同的领域作出了杰出的贡献，取得了非凡的成就。

### 1. 刘邦

汉高祖刘邦，汉朝开国皇帝，是徐州沛县人。推翻秦朝后，刘邦和项羽展开了4年的较量，争夺天下主权。最终刘邦在这场大战中胜出，建立了对后世影响深远的西汉。

### 2. 项羽

项羽在巨鹿之战中以少胜多，一举摧毁了秦军主力，展现了他非凡的军事智慧和勇气。秦朝灭亡后，他自封为西楚霸王，选定徐州为首都。尽管在随后的楚汉战争中败亡，项羽凭借非凡的英雄气概和杰出的军事指挥才能，成为历史上虽败犹荣的典范。

archives, nine emperors came from Xuzhou, including Liu Bang, Emperor Gaozu of Han, and Sun Quan, Emperor of Eastern Wu. They either were born or rose to prominence in this region. Besides emperors, many notable figures from Xuzhou have made outstanding contributions and achieved remarkable success in various fields.

### 1. Liu Bang

Liu Bang, the founding emperor of the Han Dynasty, hailed from Pei County in Xuzhou. After overthrowing the Qin Dynasty, Liu Bang engaged in a four-year struggle with Xiang Yu for supremacy over China. Ultimately, Liu Bang emerged victorious in this great battle and established the Western Han Dynasty, which had a profound impact on subsequent history.

### 2. Xiang Yu

Xiang Yu, known for his extraordinary military prowess and bravery, defeated the Qin army in the Battle of Julu. After the fall of the Qin Dynasty, he proclaimed himself King of Western Chu and chose Xuzhou as his capital. Despite his eventual defeat in the Chu-Han War, Xiang Yu remains a historical figure admired for his heroic spirit and exceptional military leadership.

### 3. 解忧公主

解忧公主是西汉楚王刘戊的孙女，她奉汉武帝的命令和亲西域乌孙国，不仅把丰富的中原文化带到了遥远的西域，也促进了汉朝与西域各国之间的友好往来，为地区间的文化交流和民族融合奠定了基础。

### 4. 张道陵

张道陵，东汉时期沛国丰县（今徐州市丰县）人，道教创始人。他的贡献不仅在于创立了道教这一宗教体系，更重要的是，他大力推广并深化了道家思想，将其融入社会日常生活的各个方面，为后世的文化、艺术、科技等方面的发展奠定了基础。

### 5. 苏轼

苏轼，北宋著名政治家、文学家，徐州是他政治生涯的重要一站。他在40岁盛年时期担任徐州知州。期间，他亲自带领百姓抗洪救灾，受到了皇帝的嘉奖。他还积极开采煤炭、鼓励农商、兴办教育、治理社会治安问题，有力地推动了徐州的经济繁荣、文化发展和社会和谐稳定。徐州老百姓亲切地称他为"苏徐州"，并修建了苏轼纪念馆、苏堤路、苏公岛、苏公桥、苏公塔等，寄托了对他的深深怀念和敬仰之情。

### 3. Princess Jieyou

Princess Jieyou was the granddaughter of Liu Wu, King of Chu of the Western Han Dynasty. She was sent by Emperor Wu of Han to marry the ruler of the Wusun State in the Western Regions. She brought with her the rich culture of the Central Plains to the distant Western Regions and significantly enhanced the friendly relations between the Han Dynasty and the various states in the Western Regions, thus laying the foundation for cultural exchange and ethnic integration.

### 4. Zhang Daoling

Zhang Daoling, a native of Fengxian County in Peiguo (Today's Fengxian County, Xuzhou), founded Taoism in the Eastern Han Dynasty. In addition to establishing the Taoist religious system, he popularized the Taoist thought and integrated it into everyday social life. This laid the groundwork for subsequent developments in culture, art and science.

### 5. Su Shi

Su Shi, a renowned statesman and literary figure of the Northern Song Dynasty, had an important link with Xuzhou in his political career. He served as the prefect of Xuzhou at the age of 40. During his tenure, he led the people in flood control and disaster relief efforts, and earned commendation from the emperor. He also promoted coal mining, encouraged agriculture and commerce, established educational institutions, and addressed social security issues — all these contributed to Xuzhou's economic prosperity, cultural development, and social harmony and stability. The people of Xuzhou affectionately referred to him as "Su of Xuzhou" and built numerous memorials

## 八、红色文化

在解放战争时期具有决定意义的三大战役①中，淮海战役规模最大、历时最长、歼敌最多。徐州是淮海战役的核心战场之一。在这场战役中，中国人民解放军取得了决定性的胜利，为后续渡江作战和全面解放铺平了道路。为纪念在这场战役中牺牲的战士，铭记这场重大的历史事件，1959年，国务院批准在徐州云龙山修建淮海战役烈士纪念塔，并于1965年建成，毛泽东主席亲笔题写了塔名。

淮海战役烈士纪念塔周围还建有多个配套景点，淮海战役纪念馆、淮海战役全景画馆、淮海战役碑林、淮海战役总前委群雕遗迹和徐州国防教育馆等景点，共同组成了一个综合性的纪念园区。

---

① 三大战役是指1948年9月至1949年1月，中国人民解放军与国民党军队进行的三场战略决战，包括辽沈战役、淮海战役和平津战役。
The Three Major Campaigns refer to the three strategic decisive wars between the People's Liberation Army of China and the Nationalist Army from September 1948 to January 1949, including the Liaoshen Campaign, the Huaihai Campaign and the Pingjin Campaign.

in his honor, such as the Su Shi Memorial Hall, Su's Dyke Road, Lord Su's Island, Lord Su's Bridge and Lord Su's Tower, to express their deep respect and admiration for him.

## VIII. Revolutionary Culture

Among the Three Campaigns of the Liberation War,① the Huaihai Campaign was the largest, the longest, and resulted in the most enemy casualties. Xuzhou was one of the core battlefields of the Huaihai Campaign. In this campaign, the People's Liberation Army achieved a decisive victory, paving the way for subsequent operations across the Yangtze River and the liberation of the entire country. To commemorate the soldiers who sacrificed their lives in the campaign and to remember this significant historical event, the State Council approved the construction of the Memorial Tower for the Martyrs of the Huaihai Campaign on the Yunlong Mountain in Xuzhou in 1959. The tower was completed in 1965, with an inscription by Chairman Mao Zedong himself.

Near the Memorial Tower there are several related attractions, including the Huaihai Campaign Memorial Hall, the Huaihai Campaign Panorama Hall, the Huaihai Campaign Stele Forest, the Sculptures of the Generals in the Huaihai Campaign, and the Xuzhou National Defense Education Center. These sites form a comprehensive memorial park.

## 九、生态保护

潘安湖采煤塌陷地治理是徐州重要的生态工程之一。潘安湖在徐州市东北部的"百年煤城"贾汪区。130多年的开采历史让这里的土地资源和生态环境遭到了严重的破坏，煤矿采煤塌陷面积达12.6平方公里。

徐州市针对塌陷区的实际情况，采取了湿地修复、土壤改良和种树植草等措施，让这片区域恢复了生态功能，土地也得到了再利用。同时，通过精心的景观设计，将塌陷区转变为独具特色的湿地公园，实现了矿区到景区的华丽转变，取得了显著的经济效益、社会效益和环境生态效益。

## IX. Ecological Protection

The governance of the Pan'an Lake coal mining subsidence area is one of the most important ecological projects of Xuzhou. The Pan'an Lake is located in Jiawang District, known as the "Hundred-Year Coal Town", in the northeastern part of Xuzhou. After over 130 years of mining, the land resources and ecological environment were severely damaged, and coal mining subsidence covered an area of 12.6 square kilometers.

To address the conditions in the subsidence area, measures have been taken to restore wetland, improve soil, and plant tree and grass, so that the ecological functions of the region can be restored and the land be reused. Through meticulous landscape design, the subsidence area has been transformed into a unique wetland park. By transforming a mining area to a scenic spot, this project has yielded significant economic, social, and environmental ecological benefits.

## 练习

### 一、判断题

1. 徐州汉画像石既有反映先民们现实生活的题材，也有表现信仰生活的神话图腾。☐

2. 中国矿业大学从1909年起开始招收国际学生，先后接收84个国家和地区的学生来校学习。☐

3. 徐州是全国最大的工程机械制造和研发基地，享有"中国工程机械之都"的称誉。☐

4. 解忧公主是西汉楚王刘注的后裔，她奉旨下嫁西域乌孙国，同时也把中原文化传播到西域。☐

5. 毛泽东主席为淮海战役烈士纪念塔亲笔题写了塔名。☐

### 二、思考题

1. 徐州绿色低碳产业加快转型发展体现在哪些方面？

2. 项羽在楚汉战争中败亡，但他两千年来都被尊奉为盖世英雄，这是什么原因？

### 三、拓展题

拍一个短视频，把徐州的名胜古迹介绍给海内外的朋友。

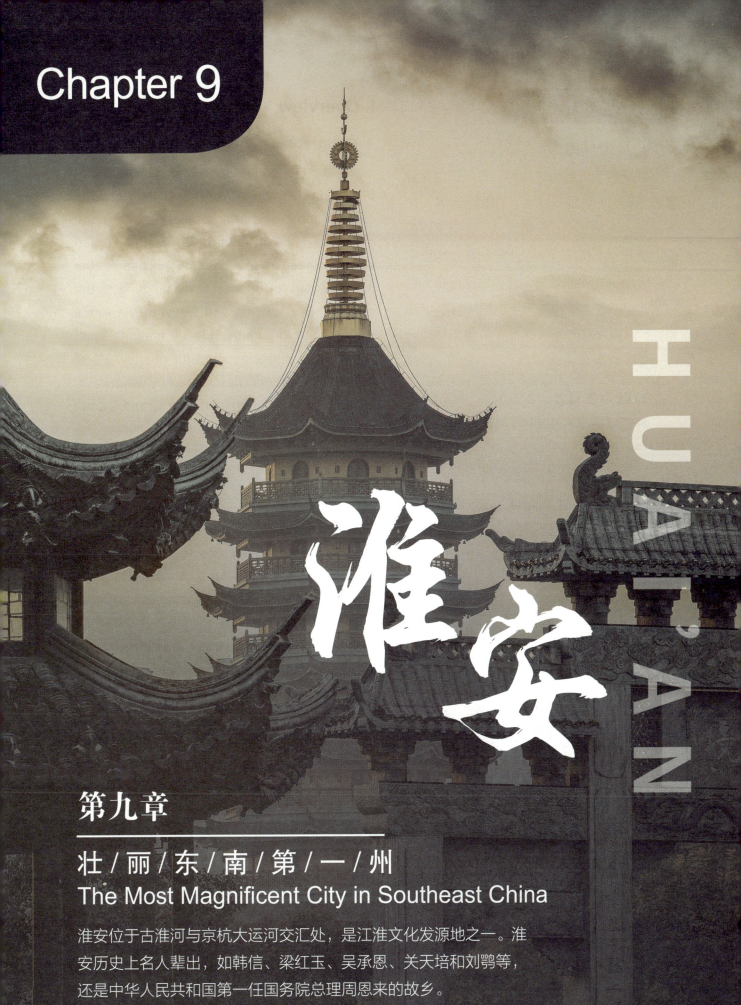

# Chapter 9

HUAI'AN

# 淮安

## 第九章

壮 / 丽 / 东 / 南 / 第 / 一 / 州

### The Most Magnificent City in Southeast China

淮安位于古淮河与京杭大运河交汇处，是江淮文化发源地之一。淮安历史上名人辈出，如韩信、梁红玉、吴承恩、关天培和刘鹗等，还是中华人民共和国第一任国务院总理周恩来的故乡。

# 一、城市概况

## 1. 地理环境

淮安位于江苏省中北部，在中国地理分界线"秦岭—淮河"线上，北邻连云港，东连盐城，南接扬州、安徽滁州，西与宿迁相连，面积达1.003万平方公里。淮安地势平坦，近七成为平原地形。这里水网密布，京杭大运河、淮河等9条河流纵贯横穿，中国第四大、江苏第二大淡水湖——洪泽湖也大部分位于境内。

## 2. 城市变迁

淮安地区早在6000年前就有先民活动的踪迹，秦朝（公元前221年—公元前207年）起开始有明确的行政建制，古时曾称"淮阴""楚州"等。"淮安"这一名称最早出现于南齐永明七年（489年）。明清两朝（1368年—1912年）在此设置淮安府，历时500余年。1949年中华人民共和国成立前夕，在此设立淮阴专区，后历经多次调整，1983年改为淮阴市，2001年更名为淮安市。

# I. Overview

## 1. Geographical Environment

Huai'an is located in the north-central part of Jiangsu Province, on the Qinling-Huaihe Line, which is the geographical dividing line of China. Huai'an covers an area of 10,030 square kilometers and borders Yancheng to the east, Suqian to the west, Lianyungang to the north, and Yangzhou and Chuzhou (in Anhui Province) to the south. Huai'an features a flat terrain, and plains account for nearly 70% of its area. The city is crisscrossed by waterways, including the Beijing-Hangzhou Grand Canal, the Huaihe River, and seven other rivers. The Hongze Lake, the fourth largest freshwater lake in China and the second largest in Jiangsu, is mostly located within its boundaries.

## 2. Development

There have been traces of human activities in the Huai'an area as far back as 6,000 years ago. Huai'an had clear administrative structures during the Qin Dynasty (221 BC — 207 BC) and was historically known as Huaiyin and Chuzhou, among other names. The name "Huai'an" first appeared in the 7th year of the Yongming era of the Southern Qi Dynasty (489 AD). During the Ming and Qing Dynasties (1368 AD — 1912 AD), Huai'an Prefecture was established and lasted for over 500 years. On the eve of the founding of the People's Republic of China in 1949, the Huaiyin special zone was founded. After several adjustments, the special zone was renamed Huaiyin City in 1983 and finally changed to Huai'an City in 2001.

### 3. 今日淮安

淮安是江苏省辖的13个地级市之一，包括4个区、3个县。近年来，淮安充分利用四通八达的地理位置优势，发挥集公路、铁路、水运、空运于一体的立体交通网络优势，发掘深厚历史文化内涵与优良生态环境中蕴含的文旅融合发展优势，全面建设长三角北部现代化中心城市。

## 二、文化印象

### 1. 历史文化名城

淮安是国家历史文化名城，自古有"壮丽东南第一州"①的美誉，拥有丰富的历史文化资源：青莲岗文化遗址、淮安府署保留了淮河下游历史变迁的重要信息；总督漕运公署遗址见证了中国古代独特的漕运文化传统；清口枢纽反映了中国古代高超的水利工程技术；河下古镇展示了保存完好的传统街巷风貌；此外，周恩来故居和周恩来纪念馆作为红色地标，传承和弘扬革命精神，是重要的爱国主义教育基地。

---

① 出自明朝姚广孝所著的《淮安览古》。
The statement comes from *Huaian Overview of Antiquity* by Yao Guangxiao of the Ming Dynasty.

## 3. Huai'an Today

Huai'an is one of the 13 prefecture-level cities under Jiangsu Province. It is comprised of four districts and three counties. In recent years, Huai'an benefits from its geographical advantage of being well-connected in all directions and having a comprehensive transport network with road, rail, water, and air routes, and explores the development prospects of culture and tourism in its rich historical and cultural resources and favorable ecological environment. All these ongoing efforts aim to build Huai'an into a modern city in the northern part of the Yangtze River Delta.

## II. Cultural Impressions

### 1. Historical and Cultural City

Huai'an, a national historical and cultural city, is known as "the most magnificent city in southeast China".① It boasts a wealth of historical and cultural resources. The Qingliangang Cultural Site and the Huai'an Yamen preserve important information about the historical changes in the lower reaches of the Huaihe River. The site of the Water Transport Governor's Office witnesses the unique tradition of grain transport in ancient China. The Qingkou Hub reflects the advanced water conservancy engineering technology of ancient China. The Hexia Ancient Town shows the well-preserved traditional streetscapes. Furthermore, the Former Residence and Memorial Hall of Premier Zhou Enlai, a historical relic of the Chinese revolution, is an important site for patriotic education.

## 2. 周恩来故里

淮安是周恩来总理的故乡。周恩来是中华人民共和国第一任总理、外交事业的创始人和主要领导人之一。他提出的"和平共处五项原则"至今仍是国际关系的基本准则之一。周恩来在淮安度过了12个春秋,童年与少年时期的经历对塑造他的优秀品格起到了重要作用。周恩来一生不忘人民,被尊称为"人民的好总理"。每年,无数游客来到淮安,追寻周总理的足迹,从他的精神中汲取前进力量。

## 三、教育交流

### 1. 高等教育概况

淮安现有普通高等学校8所,其中本科院校2所,分别为淮阴师范学院和淮阴工学院。这两所高校在学科建设、人才培养等方面各有特色,可为国际学生提供多样化的学习和文化交流机会。

### 2. 高校介绍

#### 1)淮阴师范学院

淮阴师范学院(www.hytc.edu.cn)是一所以教师教育为主要特色的省属本科院校。学校广泛开展国际合作交流,先后与15个国家和地区的60多所高校建立了友好合作关系。学校于2004年招收首批长期语言国际学生,2017年首次招收学历国际学生,现有汉语国际教育等专业面向全球招生。

## 2. Hometown of Zhou Enlai

Huai'an is the hometown of Zhou Enlai, the first premier of the People's Republic of China and one of the main leaders in the founding and development of China's diplomacy. He proposed the Five Principles of Peaceful Coexistence, which remain fundamental norms in international relations. Zhou Enlai spent 12 years in Huai'an, and the experiences of his childhood and adolescence greatly shaped his character. Zhou Enlai never forgot the people and was honored as "The People's Good Premier". Every year, countless visitors come to Huai'an to trace his footsteps and draw strength from his spirit.

## III. Education and International Exchanges

### 1. Overview of Higher Education

Huai'an has 8 general colleges and universities, including 2 undergraduate institutions: Huaiyin Normal University and Huaiyin Institute of Technology. Both universities have their own distinctive features in terms of academic disciplines and education, and can offer diverse learning and cultural exchange opportunities for international students.

### 2. Introduction to Universities

### 1) Huaiyin Normal University

Huaiyin Normal University (HNU) (www.hytc.edu.cn) is a provincial undergraduate university specializing in educating teachers. HNU has carried out extensive international cooperation and exchanges, and established friendly cooperative relations with more than 60 universities in 15 countries and regions. HNU started enrolling international students for long-term language programs in 2004 and began admitting international students for degree programs in 2017. Some academic programs, such as international Chinese language education, are open to global enrollment.

## 2）淮阴工学院

淮阴工学院（www.hyit.edu.cn）始建于1958年，是一所以工科教育为特色的省属本科院校。学校先后与20多个国家和地区的60多所高校建立了友好合作关系。2016年，学校招收了首批来自18个国家的67名国际学生，成为淮安首先招收学历国际学生的高等学府。学校的材料与化工等多个专业面向全球招生。

## 四、经济腾飞

### 1. 运河之都

从2000余年前连接长江与淮河的邗沟，到贯通南北的隋唐大运河，再到"黄金水道"京杭大运河，运河的开通与发展，给淮安地区带来了漕运的兴盛、商业的繁荣。明清时期在此设漕运总督，统管全国漕运事务；清朝雍正七年（1729年）又设江南河道总督，进一步加强了对江苏河道的治理和维护。这些举措使淮安成为当时全国最重要的漕运中心。时至今日，淮安的水利建设依然引人注目。这里有亚洲最大水上立交——淮安水上立交枢纽工程。该工程采用"上槽下洞"的特殊设计，既确保了京杭大运河的航运畅通，又满足了淮河入海水道及周边地区的泄洪排涝需求。

## 2) Huaiyin Institute of Technology

Huaiyin Institute of Technology (HYIT) (www.hyit.edu.cn), founded in 1958, is a provincial undergraduate university specializing in engineering education. HYIT has established friendly cooperative relations with more than 60 universities in over 20 countries and regions. In 2016, the university enrolled its first batch of 67 international students from 18 countries, and became the first higher education institution in Huai'an to admit international students for degree programs. Certain academic programs, including materials and chemical engineering, are open to global enrollment.

## IV. Economic Takeoff

### 1. The City of Canals

From the Hangou Canal that connected the Yangtze River and the Huaihe River over 2,000 years ago, to the Sui-Tang Grand Canal that traversed the north and south, and then to the "Golden Waterway" Beijing-Hangzhou Grand Canal, the different canals have brought prosperity to the grain transport and commercial activities of Huai'an. During the Ming and Qing Dynasties, the Water Transport Governor's Office was set up in Huai'an to oversee grain transport affairs nationwide. In the 7th year of Emperor Yongzheng's reign of the Qing Dynasty (1729), the Viceroy of Southern Rivers was established in Huai'an to further strengthen the management and maintenance of waterways in Jiangsu. As a result, Huai'an became the most important grain transport center in China at that time. Today, Huai'an boasts impressive water conservancy projects, including the Huai'an Waterway Interchange Hub Project, which is the largest waterway interchange in Asia and uses a special "upper channel and lower culvert" design to ensure the smooth navigation of the Beijing-Hangzhou Grand Canal while meeting

## 2. 千年淮盐

盐是"百味之首"，拥有2000余年历史的淮盐更是其中精品。淮安自古便是淮盐生产与转运的重镇。20世纪80年代，淮安发现特大盐矿，并积极把自然资源优势转化为经济发展动力。现在，淮安在继承传统的同时不断创新，以"高端、绿色、循环、集约"为导向，大力发展盐化新材料产业。"千年淮盐"在新时代开启了可持续发展的新篇章。

## 五、特色美食

### 1. 淮扬风味

发源于淮安与扬州地区的"淮扬菜"是中国四大菜系之一。淮扬自古繁华富庶，淮扬菜自然十分讲究：选料严谨、制作精细。淮扬位于中国南北交界处，这使淮扬菜能够融合南北烹饪的精华，既有南方菜的雅致，也有北方菜的醇厚。1949年中华人民共和国成立时的"开国第一宴"，就选择了"南北咸宜"的淮扬菜。这些年，淮扬菜还通过各种国际活动，积极推动中国美食走向全球。可以说，淮安之所以能够入选"世界美食之都"，淮扬菜发挥了至关重要的作用。

### 2. 经典美味

来到淮安，既可以品尝软兜长鱼、平桥豆腐这类传统名菜，也可以试试以"淮点三绝"——汤包、淮饺、烫面饺为代表的特色小吃。在街头还能看到一种细如金线的点心——茶馓。这种点心香脆松口，很适合用来招待宾客或赠送亲友。

the flood discharge needs of the Huaihe River outfall waterway and its surrounding areas.

## 2. The Huai Salt

Salt is often referred to as the "king of flavors". The Huai salt, with a history of over 2,000 years, is regarded as a premium product. Historically, Huai'an was an important center for the production and transportation of the Huai salt. Since a large salt mine was discovered in Huai'an in the 1980s, these natural resources have driven economic development. Now, Huai'an is continuously innovating while preserving its traditions. It is vigorously developing the salt-based new materials industry in a "high-end, green, circular, and intensive" direction. The millennia-old Huai salt is embarking on a new chapter of sustainable development in the new era.

## V. Specialty Food

### 1. Huaiyang Flavor

"Huaiyang cuisine", which originated in the area of Huai'an and Yangzhou (collectively called Huaiyang), is one of China's four major culinary styles. The Huaiyang area has been prosperous and affluent since ancient times, and Huaiyang cuisine has been renowned for its meticulous selection of ingredients and refined cooking techniques. Since the Huaiyang area is located at the junction of southern and northern China, Huaiyang cuisine blends the essence of southern and northern cooking styles, featuring the elegance of southern dishes and the richness of northern dishes. In 1949, when the People's Republic of China was founded, Huaiyang cuisine, enjoyed by both southerners and northerners, was chosen as the first course for the "National Banquet". Over the years, Huaiyang cuisine, as an example of the Chinese culinary culture, has been introduced to the world through various

## 六、历史名人

### 1. 韩信

韩信，淮阴（今属淮安市）人，是中国西汉的开国重臣、杰出的军事家，被誉为"汉初三杰"之一。韩信拥有非凡的军事才能，被赞为"兵仙"。韩信的一生极为传奇，为后人留下了"多多益善""背水一战""推陈出新""成也萧何，败也萧何"等众多成语典故，这种文化现象在中国历史上十分罕见。

international events and plays a crucial role in helping Huai'an to be selected as a "City of Gastronomy" by UNESCO.

### 2. Classic Delicacies

In Huai'an, you can enjoy famous traditional dishes such as shredded stir-fried eel and Pingqiao tofu, as well as special snacks like the "Three Delicacies of Huai'an" — soup dumplings, wontons, and hot-water dough dumplings. On the streets, you can also find a delightful snack named Cha San, which is a kind of deep-fried thin crispy noodles resembling gold threads. It is an ideal treat for guests and a good gift for family and friends.

## VI. Historical Figures

### 1. Han Xin

Han Xin, a native of Huaiyin (now part of Huai'an), was a founding statesman and an outstanding military strategist of the Western Han Dynasty. He was acclaimed as one of the "Three Heroes of the Early Han Dynasty" and was praised as the "God of War" for his extraordinary military talent. Han Xin's legendary life gave rise to a large number of idioms, such as "the more, the better", "fighting with one's back to the river", "to innovate by discarding the outdated", and "to succeed or to fail for the same reason". The phenomenon of many idioms originating from a single individual is rare in Chinese history.

### 2. Wu Cheng'en

Wu Cheng'en, a novelist of the Ming Dynasty, was originally from Lianshui (now part of Huai'an) and later settled in Shanyang (now part of Huai'an). He is best known for writing *The Journey to the West*, one of China's Four Great Classical Novels. Wu Cheng'en skillfully integrated the essence of Huai'an's canal culture — communication, openness,

**2. 吴承恩**

吴承恩，明代小说家，祖籍涟水（今属淮安市），后定居于山阳（今属淮安市），他最为人所知的成就，是创作了中国古典四大名著之一的《西游记》。吴承恩巧妙地将运河文化的精髓——交流、开放、融合、进取融入《西游记》，形成了作品独特的艺术魅力。此外，中国古典四大名著中《水浒传》的作者施耐庵、《三国演义》的作者罗贯中，都曾长期在淮安生活与创作，这两部文学著作与淮安的关系也非常密切。

integration, and progress — into *The Journey to the West* to create the unique artistic charm of this work. Additionally, other authors of China's Four Great Classical Novels, namely Shi Nai'an, who wrote *The Water Margin*, and Luo Guanzhong, who wrote *The Romance of the Three Kingdoms*, also lived and wrote in Huai'an for a long time, linking these two literary masterpieces to this city.

## 练习

### 一、判断题

1. 淮安市位于江苏省中北部、中国南北分界线"秦岭—淮河"线以北。☐

2. 淮安是周恩来总理的故乡，已被列入"国家历史文化名城"。☐

3. 淮安虽是盐运重镇，却并无盐矿资源。☐

4. 淮阴工学院以工科见长，淮阴师范学院则以教师教育为主要特色。☐

5. 中华人民共和国成立时的"开国第一宴"是淮扬菜。☐

6. 中国古典四大名著之一《水浒传》的作者是吴承恩。☐

### 二、思考题

1. 如果想了解淮安的传统街巷风貌，你建议去哪儿参观游览？

2. 淮安水上立交枢纽工程"上槽下洞"的结构有何意义？

3. 淮扬菜有什么特点？

### 三、拓展题

1. 在中国的饮食文化中，有"四大菜系"之说，淮扬菜正是其中之一。你知道其他三大菜系是什么吗，分别具有什么特点？

2. "多多益善""背水一战""推陈出新""成也萧何，败也萧何"这四个成语均与西汉军事家韩信有关。请你查一查这些成语的出处与含义。

# Chapter 10

连云港

LIANYUNGANG

第十章

新 / 亚 / 欧 / 大 / 陆 / 桥 / 东 / 方 / 起 / 点

The Eastern Starting Point of the New
Eurasian Land Bridge

连云港古称"海州"，因面向连岛、背靠云台山，又因为是海港而
得名。作为陆上与海上丝绸之路的交汇点，这里既拥有江苏最大的
岛屿——东西连岛，也有江苏第一高峰——云台山玉女峰。

## 一、城市概况

### 1. 地理环境

连云港位于江苏东北端，东临黄海，土地总面积7615平方公里，海域面积7516平方公里。境内地势由西北向东南倾斜，地貌类型多样、自然资源丰富：平原、丘陵、山地、海岛兼有，森林、湖泊、河流、海洋具备。这里既有江苏第一大岛——面积6.07平方公里的东西连岛，也有江苏第一高峰——海拔624.4米的云台山主峰玉女峰。

### 2. 城市变迁

连云港自秦朝起开始有明确的行政建置，古称"朐县""海州"。随着时代的发展，海州逐渐成为重要的海上门户，清朝康熙二十四年（1685年）在此设立了江海关，是清初四大海关之一。步入20世纪，贯穿中国东中西部的陇海铁路的东端港口在此建成，因面向连岛、背靠云台山，取名连云港。后来这座城市也因港得名，称为连云港市。

## I. Overview

### 1. Geographical Environment

Lianyungang is located at the northeastern end of Jiangsu Province and faces the Yellow Sea to the east. It has a land area of 7,615 square kilometers and a sea area of 7,516 square kilometers. The terrain slopes from northwest to southeast, with diverse landforms and abundant natural resources: plains, hills, mountains, and islands, as well as forests, lakes, rivers, and the sea. It boasts Jiangsu's largest island, the Lian Island, which covers 6.07 square kilometers, and Jiangsu's highest peak, the Yunv Peak of the Yuntai Mountain, standing at 624.4 meters.

### 2. Development

Lianyungang, historically known as Quxian and Haizhou, had clear administrative structures in the Qin Dynasty. Over time, Haizhou became an important maritime gateway. In the 24th year of Emperor Kangxi's reign of the Qing Dynasty (1685), the Jianghai Customs was established in Lianyungang and became one of the four major customs offices in the early Qing Dynasty. In the 20th century, the eastern port of the Longhai Railway, which connects eastern, central, and western parts of China, was built here. Facing the Lian Island and backed by the Yuntai Mountain, the port was named Lianyungang. Later, the city became known as Lianyungang due to its prominent port.

### 3. 今日连云港

　　连云港作为中国首批沿海开放城市之一，凭借"一带一路"交汇点的区位优势，连接东西、沟通南北、海陆转换、辐射全球，大力发展新医药、新材料、新能源等新兴产业。2023年，恰逢"一带一路"倡议提出十周年的历史节点，连云港成功举办首届中欧班列国际合作论坛，积极搭建国际经济文化交流的平台。

## 二、文化印象

### 1. 西游胜境

　　在连云港丰富的文化资源中，最出名的当属《西游记》。《西游记》是中国古典四大名著之一，主角孙悟空更是家喻户晓。尽管作者吴承恩出生于淮安，但其母亲是海州（今连云港）人。他从小就多次探访海州，最终以云台山为原型，创作了孙悟空的老家——花果山。现今的花果山风景区拥有玉女峰、水帘洞、三元宫等景观，每年都吸引着大量游客前来游览。《西游记》中的很多描写都能在这里得到印证。

### 3. Lianyungang Today

As one of the first group of China's coastal open cities, Lianyungang, a hub of the Belt and Road Initiative, leverages its advantages to connect the east and west, bridge the north and south, facilitate sea-land transport, and exert its influence globally. In recent years, Lianyungang has vigorously developed emerging industries such as new medicine, new materials, and new energy. In 2023, marking the 10th anniversary of the Belt and Road Initiative, Lianyungang successfully held the first China-Europe Railway Express Cooperation Forum in an effort to build a new platform for international economic and cultural exchanges.

## II. Cultural Impressions

### 1. The Journey to the West

Among the rich cultural resources of Lianyungang, *The Journey to the West* is undoubtedly the most famous. *The Journey to the West* is one of China's Four Great Classical Novels, and the main character Sun Wukong, also known as the Monkey King, is a household name. Although the author Wu Cheng'en was born in Huai'an, his mother was from Haizhou (now Lianyungang). He visited Haizhou many times during his childhood and finally took the Yuntai Mountain as the inspiration for Sun Wukong's home — the Huaguo Mountain. Today, the Huaguo Mountain Scenic Area features popular attractions such as the Yunv Peak, the Water Curtain Cave, and the Sanyuan Temple. Many details in this area fit the descriptions in *The Journey to the West*.

### 2. City of Crystal

A famous specialty of Lianyungang is the Donghai Crystal. Donghai County, located in the western part of Lianyungang, boasts the greatest crystal reserves and the highest crystal quality in China. As a result, Donghai has

### 2. 水晶之都

连云港还有一张闪亮的名片——东海水晶。东海县在连云港西部，水晶储量与品质均居全国之首，是中国最大的水晶市场、世界水晶交易重要集散地，有"世界水晶之都""中国水晶之都"称号。2013年开放的中国东海水晶博物馆，是中国目前唯一以水晶为主题的博物馆。

## 三、教育交流

### 1. 高等教育概况

连云港现有普通高等学校5所，其中本科院校2所，分别为江苏海洋大学、南京医科大学康达学院。连云港一直坚持高等教育的对外开放，积极深化国际交流合作，推进共建"一带一路"教育行动，共享教育改革发展的成果与经验。

### 2. 高校介绍

江苏海洋大学（www.jou.edu.cn）是一所以"海洋"为特色、强调海洋科学与技术发展的省属本科高校。学校目前已与多所国外高校建立合作关系，签署教育与科研合作协议。同时，学校积极推动来华留学教育高质量发展，现有海洋技术、药学等多个优势学科面向全球开放招生。

been the largest crystal market in China and a key crystal trading hub in the world. Donghai has also earned titles such as "World Crystal Capital" and "China Crystal Capital". The China Donghai Crystal Museum, opened in 2013, is currently the only museum in China themed around crystals.

## III. Education and International Exchanges

### 1. Overview of Higher Education

There are five higher education institutions in Lianyungang, including two undergraduate institutions: Jiangsu Ocean University and Kangda College of Nanjing Medical University. Lianyungang has consistently advanced the opening-up of higher education by deepening international exchanges and cooperation, promoting the high-quality development of the Education Action Plan for the Belt and Road Initiative, and sharing the achievements and experiences of educational reform and development.

### 2. Introduction to Universities

Jiangsu Ocean University (JOU, www.jou.edu.cn) is a provincial undergraduate university with "ocean" as its disciplinary focus. It emphasizes the development of marine science and technology. JOU has established cooperative relations and signed agreements of education and scientific research cooperation with many foreign universities. Additionally, JOU promotes the high-quality development of international student education, and its advantageous disciplines such as marine technology and pharmacy are open to global enrollment.

## 四、经济腾飞

### 1. "一带一路"交汇点

连云港作为新亚欧大陆桥的东方起点、江苏唯一拥有30万吨级航道的深水海港，近年来一直积极参与共建"一带一路"，推动陆海联动、东西互济。2014年，中哈（连云港）物流合作基地成立，成为"一带一路"倡议落地的首个经贸合作实体项目，现已成为亚欧跨境运输的重要集结中心。2019年设立的中国（江苏）自由贸易试验区覆盖南京、苏州、连云港三个片区。其中，连云港首创国际班列过境集装箱"车船直取"零等待模式。这一模式极大地提升了效率、降低了成本，现已向全国口岸推广。

### 2. 中华药港

连云港是中国最大的民营生物医药研发和生产聚集地，汇集了众多行业内知名企业，研发实力雄厚，不仅对当地经济发展贡献显著，在国内医药市场中也占据重要位置。在2023年中国医药研发产品线最佳工业企业榜单中，连云港共有四家药企进入前十名。近年来，连云港全力打造"中华药港"，推动医药产业从"领跑全国"向"参与全球竞争"转变。

## IV. Economic Takeoff

### 1. Hub of the Belt and Road Initiative

As the eastern starting point of the New Eurasian Land Bridge and the only deep-water port in Jiangsu with a 300,000-ton capacity channel, Lianyungang has been actively participating in the joint construction of the Belt and Road Initiative and promoting land-sea linkage and east-west mutual benefit in recent years. The China-Kazakhstan (Lianyungang) Logistics Cooperation Base, founded in 2014, is the first economic and trade cooperation project implemented under the Belt and Road Initiative, and it is now a key center for Asia-Europe cross-border transportation. The China (Jiangsu) Pilot Free Trade Zone, established in 2019, covers three areas: Nanjing, Suzhou and Lianyungang. The Zero-wait Vehicle-to-ship Direct Access Mode for international train transit containers, invented in Lianyungang, has greatly improved efficiency, reduced costs and been promoted to ports nationwide.

### 2. Chinese Medicine Port

Lianyungang boasts China's largest private biopharmaceutical research and production cluster, where many well-known companies with research and development capabilities contribute to the local economy and occupy an important position in the domestic pharmaceutical market. In the list of China's best industrial enterprises in the pharmaceutical R&D pipeline for 2023, four companies from Lianyungang were ranked among the top ten. In recent years, Lianyungang has been striving to build the "Chinese Medicine Port", advancing the pharmaceutical industry from "leading the nation" to "participating in global competition".

## 五、特色美食

### 1. 胸海风味

连云港菜又叫胸海菜。靠山吃山，靠水吃水，不同的地理环境自然孕育出不同的风味。连云港位于中国南北方的过渡地带，这使胸海菜自然融汇了南北风味。此外，连云港依山傍海，又让胸海菜在选材上可以兼具山海、无所不包：云台山茂密的森林提供了多样的山珍，黄海广阔的海域带来了丰富的海味。

### 2. 经典美味

胸海菜有时注重保留食材的自然风味，对虾只需水煮，梭子蟹只要清蒸；有时则在烹饪技巧上精益求精，创造出油爆乌花、豉香黄鱼这类风味更为丰富的菜品。在连云港街头，还有桃林烧鸡、板浦凉粉、赣榆煎饼等美味小吃，深受人们喜爱。

## V. Specialty Food

### 1. Quhai Flavor

Lianyungang cuisine is also known as Quhai cuisine. "Live by the mountain, eat from the mountain; live by the water, eat from the water." Different geographical environments naturally give birth to different flavors. Lianyungang is located in the transitional zone between the south and the north of China, and Quhai cuisine naturally blend southern and northern flavors. In addition, Lianyungang is surrounded by mountains and the sea, which provide a diverse range of ingredients, including mountain delicacies from the Yuntai Mountain and seafood from the Yellow Sea.

### 2. Classic Delicacies

Quhai dishes, such as boiled shrimp and steamed crabs, highlight the natural flavors of the ingredients. On the other hand, dishes like the stir-fried squid in a flower-cut style and the yellow croaker with fermented black bean sauce, showcase a richer range of flavors through their superb cooking techniques. When visiting Lianyungang, be sure to try the popular street foods including Taolin roast chicken, Banpu bean jelly, and Ganyu baked pancakes.

## 六、历史名人

### 1. 徐福

徐福是秦朝齐地琅琊郡（今连云港赣榆）人。秦始皇追求长生不死，派徐福率船队出海，为他寻找长生不死的仙药。徐福自然未能寻到仙药，却在东渡过程中发现了一片"平原广泽"，即现在的日本。徐福一行人带去了秦朝先进的文化和科技，促进了当地的社会发展。因此，徐福也被视为开启中日文化交流历史的第一人。

### 2. 李汝珍

李汝珍是清朝的小说家、文学家，19岁时随兄来到海州（今连云港），并在此度过了人生的大部分时光。李汝珍博学多才，"消磨了三十多年层层心血"，融入海州独特的地方风物，创作出了长篇小说《镜花缘》。这部经典自问世以来，一直引起各方关注，中国著名文学家、思想家鲁迅称其为"博物多识之作"，苏联学者费施曼女士称赞其为"一部熔幻想小说、历史小说、讽刺小说和游记小说于一炉的杰作"。

## VI. Historical Figures

### 1. Xu Fu

Xu Fu was a native of Langya Commandery in the Qi territory (now Ganyu, Lianyungang) during the Qin Dynasty. Qin Shihuang, the first emperor of the Qin Dynasty, sought immortality and sent Xu Fu on a voyage in search of the elixir of immortality. Xu Fu did not find the elixir but discovered a vast plain with extensive marshlands, now known as Japan. Xu Fu and his team brought advanced culture and technology from the Qin Dynasty to promote local social development. Therefore, Xu Fu is considered the first person to initiate the cultural exchange between China and Japan.

### 2. Li Ruzhen

Li Ruzhen was a novelist and literary scholar of the Qing Dynasty. At the age of 19, he followed his brother to Haizhou (now Lianyungang), where he spent most of his life. Erudite and versatile, Li Ruzhen spent decades writing his novel *Flowers in the Mirror*, which incorporated the distinctive landscapes and customs of Haizhou. This novel has won much acclaim since its publication. Lu Xun, a great Chinese writer, called it "a work rich in knowledge and insight"; the Soviet scholar Ms. Olga Fishman praised it as "a masterpiece combining fantasy, history, satire, and travel".

## 练习

### 一、判断题

1. 连云港因面向连岛、背靠云台山而得名。　☐

2. 东海县位于连云港市东部，享有"世界水晶之都""中国水晶之都"称号。　☐

3. 连云港只有江苏海洋大学这一所本科院校，该校强调海洋科学与技术发展。　☐

4. 江苏省目前拥有多个具备30万吨级航道的深水海港，连云港是其中之一。　☐

5. 连云港菜又叫朐海菜，既融汇南北，又兼具山海。　☐

6. 徐福东渡的初衷是为秦始皇寻求长生不死之药。　☐

### 二、思考题

1. 吴承恩是怎么创作出《西游记》中孙悟空的老家花果山的？

2. 连云港医药产业有什么发展目标？

3. 《镜花缘》这本书有什么特点？

### 三、拓展题

1. 近年来，连云港一直积极融入共建"一带一路"，首创的国际班列过境集装箱"车船直取"零等待模式，已向全国口岸推广。请你查一查，"车船直取"模式是怎么操作的，相较于传统模式有何优势？

2. 徐福被视为开启中日文化交流历史的第一人。除了他，你还知道哪些为中外文化交流作出贡献的历史人物，他们主要做了什么？

# Chapter 11

盐城

YAN CHENG

第十一章
———————
黄 / 海 / 明 / 珠　湿 / 地 / 之 / 都
Pearl of the Yellow Sea, Capital of Wetlands

盐城因其周围布满盐场而得名。它位于黄海之滨，拥有江苏最长的海岸线。其东部的海岸型湿地被列为世界重点湿地保护区，区内建有全球首个野生麋鹿保护区及国家级珍禽自然保护区。

## 一、城市概况

### 1. 地理环境

盐城地处江苏沿海中部，东临黄海，土地面积约1.7万平方公里，海域面积1.9万平方公里。盐城有江苏最长的海岸线，占全省海岸线长度的56%。盐城全市都是平原，西北和东南部高，中部和东北部低。气候受海洋影响较大，四季分明，年平均气温在15℃左右，空气温暖而湿润，雨水丰沛。

### 2. 城市变迁

盐城有2000多年建城史，早在西周时期，这片土地被称为"淮夷"，西汉时期盐渎县的建立，标志着盐城作为行政区域的开端。东晋（公元411年）时，因"环城皆盐场"而改名为"盐城"，1983年设立为地级市，2023年有常住人口660多万。在行政规划上，盐城下辖1个县级市，5个县和3个市辖区，此外还设有国家级经济技术开发区、国家级高新技术开发区、盐南高新技术产业开发区。

## I. Overview

### 1. Geographical Environment

Yancheng, located in the central coastal area of Jiangsu Province and bordered by the Yellow Sea to the east, has a land area of approximately 17,000 square kilometers and a sea area of 19,000 square kilometers. Yancheng boasts the longest coastline in Jiangsu, accounting for 56% of the province's total coastline length. The entire city of Yancheng is a plain, with higher elevations in the northwest and southeast, and lower elevations in the central and northeastern parts. The maritime climate features distinct seasons and an annual average temperature of around 15°C. The air is warm and humid, and rainfall is abundant.

### 2. Development

The town of Yancheng appeared over 2,000 years ago. As early as the Western Zhou Dynasty, this place was known as "Huaiyi". The establishment of Yandu County during the Western Han Dynasty marked the beginning of Yancheng as an administrative region. In 411 AD, during the Eastern Jin Dynasty, the county was renamed "Yancheng" — a town surrounded by salt fields. It was established as a prefecture-level city in 1983. As of 2023, Yancheng has a permanent population of over 6.6 million. Administratively, Yancheng governs one county-level city, five counties, and three urban districts. Additionally, it has a national-level economic and technological development zone, a national-level high-tech development zone, and the Yannan High-Tech Industrial Development Zone.

### 3. 今日盐城

盐城是长三角一体化中心区城市之一，淮河生态经济带的出海门户以及中韩产业园地方合作城市。盐城交通便捷，拥有南洋国际机场和盐城港两个一类开放口岸，共同构建了盐城海陆空立体化交通网络的核心，加速了人流、物流、信息流的高效流通。汽车制造、钢铁工业、新能源和电子信息四大主导产业构建了盐城多元化、高技术含量的现代产业体系。2020年，随着盐通高铁的顺利通车，盐城正式融入"上海1小时经济圈"，这极大地缩短了盐城与长三角核心城市的距离，为盐城带来了前所未有的发展机遇。

## 二、文化印象

盐城坐落于黄海之滨，有"黄海明珠"的美誉。这座城市拥有广阔的滨海平原，加上大面积的湿地和滩涂资源，塑造了盐城鲜明的地域文化。

### 1. 白色文化

"白色文化"指海盐文化。盐城一直是中国海盐生产中心之一，海盐不仅塑造了盐城的经济基础，也深深影响了当地的历史文化、风俗习惯乃至城市精神。盐城人民在长期的盐业生产中形成的吃苦耐劳、团结协作精神，是海盐文化在人文层面的深刻体现。从"盐都""盐城"等地名，到盐雕艺术这样的非物质文化遗产，都彰显了海盐在盐城历史上的核心地位。2008年，第一座国家

### 3. Yancheng Today

Yancheng is one of the central cities in the Yangtze River Delta Integration Zone as it serves as a gateway to the Huaihe River Ecological Economic Belt and a local cooperation city for the China-Korea Industrial Park. Yancheng boasts convenient transportation as Nanyang International Airport and Yancheng Port form the core of Yancheng's integrated sea, land, and air transportation network, thus enhancing the efficient flow of people, goods, and information. The city has developed a diversified and high-tech modern industrial system, with four leading industries: automobile manufacturing, steel industry, new energy, and electronic information. Upon the opening of Yancheng-Nantong High-Speed Railway in 2020, Yancheng was officially included in the one-hour economic circle of Shanghai. Since the distance between Yancheng and the core cities of the Yangtze River Delta is greatly reduced, it may enjoy unprecedented development opportunities.

## II. Cultural Impressions

Yancheng, located on the coast of the Yellow Sea, is known as the "Pearl of the Yellow Sea". The city boasts vast coastal plains, extensive wetland and mudflat resources, which have shaped Yancheng's distinctive regional culture.

### 1. White Culture

"White Culture" refers to the sea salt culture. Yancheng has long been one of the sea salt production centers in China. Sea salt has not only shaped the economic foundation of Yancheng but has also deeply influenced its historical culture, customs, and local people's spirit — hard work, perseverance, and unity developed through long-term sea salt production, an embodiment of Yancheng's sea salt culture on a humanistic level. Sea

级盐类专题博物馆——中国海盐博物馆在盐城开馆，更是对海盐文化的一种集中展示和传承。

### 2. 红色文化

"红色文化"指新四军文化。1941年，新四军在此重建军部，标志着盐城成为华中敌后抗战的政治和文化中心，也奠定了盐城作为革命老区的地位。盐城有全国最全面、系统展示新四军抗战历程的大型综合性纪念馆——新四军纪念馆。

### 3. 绿色文化

"绿色文化"指生态文化。盐城黄海湿地作为世界自然遗产的典范，正是这种文化的生动体现。盐城的绿色文化围绕湿地、海洋、森林三大生态系统展开，通过建立和维护自然保护区，如珍禽丹顶鹤和麋鹿国家级自然保护区，展现了人与自然和谐共生的可能性。盐城黄海湿地是西太平洋最大的湿地，盐城也因此获得"国际湿地城市"称号。

### 4. 蓝色文化

"蓝色文化"指海洋文化。盐城在中国东部沿海，拥有江苏最长海岸线、最大滩涂，"蓝色文化"体现在盐城与海洋的紧密联系中，是当地社会、经济、文化发展的重要基础。港口风光、渔港风情、沿海风电场、海鲜美食、沿海观光带共同塑造了盐城作为海滨城市独有的风貌和气质。

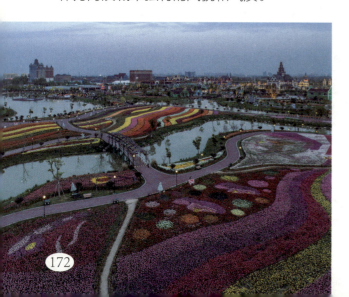

salt plays a central role in Yancheng's history, as can be seen in place names like "Yandu" and "Yancheng" as well as intangible cultural heritage such as salt carving art. In 2008, the opening of the first national sea salt museum, the China Sea Salt Museum in Yancheng, marked a dedicated inheritance of Yancheng's sea salt culture.

### 2. Red Culture

"Red Culture" refers to the legacy of the New Fourth Army. In 1941, the New Fourth Army rebuilt its headquarters in Yancheng and made the city a political and cultural center of the counter-Japanese resistance in central China. This also established Yancheng's status as a revolutionary base. Now, the city is home to the New Fourth Army Memorial Hall, a comprehensive museum that showcases the history of the New Fourth Army's resistance during the war.

### 3. Green Culture

"Green Culture" refers to ecological protection. The Yellow Sea Wetland in Yancheng, as a World Natural Heritage Site, is a good example. Yancheng's ecological protection focuses on three ecological systems: wetland, sea and forest. By establishing and maintaining nature reserves such as the National Nature Reserves for the endangered red-crowned crane and milu deer, Yancheng tries to achieve a harmonious coexistence between human and nature. Since the Yellow Sea Wetland in Yancheng is the largest wetland in the west of the Pacific, Yancheng has been called an "International Wetland City".

### 4. Blue Culture

"Blue Culture" refers to the maritime culture. Located on the eastern coast of China, Yancheng boasts the longest coastline and the largest mudflat in Jiangsu Province. Yancheng's

## 三、教育交流

盐城共有6所普通高校，其中盐城师范学院、盐城工学院等4所院校招收国际学生。

### 1）盐城师范学院

盐城师范学院（www.yctu.edu.cn）创建于1958年，是一所综合性的本科院校，拥有经济学、法学、教育学、文学、历史学、理学、工学、农学、管理学、艺术学等10大学科门类。学校长期招收汉语进修生和交换生，2018年起，学校开始面向全球招收国际贸易等多个专业的本科生。

### 2）盐城工学院

盐城工学院（www.ycit.cn）1996年由两所学校合并组建而成，是一所以工为主，理、工、文、艺、经、管、农多学科协调发展的高等教育机构。2018年，学校获批成为硕士学位授予单位。2022年，获江苏省博士学位授予立项建设单位资格，显示出学校在提升教育层次和科研能力方面的进展。学校招收经济类、计算机类等本科专业国际学生。

maritime culture, reflected in its close link with the sea, serves as an important foundation for the city's social, economic, and cultural development. Yancheng's unique character and charm as a seaside city are shaped by its coastal scenery, fishing harbor ambiance, coastal wind farms, seafood cuisine, and coastal sightseeing areas.

## III. Education and International Exchanges

There are six universities in Yancheng, and four of them, including Yancheng Teachers University and Yancheng Institute of Technology, enroll international students.

### 1) Yancheng Teachers University

Yancheng Teachers University (www.yctu. edu.cn), established in 1958, is a comprehensive undergraduate institution which offers programs across ten academic disciplines: economics, law, education, literature, history, science, engineering, agriculture, management, and arts. It has a long history of enrolling Chinese language students and exchange students. Since 2018, some of its undergraduate programs including international trade are open to students from around the world.

### 2) Yancheng Institute of Technology

Yancheng Institute of Technology (www. ycit.cn), founded in 1996 through the merger of two colleges, is a higher education institution with a focus on engineering among a range of disciplines in science, engineering, literature, art, economics, management, and agriculture. In 2018, the university was approved to confer master's degrees. In 2022, it was granted the qualification to develop doctoral degree programs in Jiangsu Province, a testament to the institution's progress in advancing education and research capabilities. It enrolls international students in undergraduate programs such as economics and computer science.

## 四、经济腾飞

### 1. 中韩（盐城）产业园

中韩（盐城）产业园成立于2017年，不仅是韩国企业在中国投资与发展的重要产业集聚区，也是中韩贸易往来与物流集散基地。该产业园总规划面积50平方公里，成功吸引了现代起亚汽车、LG集团、京信电子在内的1000多家韩国企业，吸引外资总额已突破100亿美元。产业园凭借优越的地理位置、完善的基础设施以及一系列优惠政策，持续促进中韩的经济合作，为双方互利共赢搭建了一个综合性平台。

### 2. 绿色经济

盐城依托湿地、海洋、森林三大自然生态资源，以及"世界自然遗产"的国际影响力，正在努力构造以生态为核心竞争力的城市发展战略。围绕盐城黄海湿地世界自然遗产，以及其他多个国家级自然保护区，盐城开发了一系列生态旅游产品和路线，展现自然之美和生物的多样性。

## IV. Economic Takeoff

### 1. China-Korea (Yancheng) Industrial Park

The China-Korea (Yancheng) Industrial Park, founded in 2017, serves as a key industrial cluster for Korean enterprises investing and developing in China. It also functions as a base for China-Korea trade and logistics. The park covers a planned area of 50 square kilometers and has attracted over 1,000 Korean companies, including Hyundai-Kia Motors, LG Group, and Kyungshin Electronics. The total foreign investment in the park has surpassed $10 billion. Thanks to its advantageous location, well-developed infrastructure, and a range of preferential policies, the industrial park continuously promotes the economic cooperation between China and Korea, and helps to create a comprehensive platform for mutual benefit and win-win outcomes.

### 2. Green Economy

Taking advantage of its natural resources in wetland, sea, and forest, as well as the international influence of its "World Natural Heritage" status, Yancheng is working to develop a growth strategy centered around ecological competitiveness. The city has developed a range of eco-tourism products and routes based on the Yellow Sea Wetland (World Natural Heritage Site) and other national nature reserves to showcase its natural beauty and biodiversity.

## 五、特色美食

### 1. 东台鱼汤面

东台鱼汤面以白汤面和鱼汤为主要原料，通常选用新鲜的河鱼，慢火熬煮出乳白色的汤汁，配上葱花、姜丝、胡椒粉等佐料，一碗面汇聚了汤的醇厚、鱼的鲜美，更有丰富的营养。

### 2. 建湖藕粉圆

传统藕粉圆是一道传统特色小吃，用白糖、枣泥、芝麻粉、桂花等香甜的馅料混合，搓成小丸子形状，再在外层裹上优质的藕粉，在开水中多次汆(cuān)制而成。藕粉圆外层晶莹剔透，略有韧性，吃起来有弹性、甜而不腻。

### 3. 伍佑醉螺

伍佑醉螺是盐城的地方传统名吃，以盐城滩涂上盛产的优质泥螺为原料，加上特制的卤汤和曲酒进行腌制。这种腌制方法不仅保留了泥螺原有的鲜味，还让泥螺酒香浓郁，形成了咸甜适中的独特风味。

## V. Specialty Food

### 1. Dongtai Fish Soup Noodles

Dongtai fish soup noodles feature white soup noodles and fish broth as the main ingredients. Fresh river fish is slowly cooked to create a creamy broth, seasoned with scallions, ginger slices, and pepper, and then made into a bowl of noodles that combine the rich flavor of the broth with the freshness of the fish. It is both delicious and nutritious.

### 2. Jianhu Lotus Root Powder Balls

Jianhu lotus root powder balls are a classic snack. The filling is made by mixing sweet ingredients like white sugar, jujube paste, sesame powder, and osmanthus flowers, and then rolled into small balls, which are coated with high-quality lotus root powder and blanched in boiling water. The balls made in this way are translucent and elastic on the outside and taste delightfully chewy and sweet.

### 3. Wuyou Wine-saturated Snails

Wuyou wine-saturated snails are a traditional delicacy from Yancheng. High-quality mud snails, abundant in the region's mudflats, are used as the main ingredient. The snails are marinated with a special brine and rice wine. In this way, the original freshness of the snails is preserved, while an aromatic flavor from the wine is added to create a unique taste that's both salty and sweet.

## 六、生态保护

### 1. 江苏大丰麋鹿国家级自然保护区

江苏大丰麋鹿国家级自然保护区位于盐城市大丰区，是全球占地面积最大、野生麋鹿种群数量最多、麋鹿基因库最大的自然保护区。保护区由林地、芦荡、草滩、沼泽地、盐碱裸露地组成，属于典型的黄海滩涂型湿地生态系统，为麋鹿和其他众多野生动物提供了理想的栖息地。中华麋鹿园作为保护区对外开放的部分，通过生态旅游方式向公众传播自然保护的意识，是结合自然保护与可持续旅游的典范。

### 2. 江苏盐城湿地珍禽国家级自然保护区

江苏盐城湿地珍禽国家级自然保护区是中国最大的滩涂湿地保护区之一，主要保护丹顶鹤等珍稀鸟类以及它们赖以生存的滩涂湿地生态系统。保护区地跨多个县市，是丹顶鹤等许多候鸟迁徙路线上的重要停歇地。其对外开放部分，盐城丹顶鹤湿地生态旅游区是国家4A级景区。

## VI. Ecological Protection

### 1. Jiangsu Dafeng Milu Deer National Nature Reserve

Jiangsu Dafeng Milu Deer National Nature Reserve is located in Dafeng District, Yancheng, Jiangsu Province. It is the largest nature reserve in the world in terms of land area, population of wild milu deer and the milu deer gene pool. The reserve comprises forests, reed marshes, grasslands, swamps and saline-alkaline barren lands, representing a typical mudflat wetland ecosystem of the Yellow Sea. This diverse habitat provides an ideal environment for milu deer and many other wildlife species. The Chinese Milu Park (national 5A-level scenic spot), an open section of the reserve, promotes environmental awareness through eco-tourism and serves as a model for combining nature conservation with sustainable tourism.

### 2. Jiangsu Yancheng Wetland National Nature Reserve, Rare Birds

Jiangsu Yancheng Wetland National Nature Reserve, Rare Bird, located in Yancheng, Jiangsu Province, is one of the largest mudflat wetland reserves in China. It is primarily dedicated to protecting rare birds such as the red-crowned cranes and their mudflat wetland habitats. The reserve spans multiple counties and cities and serves as a crucial stopover for many migratory birds, including the red-crowned cranes. The open section, the Yancheng Red-Crowned Crane Wetland Eco-Tourism Area, is recognized as a national 4A-level scenic spot.

## 3. 江苏黄海海滨国家森林公园

江苏黄海海滨国家森林公园占地近7万亩，园内有各类植物628种、鸟类342种和兽类近30种。这里的空气质量极佳，负氧离子含量达到每立方厘米4000个，是一个真正的"绿色氧吧"。公园的森林覆盖率超过90%，是中国最大的平原森林，这为众多动物提供了理想的栖息环境，也在维持生态平衡、净化空气等方面发挥着重要作用。公园的开放部分，江苏东台黄海森林生态旅游度假区是国家4A级景区。

## 3. Jiangsu Yellow Sea Coastal National Forest Park

Jiangsu Yellow Sea Coastal National Forest Park covers an area of nearly 4,667 hectares and is home to 628 plant species, 342 bird species, and nearly 30 animal species. It has excellent air quality and is praised as a "green oxygen bar", with a negative oxygen ion concentration reaching 4,000 per cubic centimeter. Boasting a forest coverage rate of over 90%, the park is the largest flatland forest in China. The vast forest provides an ideal habitat for wildlife and plays a crucial role in maintaining ecological balance and purifying the air. The park's open section, the Jiangsu Dongtai Yellow Sea Forest Eco-Tourism Resort, is a national 4A-level scenic spot.

**练习**

**一、判断题**

1. 盐城有2000年的建城历史，古称盐渎。☐

2. 盐城位于江苏沿海中部，东临黄海。☐

3. 江苏黄海海滨国家森林公园占地约4667公顷。☐

**二、思考题**

1. 盐城这个名字是怎么来的？和盐有什么关系？

2. 请问盐城的四色文化指的是哪四种文化？

3. 你见过麋鹿吗？麋鹿俗称"四不像"，你知道是哪"四不像"吗？

**三、拓展题**

1. 盐城湿地资源丰富，"盐城黄海湿地自然遗产"是中国第一块潮间带世界自然遗产。请选择一个你感兴趣的湿地公园进行一次实地探访，通过小视频的方式做一次小组主题汇报。

2. 盐城市有一个县的名字与"后羿射日"的故事有关。请查阅相关资料并向你的同学讲述该故事的主要内容。

# Chapter 12

宿迁

SUQIAN

第十二章

第 / 一 / 江 / 山 / 春 / 好 / 处
Spring over the Gorgeous Landscape

宿迁是江苏最年轻的地级市，境内有洪泽湖、骆马湖，以及穿城而过的大运河和古黄河，是全国唯一拥有"两河两湖"独特地理标识的地级市。乾隆皇帝六次南巡有五次驻跸宿迁，并赞誉其为"第一江山春好处"。宿迁还以"名酒之乡""水产之乡""花木之乡"和"杨树之乡"而闻名。

## 一、城市概况

### 1. 地理环境

宿迁位于江苏北部，1996年经国务院批准设立为地级市，这使它成了江苏最年轻的地级市。宿迁地理位置优越，恰好在徐州、淮安和连云港三市的中心位置，与安徽接壤。宿迁有丰富的水资源，境内有洪泽湖和骆马湖两大淡水湖，京杭大运河从市中心区域流过，是促进宿迁经济发展和文化交流的重要纽带。宿迁的地貌以平原为主，河网密布，四季分明，气候适宜，这种自然条件非常有利于农作物的生长，自古便是"鱼米之乡"。

### 2. 城市变迁

宿迁有着5000多年的文明史和2700多年的建城史。公元前113年，古泗水国曾在这里建都。秦朝以后，这里先后叫"下相县""宿豫县"等，最终在唐朝宝应元年（公元762年）改为"宿迁"，这一名字沿用至今。

宿迁是秦末英雄项羽的出生地，正因为如此，宿迁也被称为"项王故里"。清乾隆皇帝对宿迁尤为喜爱，六下江南中有5次留宿在此地，并赞叹宿迁为"第一江山春好处"。

## I. Overview

### 1. Geographical Environment

Suqian, located in the northern part of Jiangsu Province, was established as a prefecture-level city in 1996 by China's State Council, so it is the youngest city of this level in the province. Suqian is positioned strategically between Xuzhou, Huai'an, and Lianyungang, and shares a border with Anhui Province. It is known for its abundant water resources, including the Hongze Lake, the Luoma Lake, and the Beijing-Hangzhou Grand Canal, which have contributed significantly to the city's economic growth and cultural exchanges. The city's landscape features plains, dense river networks, and a temperate climate with four distinct seasons. Therefore, it is an ideal environment for agriculture and enjoys the reputation of a "land of fish and rice".

### 2. Development

Suqian boasts a rich history. Civilization appeared in the region over 5,000 years ago, and the earliest city appeared more than 2,700 years ago. In 113 BC, the ancient Sishui Kingdom built its capital in this area. After the Qin Dynasty, it was named first "Xiaxiang County" and then "Suyu County" before being officially renamed "Suqian" in the first year of Baoying during the Tang Dynasty in 762 AD, a name that remains in use to this day.

Suqian is also known as the hometown of King Xiang because it is the birthplace of Xiang Yu, the heroic commander of the late Qin Dynasty. Emperor Qianlong of the Qing Dynasty seemed to have a strong passion for Suqian, as he stayed there on five out of his six tours to the south of the Yangtze River. He even praised Suqian as a wonderful place with "spring over the gorgeous landscape".

## 3. Suqian Today

Today, Suqian has a total area of 8,555 square kilometers and a population of nearly 5 million. It boasts a strategic geographical location, a well-developed transportation network, and the largest port on the Beijing-Hangzhou Grand Canal, which gives the city a great advantage in water transportation. Several highways and railways run through the city, providing easy access to important cities in and outside Jiangsu Province. Suqian is a 40-minute drive from Xuzhou Guanyin International Airport, which offers numerous domestic flights. In addition to economic growth, Suqian prioritizes ecological conservation and improvement of its residents' lives, in an effort to create a beautiful and sustainable urban environment. The city has been conferred prestigious titles such as National Civilized City, Chinese Habitat Environment Award City, and National Sanitary City.

## II. Cultural Impressions

The Western Chu culture is seen as the epitome of Suqian's regional culture and reflects the spiritual values and principles cherished by the local community. The unwavering determination and resilience displayed by Xiang Yu, King of Western Chu, have long been a source of inspiration for the people of Suqian, instilling in them a sense of righteousness, a willingness to lead, a commitment to their word, and the bravery to shoulder responsibilities.

The liquor culture of Suqian and the Western Chu culture have a symbiotic relationship. Reputed as the "liquor capital", Suqian stands out as a prominent region in the production of Chinese baijiu for it boasts a long liquor-making history, brewing techniques passed down through generations, and renowned liquor brands like Yanghe and

## 3. 今日宿迁

如今的宿迁总面积8555平方公里，常住人口接近500万，地理位置和交通网络优势都十分明显：拥有京杭大运河沿线第一大港，为宿迁的水上运输提供了极大的便利；多条高速公路和铁路贯穿而过，从宿迁乘坐高铁可以到达江苏省内外的许多重要城市；从宿迁乘车至徐州观音国际机场仅需40分钟，有良好的航空出行条件。宿迁在追求经济发展的同时，也注重生态环境的保护和居民生活质量的提升，努力打造环境优美又宜居的城市环境，先后获得全国文明城市、中国人居环境奖城市和国家卫生城市等荣誉。

## 二、文化印象

西楚文化是宿迁的代表性地域文化，是当地人民精神气质和价值观念的体现。西楚霸王项羽的勇猛和不屈的精神，激励着宿迁人民千百年来发愤图强、敢为人先、信义守诺、勇于担责。

宿迁的酒文化与西楚文化相扶相生、相得益彰。作为"酒都"，宿迁是中国白酒的核心产地之一，以悠久的酿酒历史、世代相传的酿造技术和知名白酒品牌而著称。洋河、双沟等著名白酒品牌都出自宿迁。2012年，宿迁被正式授予"中国白酒之都"的称号。

## 三、教育交流

宿迁目前设有3所高校，分别是宿迁学院、宿迁职业技术学院和宿迁泽达职业技术学院。包括国际学生在内，有全日制在校生近3万人。

宿迁学院是宿迁唯一的一所本科院校，学校注重应用型教育，致力于培养高素质应用型人才。学校与多家企业建立了紧密的产学研合作关系，为学生提供了实践和就业平台。同时，学校积极展开国际交流，与多个国家和地区的20余所高校开展校际合作交流，有助于拓宽学生的国际视野。

## 四、经济腾飞

电子商务、新能源、高端纺织、白酒是宿迁的四个标志性产业，在宿迁的经济发展中扮演着关键角色。电子商务是宿迁第一个达到千亿元规模的产业。宿迁拥有全国最大的商务呼叫中心，吸引了京东、小米、360等知名企业入驻，电子商务相关从业人数超过60万人。截至2022年底，电子商务交易额达到2200亿元。宿迁在新能源领域形成了较为完整的产业链，高端纺织产业和白酒产业则是宿迁的传统优势产业。

Shuanggou. In recognition of its significant contributions, Suqian was officially awarded the title of "China's Liquor Capital" in 2012.

## III. Education and International Exchanges

At present, there are three higher education institutions in Suqian: Suqian College, Suqian Vocational and Technical College, and Suqian Zeda Vocational and Technical College. These colleges boast nearly 30,000 full-time students, including international students.

Suqian College, dedicated to nurturing vocational talent, is the sole institution in Suqian that awards bachelor's degrees. The college has forged strong partnerships with various enterprises in order to guarantee practical training and promote employment for graduates. Additionally, Suqian College actively engages in international exchanges and collaborations with over 20 universities worldwide, so that its students can be granted a global view.

## IV. Economic Takeoff

Suqian's economic development is driven by four main industries: e-commerce, new energy, high-end textiles, and liquor production. E-commerce is the leading industry in Suqian and has achieved remarkable success, with a scale of 100 billion yuan annually and a workforce of over 600,000 professionals. The city is home to the largest business call center in the country and attracts renowned companies like JD.com, Xiaomi, and 360. The e-commerce transaction volume in Suqian reached 220 billion yuan by the end of 2022. Suqian has also established a comprehensive industrial chain in the new energy sector, while high-end textiles and liquor production remain long-standing pillars of the city's economy.

## 五、特色美食

宿迁的美食蕴含着深厚的文化内涵，风味独特。其中最为当地人津津乐道的是传统名小吃水晶山楂糕、宿迁非物质文化遗产乾隆贡酥（烧饼）和王家熏肉。

## V. Specialty Food

Suqian's local dishes are delectable and filled with cultural significance. Traditional snacks like crystal hawthorn cake, Qianlong tribute cake, and Wang Family's bacon are highly praised for their historical importance and unique flavors, and are popular choices among both residents and visitors. Each bite of these delicacies provides a taste of Suqian's rich culinary heritage and traditions.

### 练习

#### 一、判断题

1. 宿迁位于江苏省南部，是江苏省最年轻的地级市。☐
2. 因秦末英雄项羽出生于宿迁，宿迁也被称为"项王故里"。☐
3. 西楚文化和酒文化是宿迁的代表性地域文化。☐

#### 二、思考题

1. 宿迁的标志性产业有哪些？
2. 宿迁的特色美食有哪些？

#### 三、拓展题

实地探访宿迁的电子商务园区，并通过视频介绍电子商务的具体运作过程，分析电子商务对实体产业的推动作用。

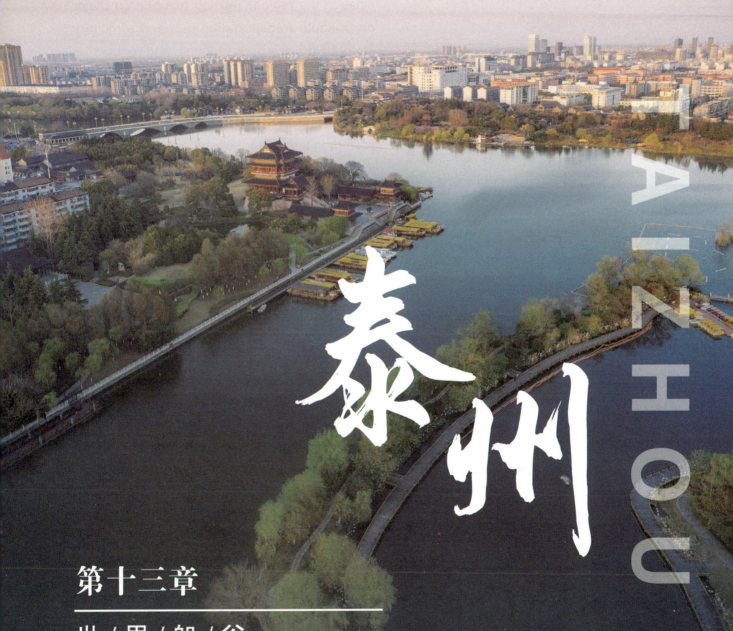

# Chapter 13

泰州

TAIZHOU

第十三章

世 / 界 / 船 / 谷
Global Shipbuilding Valley

泰州拥有超过 2100 多年的建城历史，作为苏中地区的重要城市之一，千百年来以其安定祥和著称，被誉为"祥泰之州"。如今，凭借蓬勃发展的农业、便捷的交通运输网络以及丰富的河鲜资源，泰州已成功塑造了一张融合现代农业、交通枢纽与美食文化的独特城市名片。

## 一、城市概况

泰州位于江苏中部，是一座有着2100多年历史的古城。作为苏中地区的重要城市之一，泰州地处长江北岸，自古以来便是连接南北的水陆交通枢纽和军事战略要地，被誉为"水陆要津，咽喉据郡"。

泰州境内地势平坦，河流密布，是典型的平原水乡。城市四季分明，气候温和，春天欣赏千垛菜花，秋天漫步古银杏林都是热门的旅游项目。

泰州水陆空交通便捷，为城市经济发展和居民生活提供了极大的便利。新长、宁启铁路的建成通车，加强了泰州与全国各地的联系。盐靖、京沪、沪陕等多条高速公路构成了泰州与周边乃至全国范围内的高速交通网络。泰州港作为重要的内河港口，对推动区域物流起着关键作用。扬州泰州国际机场，有飞往日本、韩国、泰国等多个国家和地区的航线以及30多条国内航线。

## I. Overview

Taizhou, located on the north bank of the Yangtze River in the central part of Jiangsu Province, is an ancient city with a history of over 2,100 years. As one of the most important cities in the region, Taizhou has been a major north-south transportation hub and a military stronghold since ancient times, and reputed as the "land-water junction and strategic county".

Taizhou is a plain with many rivers, and has a mild climate with distinct seasons. The canola flowers in spring and the ancient ginkgo forests in autumn are popular tourist attractions of Taizhou.

The convenient transportation of Taizhou benefits the city's economic development and residents' lives. Thanks to the opening of the Xinchang (Xinyi-Changxing) and Ningqi (Nanjing-Qidong) railways, the connection between Taizhou and other cities has been strengthened. The Yancheng-Jingjiang, Beijing-Shanghai, Shanghai-Shaanxi and other highways form a high-speed transportation network between Taizhou and its surrounding areas and across the entire country. As an important inland port, Taizhou Port plays a crucial role in promoting regional logistics. Yangzhou Taizhou International Airport offers direct flights to countries such as Japan, the Republic of Korea, Thailand, and more than 30 domestic cities.

## II. Cultural Impressions

Bordering the Huaihe River to the north, the Yangtze River to the south, and the Yellow Sea to the east, Taizhou boasts a unique "culture of river and sea", which is reflected in the names of many places and historical relics in Taizhou, such as the important port of Gaogang, the subordinate city Jingjiang, the iconic building Sea View Tower, as well as historical relics such as

## 二、文化印象

泰州北接淮河、南近长江、东临黄海，这样的自然环境形成了独特的江海文化。在泰州的地名和历史遗迹中，可以看到水文化的深刻影响，蕴含着"江"和"海"元素的名称特别多，如重要港口高港、下辖靖江市、标志性建筑望海楼，还有海陵仓、江海会祠、古盐运河等历史遗迹，无一不深深烙印着泰州独有的江海文化特色。江、淮、海三水的交汇带来了丰富的资源和独特的风貌。农业的发展、运输的通达、丰富的河鲜为泰州打造了一张集现代农业、交通枢纽与美食文化于一体的城市名片。长江国家文化公园泰州段的建设，标志着泰州在文化遗产保护、生态文明建设和社会经济发展之间开启了"人水和谐"共生格局的新探索。

## 三、教育交流

泰州目前有7所高校，其中本科学校5所，专科学校两所。

### 1）泰州学院

泰州学院（www.tzu.edu.cn）是全日制省属公办普通本科高等学校，学科涵盖经济学、法学、教育学、文学、理学、工学、管理学、艺术学等8个门类33个本科专业。学院积极开展国际交流合作，与美国、德国、加拿大等多个国家和地区的高校和科研机构建立了友好合作关系。

### 2）江苏农牧科技职业学院

江苏农牧科技职业学院（www.jsahvc.edu.cn）是一所公办专科高等院校，专注培养农牧科技领域类技术技能型人才。学校牵头组建国际农牧业高等职业教育联盟，与全球58所海外教育及研究机构开展合作。学校累计培养了来自43个国家的国际学生1200余名。目前，学校有来自10多个国家的全日制国际学生173人。

the Hailing Warehouse, the Jianghai Ancestral Hall and the Ancient Salt Canal. The convergence of the Yangtze River, the Huaihe River, and the Yellow Sea endows Taizhou with abundant resources and unique scenery. Today, Taizhou is well-known for its modern agriculture, convenient transportation, and local cuisine of freshwater delicacies. The construction of the Taizhou section of the Yangtze River National Cultural Park marks an exploration of the idea of "Harmony between Human and Water" in Taizhou's cultural heritage protection, ecological civilization construction, and socio-economic development.

## III. Education and International Exchanges

There are seven higher education institutions in Taizhou, including five undergraduate universities and two vocational colleges.

### 1) Taizhou University

Taizhou University (www.tzu.edu.cn) is a full-time provincial institution of higher education. It offers 33 undergraduate programs covering 8 disciplines, including economics, law, education, literature, science, engineering, management science, and art. It engages in international exchange and cooperation actively, and has set up friendly cooperative relationships with higher education institutions and research institutes in the United States, Germany, Canada, etc.

### 2) Jiangsu Agri-animal Husbandry Vocational College

Jiangsu Agri-animal Husbandry Vocational College (www.jsahvc.edu.cn) trains personnel specializing in agriculture and husbandry science and technology. It takes the lead in establishing the Higher Vocational Education International Alliance for Agri-animal Husbandry (HVEIAA) and cooperates with 58 overseas institutions. It has trained over

## 四、经济腾飞

医药产业，民营高端船舶制造是泰州的两大优势产业。

泰州被誉为"医药名城"，拥有全国首个医药类国家级高新技术产业开发区——泰州医药高新技术产业园区（又称"中国医药城"）。这里汇聚了扬子江药业集团等一批全国医药百强企业，现有海内外医药企业1200多家，包括阿斯利康、雀巢健康科学、勃林格殷格翰等。

泰州是全国最大的民营造船基地，也是国内唯一交船完工量超千万载重吨的地级市，拥有扬子江船业、新时代造船等全球领先的造船企业，以及亚星锚链、振华泵业、南极机械等一批高水平的船舶配套（船配）企业。这些企业共同构建了一个从设计、建造到配套服务的完整造船产业链，推动泰州成为全球"船谷"。

1,200 international students from 43 countries. Currently, there are 173 full-time international students from over 10 countries in the college.

## IV. Economic Takeoff

Pharmaceutics and private high-end shipbuilding are the advantageous industries in Taizhou.

Reputed as the "pharmaceutical city", Taizhou boasts the first national-level high-tech industrial development zone for pharmaceutics in China — Taizhou Pharmaceutical High-tech Industrial Park (also known as "Pharmaceutical City of China"). A group of China's top 100 pharmaceutical enterprises including Yangtze River Pharmaceutical Group and more than 1,200 domestic and foreign pharmaceutical enterprises, such as AstraZeneca, Nestle, and Boehringer Ingelheim, have settled in Taizhou Pharmaceutical High-tech Industrial Park.

Taizhou is the largest private shipbuilding base in China and the only prefecture-level city in China to produce a yearly tonnage of over 10 million deadweight tons. It has global leading enterprises such as Yangzijiang Shipbuilding Group and New Times Shipbuilding as well as high-level supporting enterprises such as Asian Star Anchor Chain, Jiangsu Zhenhua Pump Industry, and Jiangsu Antarctic Machinery. These enterprises have jointly built a complete shipbuilding industry chain from design, construction to supporting services, thus turning Taizhou into a global "shipbuilding valley".

## V. Specialty Food

The steamed buns stuffed with pork and crab roe are juicy, the baked cakes of Huangqiao are crispy, and the Eight Delicacies of the Qinhu Lake are fresh and delicious — all these are authentic Taizhou flavor.

The steamed buns stuffed with pork and crab roe are famous for their thin wrapper and

## 五、特色美食

蟹黄汤包的细腻鲜美、黄桥烧饼的香酥可口、溱湖八鲜的新鲜美味，每一道美食都能让人感受到地道的泰州风味。

蟹黄汤包以皮薄、味鲜著称。因为汤汁丰富，所以直接以"汤包"命名。汤包的吃法也很特别，要"轻轻提，慢慢移，先开窗，后吸汤"。这样的吃法既能避免汤汁溅出，又能充分体验汤包的鲜美。

黄桥烧饼色泽金黄、香酥可口，不油不腻。一般有咸甜两种口味，是老少咸宜的传统点心。

溱湖出产的簖(duàn)蟹、银鱼、青虾、甲鱼、四喜、螺贝、水禽以及水生蔬菜，统称为"溱湖八鲜"。这些食材汇集了溱湖水域的水产品和水生植物，是泰州最具代表性的菜品之一。

## 六、名胜古迹

溱湖国家湿地公园是国家5A级旅游景区，位于泰州市东北郊的溱湖，以独特的自然风光、丰富的历史文化和积极的生态保护理念而闻名。园区内水域广阔、绿树环绕、水草丰茂。作为江苏首家国家级湿地公园，这里是众多野生动物的栖息地，包括珍贵的麋鹿、丹顶鹤以及各类水鸟。游客可以在栈道上漫步，也可以坐船在水道中穿行，欣赏优美的湿地风光，是拥抱自然、放松身心的理想场所。

fresh taste. Because of the juicy filling, a bun is simply called a "soup dumpling". The buns must be eaten carefully: lift gently, move slowly, bite open a small hole, and sip the soup. In this way, the filling will not spill, and the taste of the buns can be fully enjoyed.

The baked cake of Huangqiao is golden in color and crisp in taste. Generally, there are two flavors: salty and sweet. The baked cakes are a traditional dim sum suitable for all ages.

The Qinhu Lake is home to crabs, silver fish, green shrimp, soft-shelled turtles, freshwater carps, shells, waterfowl, and aquatic vegetables, which are collectively referred to as the "Eight Delicacies of the Qinhu Lake". They represent the aquatic produce of the Qinhu Lake, and a dish made of the Eight Delicacies is an iconic food in Taizhou.

## VI. Historical Sites and Scenic Spots

The Qinhu National Wetland Park, located in the northeast suburb of Taizhou, is a national 5A-level scenic spot. It is famous for its unique natural scenery, rich historical legacy, and active ecological protection. The vast water area in the park is surrounded by green trees and abundant water grasses. As the first national wetland park in Jiangsu, the place is a wildlife habitat for Milu deer, red-crowned cranes, and various water birds. You can take a walk on the plank path or take a boat tour through the waterways to enjoy the beautiful wetland scenery. It is an ideal place to embrace nature and relax.

## 练习

### 一、判断题

1. 泰州的地形以平原为主。　☐

2. 泰州的重点产业是纺织业。　☐

3. 溱湖八鲜是溱湖出产的八种鱼类。　☐

### 二、思考题

1. 泰州不是沿海城市，为什么有很多和海有关的地名？

2. 查一查，除了医药产业和民营高端船舶制造之外，泰州还有哪些优势产业。

### 三、拓展题

参观溱湖国家湿地公园，了解泰州在湿地保护方面做出的努力，拍一个小视频或做一个PPT，进行小组汇报。

# 练习答案　Keys

## Part 1　江苏概况

练习（17页）

1. ✕　2. ✕　3. ✕　4. ✓　5. ✓　6. ✕　7. ✕　8. ✓　9. ✓　10. ✓

## Part 2　城市名片

### 第一章　南京：六朝古都

练习一（33页）

1. ✓　2. ✕　3. ✓

练习二（43页）

1. ✕　2. ✓　3. ✕　4. ✓　5. ✕

### 第二章　苏州：人间天堂

练习一（58页）

1. ✕　2. ✓　3. ✓

练习二（64页）

1. ✓　2. ✓　3. ✕　4. ✓　5. ✕

### 第三章　无锡：太湖明珠

练习（75页）

1. ✕　2. ✕　3. ✓　4. ✕

### 第四章　常州：中华龙城

练习（94页）

1. ✕　2. ✕　3. ✓　4. ✓　5. ✕

### 第五章　镇江：城市山林

练习（109页）

1. ✕　2. ✓　3. ✕　4. ✕　5. ✓

**第六章 扬州：淮左名都**

练习（121页）

1. ✕   2. ✓   3. ✕   4. ✓

**第七章 南通：中国近代第一城**

练习（134页）

1. ✕   2. ✓   3. ✕   4. ✕   5. ✓

**第八章 徐州：楚韵汉风**

练习（152页）

1. ✓   2. ✕   3. ✓   4. ✕   5. ✓

**第九章 淮安：壮丽东南第一州**

练习（160页）

1. ✕   2. ✓   3. ✕   4. ✓   5. ✓   6. ✕

**第十章 连云港：新亚欧大陆桥东方起点**

练习（168页）

1. ✓   2. ✕   3. ✕   4. ✕   5. ✓   6. ✓

**第十一章 盐城：黄海明珠　湿地之都**

练习（178页）

1. ✓   2. ✓   3. ✓

**第十二章 宿迁：第一江山春好处**

练习（183页）

1. ✕   2. ✓   3. ✕

**第十三章 泰州：世界船谷**

练习（190页）

1. ✓   2. ✕   3. ✕